# CONWAY'S ALL THE WORLD'S BATTLESHIPS

# CONWAY'S
## ALL THE WORLD'S
# Battleships
## 1906 to the Present
### Edited by Ian Sturton

Naval
Institute
Press

# Contributors

Przemyslaw Budzbon *Russia and Soviet Union*

N J M Campbell *Germany 1906–22*

Aldo Fraccaroli *Italy 1906–22*

Norman Friedman *United States of America, Japan 1906-22*

Pierre Hervieux *France 1922–46*

Anthony Preston *Great Britain*

John Roberts *Italy 1922–46*

Robert Scheina *Latin America*

Erwin Sieche *Germany 1922–46*

Adam Smigielski *France 1906–22*

Ian Sturton *Japan 1922–46, Netherlands, Spain, Turkey, Greece*

Previous Page: Jubilee Fleet Exercises with *Renown, Hood* and *Valiant* – June 1935. *CPL*

Opposite: Return of *Royal Sovereign*, February 1949, by the Soviets. *CPL*

Published and distributed in the United States of
America and Canada by the Naval Institute Press,
Annapolis, Maryland 21402

Library of Congress Catalog Card No. 87–62393

ISBN 0-87021- 017-3

First published in Great Britain 1987 by
CONWAY MARITIME PRESS LTD
24 Bride Lane, Fleet Street,
London EC4Y 8DR
ISBN 0 85177 448 2

Line drawings by Przemyslaw Budzbon,
Adam Sonigielski, Marek Twardowski
and Ian Sturton.

Manufactured in the United Kingdom

# Contents

# Argentina

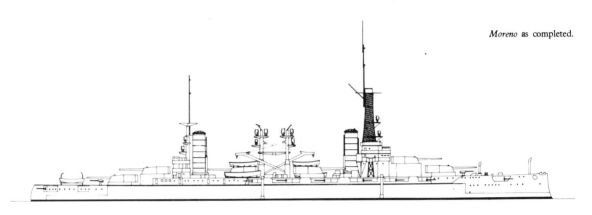

*Moreno* as completed.

The *Rivadavia* class was authorised in 1908 primarily as a response to the *Minas Gerais* class being constructed in Brazil. An intense internal debate took place in Argentina concerning the need to purchase two such expensive dreadnoughts, costing £2.2 million each. Argentina's recent border disputes with Brazil, Chile, and Uruguay helped win the day for those in favour.

The Argentine method for acquiring the best possible design stirred controversy among the building nations. In 1908 Rear-Admiral Onofre Betbeder set up office in London and requested all interested parties to submit plans for the construction of two dreadnoughts with the option to build a third. The guidelines were sketchy to allow the bidders to develop the best possible plans. Fifteen companies submitted plans. The Argentinians reviewed the submissions, chose the best features from each, and gave the revised guidelines to the competing firms. This process was then repeated. The competitors were in a furore and considered this as a looting their trade secrets.

The contract was awarded to Fore River Shipbuilding Corporation of Quincy, Massachusetts, at a saving of more than £224,000 per ship over the nearest competitor. European builders were shocked because the United States, which then lagged far behind Great Britain and Germany in the dreadnought race, was not considered to be a serious competitor.

The *Rivadavia* class closely paralleled American battleships in appearance and design. The machinery was

placed amidships with the boilers grouped in separate rooms equally forward and abaft the engine room. This arrangement reduced trimming problems and separated machinery vitals into three separate compartments.

The 'en echelon' 12in amidships turrets could in theory fire on a 180-degree arc on the side of the ship where located and 100 degrees on the opposite side. The secondary 6in guns were mounted on the upper deck behind 6in armour. The 16 4in QF guns were for protection against torpedo attack; 8 of these guns were mounted in the between decks, 4 on the gun deck aft, and 4 on the upper deck forward. The 8 remaining guns were located on the weather deck – 6

on the superstructure deck and 2 on the upper deck aft. The 4in guns were not protected by armour. Two submerged side-loading TT were located in the torpedo room forward, firing broadside. The ships' magazines stowed 120 rounds of 12in shell per gun, 300 rounds for each 6in, 350 rounds per 4in gun, and 16 Whitehead torpedoes.

The ships were initially fitted with two 15ft Barr & Stroud rangefinders mounted in revolving armoured towers above the forward and after CT for controlling the 12in guns. Two 9ft Barr & Stroud rangefinders were mounted on the platform on top of the king posts for the boat booms.

Typical of American-built dreadnoughts, protection received special

attention. The main belt was 12in amidships tapering to 5in and 4in at the stem and stern respectively. The belt extended 5ft above and 6ft below the normal waterline. The turret armour was 12in on the face, 9in on the sides, 9.5in on the rear and 4in on the top. The forward and aft CT were 12in and 9in respectively. The protective deck extended the ship's length 24in above the waterline amidships, sloping down to the lower edge of the main belt armour. The protective deck varied from 20lb medium steel to 80lb of nickel steel. The inner bottom extended most of the length of the ships. An inner skin was fitted around the magazines, boilers, and machinery. This was for added protection against mines and torpedoes.

## RIVADAVIA class *battleships*

| | |
|---|---|
| **Displacement:** | 27,940t normal; 30,600t full load |
| **Dimensions:** | 594ft 9in oa, 585ft pp × 98ft 4½in × 27ft 8½in normal |
| | *181.3m, 178.3m × 30.0m × 8.5m* |
| **Machinery:** | 3 shafts, Curtiss geared turbines, 18 Babcock and Wilcox boilers, 40,000shp = 22.5kts. Coal 4000t, oil 600t. Range 7000nm at 15kts, 11,000nm at 11kts. |
| **Armour:** | Belt 12in–10in (305mm–254mm), casemate 9.3in–6.2in (237mm–158mm), turrets 12in (305mm), CT 12in (305mm) |
| **Armament:** | 12–12in (305mm)/50 (6 × 2), 12–6in (152mm)/50, 16–4in (102mm)/50 QF, 2–21in (533mm) TT |
| **Complement:** | 1130 (130 officers and 1000 men) |

| Name | Builder | Laid down | Launched | Comp | Fate |
|---|---|---|---|---|---|
| RIVADAVIA | Fore River | 25.5.10 | 26.8.11 | 12.14 | Sold 8.2.56 |
| MORENO | New York SB | 9.7.10 | 23.9.11 | 3.15 | Sold 8.2.56 |

The electrical plant consisted of 4375kW turbogenerators located under the midship magazines forward and aft of the engine rooms. Two 75kW generators run off of diesel engines provided electricity when the boilers were cold. An 8kW Telefunken radio had an optimum range of 1500km.

The USN Board of Inspection and Survey for Ships made the following observations concerning *Rivadavia* on 21 October 1913. 'On the high speed runs the vessel made the exact contract speed, 22.5 knots; but it is believed that she can do a little better … She … handles remarkably well … The Board prefers our adopted centerline arrangement of turrets [*Wyoming* class]. While theoretically the *Rivadavia* has an ahead and astern fire of six guns, this is not so in reality, as it is almost certain that the blast from the waist turret guns would dish in the smokepipes and damage the uptakes … The Bethlehem Steel Company designed and made special [12in guns] breech-blocks, all of which were rejected, and the regular US Navy type of breech-block was finally made and installed. **With comparatively minor modifications the vessel would practically meet the requirements of our own vessels.'**

A third dreadnought was authorised in 1912 in response to Brazil's third dreadnought, the *Rio de Janeiro*. Since neither this ship nor the Brazilian *Riachuelo* ever materialised, Argentina's third dreadnought was never laid down. *Rivadavia* and *Moreno* were extensively modernised in the United States between 1924 and 1926. They were converted to oil-firing and received a new fire control system. Inactive in the latter years of their careers, they were sold for scrap on 8 February 1956.

# Austria-Hungary

Influenced by the impending construction of the first Italian dreadnought, the Austrian C-in-C, Montecuccoli, announced on 20 February 1908 that Austria-Hungary would build a new generation of battleships displacing 18,000–19,000t. In March 1908 Germany launched her first dreadnought (*Nassau*) and took the next step in the naval arms race by approving the Second Naval Amendment. Italy therefore postponed the keel laying of her first dreadnought obviously because Cuniberti and his chief naval engineer Edoardo Masdeo had to rethink the parameters of their design. In October 1908 the Austrian Naval Section issued orders for preliminary design studies and furthermore offered a prize in a design competition open to Austro-Hungarian naval architects. The results of both were to be overtaken by events during the next half-year. When in March 1909 the STT yard presented five different design studies, it had just become public that the Italians had gone their own way by adopting triple turrets for their *Dreadnought A* (later the *Dante Alighieri*). The further development of the new Austrian battleship became problematical for the naval authorities, so they decided to adopt the triple turret as well, at the same time asking their German ally for information on the design of their newest type, the *Kaiser* class. This they duly received in April 1909 by special permission of the German Emperor. Nevertheless it seems that Austria-Hungary did not take into consideration German design philosophy and experience, since the basic *Tegetthoff* design had been accepted on 27 April 1909.

Italy had begun construction of *Dreadnought A* by 6 June 1909, so the Austrian C-in-C believed that obtaining the necessary funds in the 1910 budget (to be discussed in November 1909) would not be difficult. Two of the *Radetzky* class pre-dreadnoughts had already been launched and STT urgently needed follow-up contracts to maintain their force of skilled workers, so Montecuccoli lost no time and suggested as early as August 1909 that both STT and Skoda should start construction at their own risk until the budget was approved. To everyone's

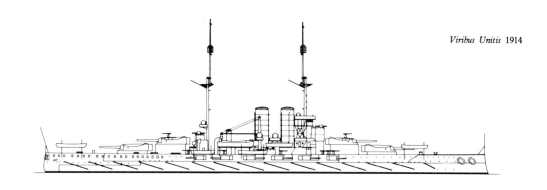

*Viribus Unitis* 1914

## TEGETTHOFF class *battleships*

| | |
|---|---|
| **Displacement:** | 20,013.5t design; 21,595t deep load (*Szent István* 20,008t; 21,689t) |
| **Dimensions:** | 495ft 5in wl, 499ft 3in oa × 89ft 8in × 29ft deep load |
| | *151.0m, 152.2m × 27.3m × 8.9m* |
| **Machinery:** | 4-shaft Parsons geared turbines, 12 Yarrow boilers, 27,000shp = 20.3kts (*Szent István* 2-shaft AEG-Curtiss turbines, 12 Babcock & Wilcox boilers, 26,400shp = ?kts; no official trials due to war). Coal 2000t max. Range 4200nm at 10kts |
| **Armour:** | Belt 280mm–150mm (11in–5.9in), deck 48mm–30mm (1.9in – 1.2in), slopes 48mm (1.9in), torpedo bulkhead 50mm (2in), main turrets 280mm–60mm (11in–2.4in), casemates 120mm (4.7in), CT 280mm–60mm (11in–2.4in) |
| **Armament:** | 12-12in (305mm)/45 K 10 (4 × 3), 12-5.9in (150mm)/50 K 10, 18–66mm/50 K 10 (from 1914 3–4 on AA mountings on turret roofs), 2-66mm/18 (landing guns), 4–21in (533mm) TT (1 bow, 1 stern, 2 beam) |
| **Complement:** | 1087 (*Szent István* 1094) |

| Name | Builder | Laid down | Launched | Comp | Fate |
|---|---|---|---|---|---|
| VIRIBUS UNITIS | STT | 24.7.10 | 24.6.11 | 5.12.12 | Sunk 1.11.18 |
| TEGETTHOFF | STT | 24.9.10 | 21.3.12 | 21.7.13 | BU 1924–25 |
| PRINZ EUGEN | STT | 16.1.12 | 30.11.12 | 17.7.14 | Sunk 28.6.22 |
| SZENT ISTVÁN | Danubius, Fiume | 29.1.12 | 17.1.14 | 13.12.15 | Sunk 10.6.18 |

surprise the funds were refused for political reasons, and Montecuccoli was forced to embark on an elaborate campaign of deception and propaganda to disguise the fact that the ships were being built without parliamentary approval. He claimed that industry was financing construction on speculation, but it certainly was not, and was very uneasy with the situation. Not until Montecuccoli took an expensive 32 million crowns credit on his own responsibility were the keels of dreadnoughts IV and V laid, on 24 July and 24 September 1910. In the meantime Italy had launched the *Dante Alighieri* and started construction of her second dreadnought and France had laid the keel of her first (*Courbet*) to match the Central Powers'

dreadnought superiority in the Mediterranean. Therefore the two Austrian dreadnoughts were already in the early stages of construction when the mutual parliamentary delegations met in March 1911 to discuss the 1911 budget.

From the technical point of view the *Tegetthoff*s were very compact and powerful ships and the first dreadnoughts in service with 12in triple turrets, although Italy was the first naval power to design a triple turret and lay down a triple-turreted ship. Obviously German design theories about underwater protection came too late, so once again the *Tegetthoff*s had Popper's underwater protection scheme incorporating a double bottom. Although the Austro-

Hungary Naval Technical Committee had organised a design competition for this type, it was entirely Popper's brainchild because he had been consultant to the main contractor, STT, since his retirement in 1907.

In spring 1914 *Viribus Unitis* and *Tegetthoff* made their only training cruise in the eastern Mediterranean. During the war they formed the 1st Division of the 1st Battle Squadron and participated in the shore bombardment of the Italian coast in May 1915 (with the exception of *Szent István*, which was nearing completion at the Pola N Yd where she had been towed after launching). In June 1918 all four were to form the backbone of a raiding force which was to attack the Otranto barrage, but *Szent István* was

*Tegetthoff* May 1914.
CPL

torpedoed and sunk off Premuda Island on 10 June 1918 by the Italian *MAS 15* during the sortie, causing the whole operation to be cancelled. *Viribus Unitis* was sunk in Pola harbour on 1 November 1918 by a limpet mine laid by two Italian frogmen, after she had been handed over to the Yugoslav National Council. *Tegetthoff* was ceded to Italy in 1919 and scrapped in 1924–25 at La Spezia. *Prinz Eugen* was ceded to France in 1919, towed to Toulon and completely disarmed and stripped of her interior fittings. She was used as an explosives target for underwater shock tests and aircraft bombs. She was finally sunk as a gunnery target on 28 June 1922 by the French battleships *Bretagne*, *Jean Bart*, *Paris* and *France*. Whether some of her guns were used in coastal batteries by the French or the Germans (Atlantic Wall) is not known.

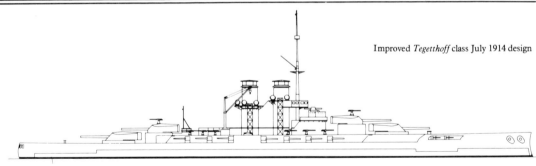

Improved *Tegetthoff* class July 1914 design

International naval literature always refers to the projected battleships VIII-XI as the 'Ersatz *Monarch* class', but in official files these ships were given only project numbers (project I, II, III and so on) or tonnage designations (22,000t battleships, 23,400t battleships and the final variant 24,500t battleship); they were finally referred to as the 'Improved *Tegetthoff* class'. On 3 June 1911 the naval authorities ordered preparatory designs for the next generation of dreadnoughts to the following alternative particulars: A 23,000t, 10–30.5cm/45, 18–15cm, 24–66mm QF; and B 24,600t, 10–34.5cm/45, 18–15cm, 24–66mm QF. The displacement limit was the result of the need to fit the future ship (with half consumable stores and full ammunition load) into floating drydock No I, which had a lifting power of 23,800t. It was believed, nevertheless, that such a design could match contemporary opponents

## Improved TEGETTHOFF class *battleships*

**Displacement:** 24,500t design
**Dimensions:** 564ft 3in wl, 568ft 3in oa × 93ft 6in × 27ft 5in (design)
*172.0m, 173.2m × 28.5m × 8.4m*
**Machinery:** 4-shaft steam turbines, 15 Yarrow boilers (9 coal-, 6 oil-fired), 31,000shp = 21kts (design). Coal 1425t, oil 1425t max. Range 5000nm at 10kts
**Armour:** Belt 310mm–140mm (12.2in–5.5in), deck 36mm (1.4in), slopes 36mm (1.4in), torpedo bulkhead 85mm (3.3in), main turrets 340mm–80mm (13.4–3.1in), casemates 150mm (5.9in), CT 320mm (12.6in)
**Armament:** 10–13.8in (350mm)/45 (2 × 2, 2 × 3), 14–5.9in (150mm)/50, 20–3.5in (90mm)/45 (12 on AA mountings), 2–47mm/47, 2–66mm/18 (landing guns), 6–21in (533mm) TT (2 × 1, 2 × 2, bow, stern and beam).
**Complement:** No figures available.

| Name | Builder | Laid down* | Launched | Comp* | Fate |
|------|---------|-----------|----------|-------|------|
| BATTLESHIP VIII | STT | 1.7.14 | — | 30.6.17 | Never laid down |
| BATTLESHIP IX | Danubius, Fiume | 1.1.15 | — | 31.12.17 | Never laid down |
| BATTLESHIP X | STT | 1.6.16 | — | 31.5.19 | Never laid down |
| BATTLESHIP XI | Danubius, Fiume | 1.6.16 | — | 31.5.19 | Never laid down |

*As proposed in secret schedule of 12.1.14

by cutting down the cruising radius – *ie* saving fuel weight – because of the geographical position of the Hapsburg Empire.

In December 1911 the Naval Technical Committee presented its design studies for 'A' and 'B', which had the following particulars: A – 22,000t, 12–30.5cm/45, 22– 15cm/50, 24–75cm/50 QF, 5 TT, and B – 23,400t, 10–34.5cm/45, 22–15cm/50, 24–75mm/50. The demand for more secondary armament was solved by using twin casemates. The Skoda 75mm/50 (3in) QF was a further development of the standard 66mm/45 (2.6in) and was offered to the Austro–Hungary Navy in 1911. A board meeting of 12 May 1912 increased the final calibre to 35cm (13.8in) to balance the loss of penetration power in the standard shell to be developed. A second reason might have been the compatibility with German ammunition (compare the calibre of the German battlecruisers of the *Mackensen* class). In January 1913 the Naval Technical Committee presented its next design: 24,500t, 10–35cm, 18–15cm. The strict weight

limit forced the designers to save every possible ton and therefore they reduced the secondary armament, omitted the aft CT and the mainmast and designed the heavy guns in triple turrets superimposed over twins. As this obviously affected stability, ammunition stowage was reduced and in July 1913 exactly the same design was presented with superimposed twin mountings. This was the last design variant, to which the 'Improved *Tegetthoffs*' obviously would have been built.

From the political point of view the history of this design was not a repeat of the *Tegetthoffs*, although for a second time industry wanted to begin construction on credit. In March 1913 the heir to the throne urged the new C-in-C, Admiral Haus, to order the new dreadnoughts, because the last of the STT-built *Tegetthoffs* had been launched 4 months previously and the yard urgently needed follow-up orders. But the Hungarian authorities stubbornly refused to allow construction on credit, arguing that the only legal way would be by providing funds in the 1914–15 budget. Even the

Emperor himself could not persuade the Hungarian ministry of finance to acquiesce, resulting in a one-year delay in dreadnought construction. The 1914–15 budget – including the new battleships VIII–IX – was not approved until 28 May 1914. At the end of June 1914 STT was ordered to build No VIII and Danubius to build No IX, but due to the outbreak of the First World War the keel laying was postponed and never took place.

Skoda, which had already begun to manufacture the 35cm guns and turrets, delivered a trial barrel for first tests in November 1914 and completed guns No 1 and 2. No 1, dubbed 'Georg', was used for a mixed long-range battery (together with a 38cm/17) operating in Northern Italy which first fired on 25 May 1916. Guns No 2 and 3 were also completed but never saw front-line action; at the end of war gun No 4 was ready for delivery at Skoda and guns No 5–11 were in different stages of production.

A last attempt to build at least one unit of the 'Improved *Tegetthoff*' class in an austere version under the limitations of war was made in May 1915.

The use of armour plate already manufactured for the triple turrets was discussed, with a view to building twin mountings for one ship with 8–35cm guns in four twin turrets; but the idea was dropped when Italy declared war.

*Tegetthoff* and *Erzherzog Franz Ferdinand* in Venice 1919. *CPL*

# Brazil

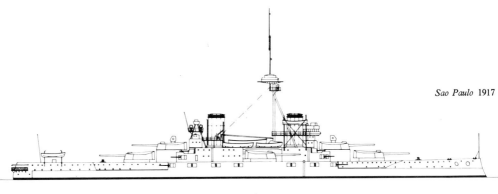

*Sao Paulo* 1917

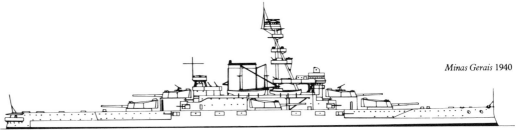

*Minas Gerais* 1940

Below: *Minas Gerais* on trials.
CPL

The class was authorised in 1906 and was the heart of the 1904 Building Programme. These ships were the largest and most powerful dreadnoughts in the world when completed. Professional magazines were full of rumours that Brazil was in fact acting as an agent for one of the leading naval powers and would turn the ships over to their real owner when completed. The English press speculated that Germany, Japan, or the United States were the real backers and the European press believed that England had actually built the ships for herself. These speculations had no foundation.

Also, expressions such as 'Pan Americanism' and 'Hemispheric Co-

## MINAS GERAIS class *battleships*

| | |
|---|---|
| **Displacement:** | 19,281t normal; 21,200t full load |
| **Dimensions:** | 543ft oa, 530ft wl, 500ft pp × 83ft × 28ft max, 25ft mean |
| | *165.5m 161.5m, 152.4m × 25.3m × 8.5m, 7.6m* |
| **Machinery:** | 2-shaft Vickers VTE, 18 Babcock boilers, 23,500ihp = 21kts. Coal 2350t, oil 400t. Range 10,000nm at 10kts. |
| **Armour:** | Belt 9in (229mm) amidships, 6in–4in (152mm–102mm) ends, casemate 9in (229mm), turrets 12in–9in (305mm–229mm), CT 12in (305mm) |
| **Armament:** | 12–12in (305m)/45 (6 × 2), 22–4.7in (120mm)/50, 8–3pdr (47mm) |
| **Complement:** | 900 |

| Name | Builder | Laid down | Launched | Comp | Fate |
|---|---|---|---|---|---|
| MINAS GERAIS | Armstrong, Elswick | 17.4.07 | 10.9.08 | 6.1.10 | Sold 1953 |
| SAO PAULO | Vickers, Barrow | 30.4.07 | 19.4.09 | 7.10 | Sold 1951 |

operation' began to appear in US naval journals overnight. Brazil, now possessing the two most powerful warships in the world, was being courted as a potential ally. A depression in the Brazilian economy coupled with the serious 22 November 1910 mutiny aboard *Minas Gerais* (named after the inland province) halted the dreadnought programme.

On 24 October 1917 Brazil declared war on the Central Powers. It was decided to send both units to Scapa Flow to join the Grand Fleet. *Minas Gerais* and *Sao Paulo* were in poor condition and lacked modern fire control equipment. *Sao Paulo* sailed for the New York N Yd in June 1918 to correct these problems. She broke down along the way and required extensive aid from US warships. *Sao Paulo*'s overhaul outlived the war and she remained in New York for two years. *Minas Gerais* underwent a similar refit following the return of her sister.

The most unusual design feature in the class was the engines. Unlike most contemporary dreadnoughts, they were powered by reciprocating engines instead of turbines. The armour plates were Krupp cemented type. The belt was 9in thick, tapering slightly fore and aft, while the same thickness was carried to the height of the upper deck over the citadel. This afforded protection to all of the barbette machinery, the boilers, magazines, and uptakes. The deck slopes were 2¼in and the aft conning tower 9in. The armour for both ships was manufactured by W G Armstrong, Whitworth & Co.

*Minas Gerais* was reconstructed between 1934 and 1937. She was converted to burn oil, new turbogenerators replaced the dynamos, and 2–4.7in AA guns were added. The two funnels were trunked into one. The ship was inactive in the latter years of her career. *Sao Paulo* was to have received a similar refit, but this was cancelled due to the poor condition of her hull and machinery; she was no more than a stationary guard ship from the 1930s until her sale. While *en route* for Europe for BU, she broke from her tow in a storm off the Azores (4 November 1951) and was lost without trace. *Minas Gerais* was BU 1954.

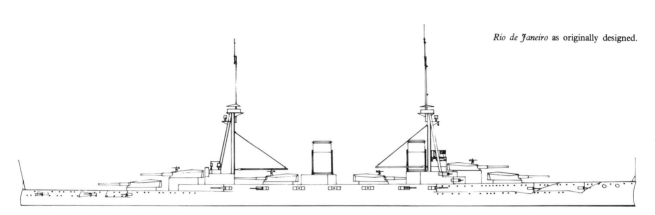

*Rio de Janeiro* as originally designed.

On 6 August 1910 Brazil astonished the naval world by announcing that she would have a third dreadnought built, *Rio de Janeiro*, to be the largest and most powerful warship in the world. The announcement was the outcome of prolonged rivalry between the 'ABC' countries of South America, Argentina, Brazil and Chile. To answer the Argentine *Moreno* and *Rivadavia* (12–12in guns), ordered in 1910 in the United States, Brazil looked at designs armed with 8–16in and 10–15in, but finally a 31,600t, 23kt design with 12–14in guns was accepted, to be built by Armstrong. The main armament was to be in twin turrets, two fore and aft and two slightly en echelon amidships. Such extravagant proposals were far ahead of any ship under construction for a major navy (the Japanese *Fuso*, the first with 12–14in guns, was not begun until March 1912). Nevertheless, the *Rio de Janeiro*'s keel was symbolically laid late in October 1910, but construction was almost immediately suspended pending confirmation by the incoming government. A strong movement in Brazil, led by the Navy League, pressed for a fourth dreadnought.

Two events undid these hopes and plans. On 22 November 1910 the *Minas Gerais* mutiny undermined public support for the Navy, and on 3 May 1911 the newly elected President Hermes Rodrigues da Fonseca shocked leading warship constructors by implying that the *Rio de Janeiro* would be an unmanageable white elephant. The contract was to be revised in favour of 'a powerful unit which will not be built on exaggerated lines such as have not yet stood the test of experience'.

The President considered that the navy needed sound reform and extra shore installations rather than more dreadnoughts. Battleship projects went ahead, however, and a Naval Mission was sent to Europe. German experts headed by the Kaiser strongly recommended a ship with the maximum number of 12in guns as the most desirable; the contract for a ship with 12–12in guns nearly went to Germany. When informed of this development, Armstrong's salesmen and designers were only too happy to revise their earlier designs, reducing tonnage and armament, and drew up plans for an immensely long 12in gun ship with seven turrets, all on the centreline. The design was accepted, and the *Rio de Janeiro* laid down again on 14 September 1911, but severe Brazilian economic difficulties led to problems in paying installments to Armstrong and in July 1912 to the ship being put up for sale. Finally, on 9 January 1914 Brazil sold the incomplete *Rio de Janeiro* to Turkey, citing the reasons as tactical incompatibility with the *Minas Gerais* class; negotiations had meanwhile been opened for a larger 15in gun ship, the *Riachuelo*.

In 1921 Great Britain offered to sell *Agincourt* (ex-*Sultan Osman I*, ex-*Rio de Janeiro*) to Brazil for £1 million. The proposal was seriously considered but decided against.

## RIO DE JANEIRO *battleship*

| | |
|---|---|
| **Displacement:** | As designed 31,600t normal |
| | As redesigned 27,500t normal |
| **Dimensions:** | 650ft pp, 690ft oa × 92ft × 26ft mean as designed |
| | *198.1m, 210.3m × 28.0m × 7.9m* |
| | 632ft pp, 671ft 6in oa × 89ft × 27ft mean as redesigned |
| | *192.6m, 204.7m × 27.1m × 8.2m* |
| **Machinery:** | 4-shaft Parsons geared turbines, 22 Babcock boilers, 45,000shp = 22kts. Coal 3000t, oil 500t |
| | (as redesigned) |
| **Armour:** | Belt 12in–6in (305mm–152mm), bulkheads 6in (152mm), barbettes 12in (305mm), CT 11in (279mm), decks 1.5in–1in (38mm–25mm) as designed |
| | Belt 9in–6in (229mm–152mm), bulkheads 6in–3in (152mm–76mm), barbettes 9in (229mm), CT 12in (305mm), decks 1.25in–1in (32mm–25mm) as redesigned |
| **Armament:** | 12–14in (356mm)/45 (6 × 2), 16–6in (152mm)/50, 14–4in (102mm)/50, 8–3pdr, 3–21in (533mm) TT sub as designed |
| | 14–12in (305mm)/50 (7 × 2), 20–6in (152mm)/50, 12–3in (76mm)/45, 8–3pdr, 3–21in (533mm) TT sub as redesigned |
| **Complement:** | 1100 (as redesigned) |

| Name | Builder | Laid down | Launched | Comp | Fate |
|---|---|---|---|---|---|
| RIO DE JANEIRO | Elswick | 14.9.11 | 22.1.13 | | Sold early 1914 while outfitting |

Launch of *Rio de Janeiro* at Elswick.
CPL

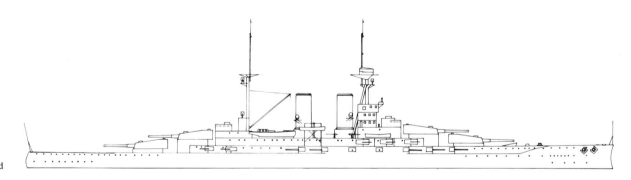

*Riachuelo* as designed

## RIACHUELO *battleship*

| | |
|---|---|
| **Displacement:** | 30,500t normal |
| **Dimensions:** | 620ft pp, 660ft oa × 94ft × 28ft mean |
| | *189.0m, 201.2m × 28.6m × 8.5m* |
| **Machinery:** | 4-shaft Parsons geared turbines, Babcock and Wilcox boilers, 40,000shp = 22.5kts. Coal 3500t, oil 700t. |
| **Armour:** | Belt 13.5in–4in (343mm–102mm), bulkheads 9in–7in (229mm–178mm), barbettes 13in–3in (330mm–76mm), turret faces 13in (330mm), CT 13in (330mm), decks 1.5in–0.75in (38mm–19mm) |
| **Armament:** | 8–15in (381mm)/45 (4 × 2), 14–6in (152mm)/50, 10–4in (102mm)/50, 4–3in (76mm) anti-balloon, 4–3pdr (47mm) saluting, 2–21in (533m) TT sub (beam) |
| **Complement:** | |

*Riachuelo* suffered the same fate as *Rio de Janeiro*. In September 1913 Brazil asked Armstrong (Elswick) shipyard to prepare alternative designs for a new battleship. Four designs were submitted, for ships displacing 31,500t–36,000t normal and fitted with 12–14in, 10 or 12–15in or 10–16in guns ('Designs A–D'). None was selected, but in February 1914 the construction of one ship was authorised, and three more designs were prepared and submitted. The ship, to be named *Riachuelo*, was ordered in May 1914 to

one of the designs (no. 781, Armstrong hull no. 879, see particulars in table), but little or no work was done prior to the outbreak of war and the keel was

not laid. It is not clear whether Brazil's economy would in practice have been strong enough to support the construction of this ship.

# Chile

---

## ALMIRANTE LATORRE class *battleships*

**Displacement:** 28,000t normal; 32,300t full load
**Dimensions:** 625ft pp, 661ft oa × 92ft × 28ft 6in mean, 30ft max
*190.5m, 201.5m × 28.0m × 8.7m, 9.1m*
**Complement:** 1176
**Other particulars:** British *Canada* class

| Name | Builder | Laid down | Launched | Comp | Fate |
|------|---------|-----------|----------|------|------|
| ALMIRANTE LATORRE (ex-*Valparaiso*, ex-*Libertad*) | Armstrong, Newcastle | 27.11.11 | 27.11.13 | 30.9.15 | Sold 1959 |
| ALMIRANTE COCHRANE (ex-*Santiago*, ex-*Constitution*) | Armstrong, Newcastle | 22.1.13 | – | – | See notes |

In 1911 Chile invited tenders for dreadnoughts to counter those ordered by Argentina, which, of course, had been ordered to counter Brazil's initial acquisitions. Although tenders were solicited in both Europe and the United States, Lt Cdr R W McNeely USN observed, 'there was being carried on in Chilean newspapers a systematic propaganda against American naval materials...' The Chilean Navy had strong ties with the Royal Navy, and it was not surprising when Armstrong was awarded the contract.

*Almirante Latorre* continued the time-honoured tradition of outclassing all preceding South American dreadnoughts in size and power. As originally designed she was to have displaced 27,400 tons normal, and carry 10–14in and 22–4.7in guns at 23kts, but following European trends the secondary armament was increased to 16–6in, for an extra 600t displacement, 6.5in draught and 0.25kts less speed.

Following the outbreak of war, *Almirante Latorre* was bought by the Royal Navy on 9 September 1914 and renamed *Canada*. *Almirante Cochrane* was purchased and taken over by the Royal Navy in 1917, renamed *Eagle* and converted into an aircraft carrier. *Canada* was repurchased by Chile in April 1920, and reverted to her prewar name. Chile also negotiated for *Eagle*, but she wanted the ship converted back to a battleship. This was impracticable. The Royal Navy offered, among other ships, two *I* class battlecruisers in her place. This proposal was not accepted. Ultimately, Chile settled for the one dreadnought.

Armour protection varied considerably throughout the ship. The belt had three thicknesses – lower 9in, middle 7in and upper 4.5in. The belt ends were 6in to 4in; this protection extended from the end of the barrel of the forward 14in gun for about 25ft and from the aft 14in gun turret for about 50ft. This left 50ft of the bow

and stern unarmoured. The secondary battery was protected by 6in of armour. The turrets were 10in–9in thick. Deck armour was as follows: shelter deck over casemates 1in, forecastle deck over 6in battery 1in, upper deck over 6in battery 1in, main deck aft 1.5in, protective deck 1in, lower deck forward 2in and aft 4in.

When completed, the range of the 14in guns was limited only by the maximum visibility. Initially, *Almirante Latorre* carried a total of 16–6in guns. The two which had been mounted on the upper deck abeam the aft funnel had to be removed. These guns had been damaged from the muzzle blasts from the 'Q' 14in turret, located just abaft the stack.

*Almirante Latorre* was modernised during 1929–31 in Devonport D Yd. She was fitted with anti-torpedo bulges, increasing beam to 103ft (31.4m), new Vickers-Armstrong turbines and boilers converted to burn oil fuel. The fuel capacity became

4300t oil, and the endurance 4400nm at 10kts. The main topmast was raised to 60ft, new fire control equipment was installed and the main armament elevation was increased. A catapult was fitted on the quarterdeck (removed c1938). The bridgework was modified and controls fitted at the ends of the upper bridge. In September 1931, just after returning to Chile, *Almirante Latorre*'s crew participated in a short-lived mutiny. In 1950 the main engines and auxiliary machinery were overhauled and the ship fitted with radar. In 1951 she suffered an engine room disaster and remained inactive during the remainder of her career.

*Almirante Latorre* on her way to the breakers.
*CPL*

# France

*Courbet* 1938–39, after her
second reconstruction. *CPL*

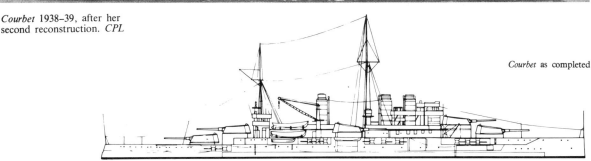

*Courbet* as completed

Authorised under the 1910 (*Courbet* and *Jean Bart*) and 1911 (remainder) programmes, these were the *Marine Nationale*'s first dreadnought-type battleships. Designed by M Lyasse. Although the armour thickness was increased by comparison with the *Danton*'s, it was thinner than was customary practice in the US and even the Royal Navy. The side armour extended comparatively far below the waterline, an arrangement due mainly to anxiety about underwater hits. Although the calibre of the medium guns – 138.6mm – was less than the generally prevalent 152mm, the slightly smaller guns had a higher rate of fire, which was important bearing in mind the problems of anti-torpedo-boat defence.

Trials results: *Courbet* 22.0kts, *Jean Bart* 22.6kts and *Paris* 21.7kts. Their 305mm guns were mounted in two pairs of twin turrets fore and aft and two twin turrets on the sides on the same frames. Ammunition carried: 100 for each 305mm gun, 275 for each 138.6mm gun together with 12 torpedoes and 30 mines (originally).

During World War One all four ships were employed in the Mediterranean. *Courbet* flew the flag of Vice-Admiral Boué de Lapeyrère and had searchlights added to a platform astern of her second funnel as well as her main mast removed to tow a kite balloon. All of the class had triple 3.6m (12ft) rangefinders installed above their CT. *Jean Bart* took a torpedo hit from the Austrian *U 12* in the Adriatic on 21 December 1914 in her wine store but the forward magazine just aft remained intact. She and *France*

## COURBET class *battleships*

**Displacement:** 22,189t standard; 23,475t normal; 25,579t full load
**Dimensions:** 541ft 4in wl, 544ft 7in oa × 88ft 7in × 29ft mean
*165.0m wl, 166.0m oa × 27.0m × 8.8m*
**Machinery:** 4-shaft Parsons turbines, 24 Belleville boilers (*France* and *Paris* fitted with Niclausse), 28,000ship = 20.0kts. Coal 906t plus oil 310t (coal 2706t plus oil 310t). Range 4200nm/1140nm at 10kts/20kts
**Armour:** Belt 270mm (10.6in) amidships, 180mm (7.1in) ends, upper belt 180mm (7.1in), main deck 70mm (2.8in), upper deck 50mm (2in), forecastle deck 30mm (1.2in), barbettes 270mm (10.6in), turrets 320mm (12.6in), casemates 180mm (7.1in), CT 300mm (11.8in) with 270mm (10.6in) roof
**Armament:** 12–12in (305mm)/45 Mod 10 (6 × 2), 22–5.5in (138.6mm)/55 Mod 10, 4–47mm, 4–17.7in (450mm) TT sub
**Complement:** 1085–1108

| Name | Builder | Laid down | Launched | Comp | Fate |
|---|---|---|---|---|---|
| COURBET | Arsenal de Brest | 1.9.10 | 23.9.11 | 19.11.13 | Scuttled 9.6.44 |
| FRANCE | A C de la Loire, St-Nazaire | 30.11.11 | 7.11.12 | July or Aug 1914 | Foundered 26.8.22 |
| JEAN BART | Arsenal de Brest | 15.11.10 | 22.9.11 | 5.6.13 | Sold for BU 14.12.45 |
| PARIS | F C de la Méditerranée La Seyne | 10.11.11 | 28.9.12 | 1.8.14 | Sold for BU 21.12.55 |

rounded off their Great War active service in the 1919 Sevastopol operation. Although the *Courbet*s were considered very carefully constructed and highly detailed in finish, they rapidly became obsolete after 1918 because no thorough modernisation work was carried out. The wetness of the foredeck in a rough sea was caused mainly by the weight of the superimposed turrets (each 561t, of which 234t was armour) and the fact that there were no drydocks long enough to allow their hulls to be lengthened.

With the exception of *France* (wrecked on an unchartered rock in Quiberon Bay), this class was refitted

1926–29. The major modifications were the trunking of the two forward funnels into a single uptake, replacing the pole foremast with a tripod, enlarging the bridgework, fitting improved fire control gear, increasing the elevation of the main armament guns to give a range of 23,000yds compared with the previous 14,500yds and increasing AA armament to 7–3in and 2–45mm. *Courbet* was also reboilered at La Seyne in 1929 with small-tube boilers originally ordered for the cancelled *Normandie* class battleships.

*Jean Bart* was renamed *Océan* in 1936 and disarmed in 1938 for service as a training ship. On 7.3.44 she was

damaged by bombs during an Allied air raid and on 15.3.44 was used for explosives trials by the Germans and sank. Subsequently salvaged, she was finally broken up during 1946–47 at Toulon. *Courbet* and *Paris* became training ships in 1939 and were taken over by the RN on 3.7.40; *Courbet* was subsequently transferred to the FNFL and served as an AA guardship while *Paris* was used as an accommodation ship. *Courbet* was expended as part of the Normandy breakwater while *Paris* was returned to France and towed to Brest in August 1945 where she served as a pontoon from 1950 until sold.

*Bretagne* in about 1938 after the reconstruction.
*CPL*

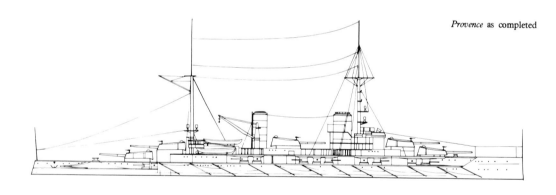

*Provence* as completed

Provided under the 1912 programme (as replacements for *Carnot, Charles Martel* and *Liberté*) and while they had the same hull and dimensions as the *Courbet* class they had a heavier main armament and a single centreline turret replaced the wing turrets amidships. *Bretagne* class battleships were comparatively well designed although their underwater protection was insufficient. Some sources state the armour belt was 250mm (9.8in) amidships. Particular attention was also paid to the weapon and command control equipment. *Bretagne* class battleships were very wet forward and were the only French ships originally fitted with Bullivant net defence, removed in 1917. They had the disadvantage of a shorter gun range than most equivalent ships at that time — the maximum range being 14,500m for the 340mm guns, although in 1917 *Lorraine*'s range was increased to 18,000m by increasing the aftermost

## BRETAGNE class *battleships*

| | |
|---|---|
| **Displacement:** | 22,189t standard; 23,558t normal; 26,180t full load |
| **Dimensions:** | 541ft 4in wl, 544ft 7in oa × 88ft 7in × 29ft 2in mean |
| | *165.0m wl, 166.0m oa × 27.0m × 8.9m* |
| **Machinery:** | 4-shafts, 2 Parsons geared turbines, 24 Niclausse boilers (*Provence* 18 Belleville, *Lorraine* 24 Guyot du Temple), 29,000shp = 20kts. Coal 900t plus oil 300t (coal 2680t plus oil 300t). Range 4700nm/2800nm at 10kts/18.75kts |
| **Armour:** | Belt 270mm (10.6in) amidships, 160mm (6.3in) ends, casemates 170mm (6.7in), main deck 70mm (2.8in), upper deck 50mm (2in), forecastle deck 30mm (1.2in), barbettes 248mm (9.8in), centre turret 400mm (15.7in), superfiring turrets 250mm (9.8in), end turrets 340mm (13.4in), CT 314mm (12.4in) |
| **Armament:** | 10-13.4in (340mm)/45 Mod 12 (5 × 2), 22-5.5in (138.6mm)/55 Mod 10, 4-47mm, 4-17.7in (450mm) TT sub (24 torpedoes), up to 30 mines |
| **Complement:** | 1124-1133 |

| Name | Builder | Laid down | Launched | Comp | Fate |
|---|---|---|---|---|---|
| BRETAGNE | Arsenal de Brest | 1.7.12 | 21.4.13 | 9.15 | Sunk 3.7.40 |
| LORRAINE | A C de St-Nazaire-Penhoët | 1.8.12 | 30.9.13 | 7.16 | BU 1954 |
| PROVENCE | Arsenal de Lorient | 1.5.12 | 20.4.13 | 6.15 | See notes |

*Lorraine*, 13 September 1944.
CPL

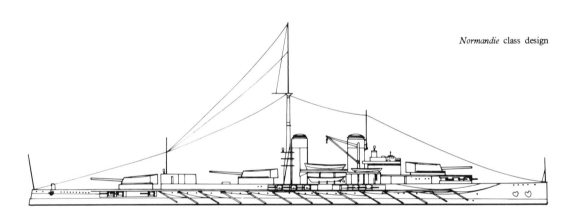

*Normandie* and *Languedoc* were ordered on 12 December 1912, *Gascogne* and *Flandre* on 30 July 1913. *Béarn* was approved as a fifth ship on 3 December 1913 to maintain the divisional formation of four battleships with three *Bretagne*s. These ships were fitted with 340mm quadruple turrets which were lighter in total than the *Bretagne*'s 5 double turrets and meant that 2 further guns could be fitted.

The originally proposed double casemate mountings for the 138.6mm guns were not adopted and the conventional single casemate mountings were retained instead. All, except *Béarn*, were designed with 2 4cyl TE on lateral shafts and 2 Parsons (*Gascogne* Rateau-Bretagne, *Languedoc* Schneider-Zoelly) direct action turbines on central shafts without reversing gear.

This class's mixed machinery was considered an unsatisfactory arrangement despite the expected lower fuel consumption than in the turbine-driven *Bretagne* class. Reciprocating engines were to be used mainly for cruising. The turbines were designed

## NORMANDIE class *battleships*

| | |
|---|---|
| **Displacement:** | 25,230t full load |
| **Dimensions:** | 559ft 9in pp, 576ft 2in wl, 579ft 5in oa × 88ft 7in × 28ft 5in |
| | *170.6m pp, 175.6m wl, 176.6m oa × 27m × 8.65m* |
| **Machinery:** | 4-shaft TE and turbines or turbines only (see notes), 21 small tube Guyot du Temple boilers (*Flandre* and *Languedoc* 28 small tube Belleville, *Béarn* 21 small tube Niclausse), 32,000shp = 21kts (an increase to 45,000shp = 22kts was planned). Coal 900t/2700t plus oil 300t. Range 6500nm/3375nm/1800nm at 12kts/16kts/21kts |
| **Armour:** | Belt 300mm (11.8in) amidships, 120mm–180mm (4.7in–7.1in) ends, upper belt 240mm (9.4in) amidships, 160mm (6.3in) ends, upper deck 50mm (2in), lower deck 50mm (2in) with slopes 70mm (2.8in), barbettes 284mm (11.2in), turrets 250mm–340mm (9.8in–13.4in), casemates 160mm–180mm (6.3in–7.1in), CT 300mm (11.8in) |
| **Armament:** | 12–13.4in (340mm)/45 Mod 12 (3 × 4), 24–5.5in (138.6mm)/55 Mod 10, 6–47mm AA, 6–17.7in (450mm) TT sub |
| **Complement:** | 1200 |

| Name | Builder | Laid down | Launched | Comp | Fate |
|---|---|---|---|---|---|
| BÉARN | F C de la Méditerranée, La Seyne | 10.1.14 | 4.20 | See notes | Converted 1923–27 to aircraft carrier |
| FLANDRE | Arsenal de Brest | 1.10.13 | 20.10.14 | — | BU from 10.24 |
| GASCOIGNE | Arsenal de Lorient | 1.10.13 | 20.9.14 | — | BU 1923–24 |
| LANGUEDOC | F C de la Gironde, Bordeaux | 18.4.13 | 1.5.16 | — | BU from 6.29 |
| NORMANDIE | A C de la Loire | 18.4.13 | 19.10.14 | — | BU 1924–25 |

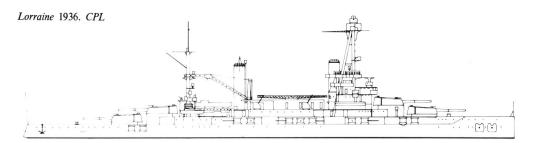

*Lorraine 1936. CPL*

turret's elevation (from 12 to 18 degrees). Similar changes to *Bretagne* and *Provence* as well as to *Lorraine*'s remaining turrets were not made before November 1918 due to the amount of work in French dockyards.

All three ships joined the *Armée Navale* in 1916, *Provence* being flagship until 1919 and beginning her service with the Athens and Salamis operations. *Lorraine* was detached to Cattaro in January and March 1919 for repatriating Austrian crews and delivering Austrian ships to France and Italy.

The range of the main armament was increased in 1921–23 by increasing the elevation from 18 deg to 23 deg, and all were converted to partial oil-firing in 1927–30, and extensively reconstructed between 1932 and 1935. This involved improved internal protection, new oil-burning small-tube boilers (for 43,000shp = 21kts), and new 13.4in guns (originally intended for the cancelled *Normandie* class) and augmented AA armament of 8–75mm/75 (8 × 1), the submerged TT and 8–5.5in guns being removed. *Lorraine*'s rebuilding went one stage further, the centre 13.4in turret being replaced by a hangar for 4 Loire-Nieuport 130 seaplanes and a catapult. The AA armament was 8–3.9in (100mm)/60 (4 × 2). Catapult and aircraft were removed in 1943, and the final light AA armament comprised 14–40mm and 25–20mm.

*Bretagne* blew up and sank on 3 July 1940 at Mers-el-Kebir (977 crew killed) under the fire of British battleships; salvaged in 1952 and BU. *Lorraine* disarmed under French control, July 1940, at Alexandria, but was fighting again by 30 May 1943. She joined the FNFL and served in the Mediterranean. Between 1945 and 1953 used as a TS and finally hulked and stricken on 17 February 1953 and BU in January 1954. *Provence* battle-damaged and beached during British action at Mers-el-Kebir was brought to Toulon for repairs November 1940 and scuttled on 27 November 1942. Raised 11 July 1943 by the Germans and had her twin 340mm turrets removed and installed as a coast battery near Toulon. Scuttled 1944 by the Germans as a blockship and was raised April 1949 and BU.

---

for steaming ahead only. However, the turbine drive (with 4 Parsons turbines only) was retained for the last of the class – *Béarn*. These ships were left unfinished when war broke out in 1914 as workers joined up and afterwards some of them were left lying incomplete for years. Equipment such as boilers earmarked for the class were fitted to other warships whereas some of the 340mm and 138.6mm guns – in so far as they were completed at all – were placed at the disposal of the Army and were put into action on various fronts. Some of the completed 340mm guns were fitted after 1918 in *Bretagne*s as replacements for their original guns.

Before these battleships were stricken and the orders cancelled, there were discussions as to whether or not they should be completed, bearing in mind recent First World War experience. Considered necessary were: increase in speed from 21–21.5kts to 24kts–25kts, which would have necessitated increasing the propulsive power to 80,000shp (replacing the machinery with new turbines); lengthening the hull and fitting torpedo bulges with a maximum width of 1m each; increasing the range of main guns from 16,000m–16,500m to 25,000m–26,000m; fitting a tripod mast with gunnery control position; improving the internal (mainly horizontal) protection; replacing the 450mm TT by 550mm. For *Béarn* the following alterations were also proposed: replacing the Niclausse boilers by 8 oil-fired boilers of latest design and replacing the turbines with new ones (80,000shp = 24–25kts), and finally an investigation into whether a completely new 340mm quadruple turret with a greater range could be developed and, if not, a discussion on the development of 400mm twin turrets.

Naval specialists were of the opinion that these ships should not be completed and this combined with a shortage of funds meant that the building programme was stopped. France already had 7 dreadnoughts at her disposal, but even so she was now on a par with Italy's navy as far as this class of ship was concerned.

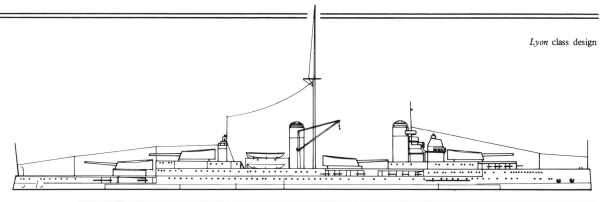

*Lyon class design*

## LYON class *battleships*

| | |
|---|---|
| **Displacement:** | 29,000t full load |
| **Dimensions:** | 623ft 4in pp, 638ft 2in oa × 95ft 2in × 28ft 5in, 30ft 2in<br>*190.0m pp, 194.5m oa × 29.0m × 8.65m, 9.2m* |
| **Machinery:** | 4-shaft turbines and VTE, boilers, 43,000shp = 23kts, see notes |
| **Armour:** | See notes |
| **Armament:** | 16–13.4in (340mm)/45 Mod 12M (4 × 4), 24–5.5in (138.6mm)/55 Mod 10, or of a new semi-automatic type to be developed, 40mm AA or 47mm AA, 6 TT sub |
| **Complement:** | ? |

Authorised under the 1912 programme to a design by M Doyère, none of them were actually started. Orders for *Lille* and *Lyon* were to have been placed on 1 January 1915 and for *Duquesne* and *Tourville* on 1 April 1915, but were not carried out. Had they been built, these ships which were an enlargement of the *Normandie*s, but more heavily armed, would have been the world's most awesome warships. A few designs had been presented to the naval staff: 27,500t, 14–340mm; 28,500t– 29,000t, 16–340mm; 27,000t, 8–380mm, 28,500t–29,000t, 10–380mm or 20–305mm (5 × 4). The amount of time taken to design a 380mm gun meant that this possibility was rejected as were two 340mm designs, one of which – a 45 calibre gun – was similar to that fitted in *Bretagne*

| Name | Builder | Laid down | Launched | Comp | Fate |
|---|---|---|---|---|---|
| DUQUESNE | Arsenal de Brest | – | – | – | – |
| LILLE | F C de la Méditerranée,<br>La Seyne | – | – | – | – |
| LYON | A C de la Loire et<br>Penhoët, St-Nazaire | – | – | – | – |
| TOURVILLE | Arsenal de Lorient | – | – | – | – |

and *Normandie*. Finally a compromise was reached which meant increasing the number of guns while retaining the 340mm calibre: two alternative projects were discussed. The first envisaged 14-340mm and the second 16-340mm. In the case of the ship with 14-340mm guns (three quadruple and one twin turret) the displacement was 27,500t on 185m wl × 28m × 8.65m hull. Finally it was decided on 24 November 1913 to adopt the second design (16-340mm/45) envisaging 4 quadruple turrets with hydraulic-electric mountings and all-round loading positions. The outbreak of the First World War put an early end to these designs and construction was not started. The question of propulsion was left undecided: it was proposed to fit combined machinery as in *Normandie* or direct drive turbines as fitted in *Béarn* and the earlier dreadnoughts. Doyere also considered the use of the geared turbines. Trials with *Enseigne Gabolde* had produced favourable results using this type of machinery. It was proposed that the class would have the same type of armour as the *Normandie* class, the difference being slightly thinner upper deck and casemates and stronger submerged sections.

---

The Naval Law of 30 March 1912 projected for the *Marine Nationale* a strength of 28 capital ships by 1920. Battlecruisers may well have been included in this figure. A specification for battlecruisers was drawn up later by the technical branch of the navy as follows: design displacement 28,000t, speed 27kts, armament 8-340mm, complement was to be no more than 1200 officers and men. Various studies were made by some French naval designers and two of the most complete designs are listed below. These ships were never ordered or even authorised.

This battlecruiser project prepared in 1913 was named after its designer. It could however only be regarded as a starting point for future work, which was never carried out. This project envisaged a fast battleship type (inspired by the British *Queen Elizabeth* class) rather than a true battlecruiser, which would be well armed and relatively lightly armoured. Even the French classification – '*cuirassé-croseur*' – suggested a new kind of ship, a forerunner of the new, fast capital ships of World War Two.

## Gille's battlecruiser design of 1913

| | |
|---|---|
| **Displacement:** | 28,100t–28,347t |
| **Dimensions:** | 672ft 7in pp × 88ft 7in × 29ft 6in |
| | *205.0m pp × 27.0m × 9.0m* |
| **Machinery:** | 4-shaft geared turbines, 52 Belleville boilers, 80,000shp = 28kts. Coal 2833t plus oil 630t for supplementary burners. Range 6300nm/4240nm/1660nm at 15kts/20.3kts/28kts |
| **Armour:** | Belt 270mm (10.6in) max |
| **Armament:** | 12-13.4in (340mm) (3 × 4), 24-5.5in (138.6mm), 6 TT sub |
| **Complement:** | 1299 |

---

Naval designer and later an admiral, M Durand-Viel prepared some designs of new capital ships according to the general specifications of the 1912 programme. There were three final designs: a slow battleship of 32,000t, 10-38mm (5 × 2) or 29,000t, 9-380mm (3 × 3) or 30,000t, 16-340mm (4 × 4) and a fast battleship of 27,500t, 10-380mm (2 × 3, 2 × 2) or 27,500t, 14-340mm (2 × 4, 3 × 2) and a battlecruiser in two variants called 'A' and 'B' (for data see above tables).

## Durand-Viel's battlecruiser design of 1913 – 'A'

| | |
|---|---|
| **Displacement:** | 27,065t designed |
| **Dimensions:** | 689ft wl × 88ft 7in × 28ft 7in |
| | *210.0m wl × 27.0m × 8.7m* |
| **Machinery:** | 4-shaft turbines, 21 Belleville boilers, 74,000shp = 27kts. Coal 1810t plus oil 1050t max. Range 3600nm at 16kts |
| **Armour:** | Very similar to *Normandie*s, but main belt 280mm (11in) max |
| **Armament:** | 8-13.4in (340mm) (2 × 4), 24-5.5in (138.6mm), 4-17.7in (450mm) TT sub |
| **Complement:** | ? |

---

## Durand-Viel's battlecruiser design of 1913 – 'B'

| | |
|---|---|
| **Displacement:** | As 'A' |
| **Dimensions:** | As 'A', but 682ft 5in wl (*208.0m*) |
| **Machinery:** | 4-shaft turbines, 18 Belleville (10 coal, 8 oil), 63,000shp = 26kts or 4-shaft geared turbines, 18 Belleville (10 coal, 8 oil), 80,000shp = 27kts. Range as 'A' |
| **Armour:** | As 'A' |
| **Armament:** | 8-14.6in (370mm) (2 × 4), 24-5.5in (138.6mm), 4-17.7in TT sub |
| **Complement:** | ? |

Sometimes classed as battlecruisers, these vessels initiated the general trend towards fast battleship designs among the major European navies. Intended as an answer to the German *Deutschland* class, they were given a high speed and comparatively light protection – the latter being only intended to defeat the German 11in AP shell with which the *Deutschland* (and later *Scharnhorst*) class were armed. *Dunkerque* was provided under the 1931 Programme and *Strasbourg* under the 1934 Programme as replacements for the battleships *France* (lost in 1922) and *Océan* (disarmed 1938) respectively, according to current treaty requirements. In outline the design was based on the British *Nelson* class with the entire main armament forward, a tower bridge structure and internal side protection. The original designed displacement was 26,500t standard, 33,000t deep load. During 2-hour full-power trials, *Dunkerque* made 31.06kts with 135,585shp and, during 8-hour full-power trials, 30.75 kts with 114,050shp. *Strasbourg* achieved similar results. The armour figures in the table are for *Dunkerque; Strasbourg* had slightly thicker armour: belt 11.8in–5.5.in (300mm–140mm), main turrets 14.2in–6.3in (360mm–160mm); decks were 0.4in (10mm) more than in *Dunkerque*. In both ships, the main armour belt was inclined at 21 degrees and was intended to resist 11in AP shells at normal inclination down to a range of 18,000yds (*Dunkerque*) or 14,000yds (*Strasbourg*). The underwater protection consisted of air and fuel compartments bounded on the inboard side by the torpedo bulkhead and outboard by a compartment filled

## DUNKERQUE class *battleships*

| | |
|---|---|
| **Displacement:** | 26,500t standard; 30,750t (*Strasbourg* 31,400t) normal; 35,500t deep load |
| **Dimensions:** | 685ft 8in pp, 703ft 9in oa × 102ft × 28ft 6in |
| | *209.0m, 214.5m × 31.1m × 8.7m* |
| **Machinery:** | 4-shaft Parsons geared turbines, 6 Indret boilers, 112,500shp = 29.5kts. Oil 6500t |
| **Armour:** | Belt 9.5in–5.5in (240mm–140mm), decks 5.5in–1.6in (140mm–40mm), torpedo bulkhead 1.6in (40mm), main turrets 13.2in–5.9in (335mm–150mm), secondary turrets 3.5in (90mm), CT 10.6in (270mm) |
| **Armament:** | 8-13in (330mm)/50 Mod 33 (2 × 4), 16-5.1in (130mm)/45 Mod 35 DP (3 × 4, 2 × 2), 8-37mm AA (4 × 2), 32-13.2mm AA (8 × 4), 4 aircraft |
| **Complement:** | 1431 |

| Name | Builder | Laid down | Launched | Comp | Fate |
|---|---|---|---|---|---|
| DUNKERQUE | Arsenal de Brest | 24.12.32 | 2.10.35 | Apr 1937 | Scuttled 27.11.42 |
| STRASBOURG | A C de St-Nazaire-Penhoët | 25.11.34 | 12.12.36 | Dec 1938 | Scuttled 27.11.42 |

with a rubber-based, water-excluding compound. The quadruple turret design was originally evolved for the cancelled battleships of the *Normandie* class and provided the 13in guns with 35° elevation giving a maximum range of 32,800yds. The turrets were spaced well apart to avoid the possibility of a single shell of torpedo neutralising them both and to minimise mutual interference due to blast effect. Ammunition stowage allowed for 800 rounds of 13in, 7865 rounds of 5.1in and 20,200 rounds of 37mm. One catapult was fitted.

Prior to the French surrender the two ships were employed mainly in covering Atlantic convoys against interference by raiders. Both were at Mers-el-Kebir (Oran) on 3 July 1940, where *Dunkerque* was heavily hit by 15in gunfire from the British fleet, one turret and machinery spaces being penetrated, and, 3 days later, by torpedo aircraft from *Ark Royal*, ex-

tensive damage being caused when a ship loaded with depth charges was torpedoed and blew up alongside. *Strasbourg* escaped and moved to Toulon where she was joined by *Dunkerque*, after temporary repairs, in February 1942. Both were scuttled at Toulon (*Dunkerque* in dry dock) in November 1942 but *Strasbourg* was salvaged by the Italian Navy in the following year. She was returned in 1944 and sunk during an Allied bombing raid on Toulon on 18.8.44. She was salvaged again in 1945 and after service as an experimental hulk for underwater tests, was sold for scrapping in May 1955. The wreck of the *Dunkerque* was removed from the drydock in 1945 and was eventually sold for scrap in 1958.

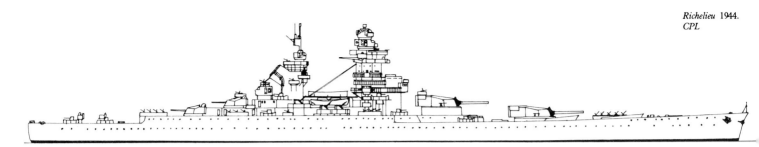

The first 2 were authorised in 1935 and the remaining pair in 1938, and were designed to carry 8-15in, 15-6in, 8-37mm and 24-13.2mm. The armament of the first two was subsequently altered owing to the exigencies of war, while more substantial changes were made to the design of the uncompleted pair. They followed the general design of the *Dunkerque* class with a high proportion (37 per cent) of displacement given over to protection (against 15in shellfire). The main belt was again internal, and inclined to the vertical; the main deck was flat on top; and the lower (splinter) deck was at the level of the waterline, but sloped down near the sides of the ship to meet the lower edge of the belt. The 380mm (1935 pattern) main armament fired a 1938lb shell at between 1 and 2 rounds per minute to a range of 50,000yds at 35° elevation. Magazine capacity was originally 832-15in and 2800-6in, but in 1943 this became 650-15in, 3000-6in and 6500-3.9in. The *Richelieu*'s machinery

*Richelieu* 1954. *CPL*

## RICHELIEU class *battleships*

| | |
|---|---|
| **Displacement:** | 38,500t (*Jean Bart* 42,807t) standard; 43,293t (*Jean Bart* 46,500t) normal; 47,548t (*Jean Bart* 49,850t) deep load |
| **Dimensions:** | 794ft pp, 813ft 2in oa × 108ft 3in (*Jean Bart* 116ft 3in over bulges) × 31ft 7in (*Jean Bart* 30ft 3in) *242.0m, 247.8m × 33.0m (35.4m) × 9.6m (9.2m)* |
| **Machinery:** | 4-shaft Parsons geared turbines, 6 Indret boilers, 150,000shp = 30kts (*Jean Bart* 165,000shp = 32kts). Oil 6796t (*Jean Bart* 6476t) |
| **Armour:** | Belt 13.6in (330mm), fore bulkhead 15in-9.8in (380mm-250mm), torpedo bulkhead 1.2in-2in (30mm-50mm), main deck 6.7in-5.9in (170mm-150mm), lower deck 2in-1.6in (50mm-40mm), main turrets 16.9in-6.7in (430mm-170mm), secondary turrets 5.1in-2.8in (130mm-70mm), CT 13.8in (340mm) |
| **Armament:** | (*Richelieu* in 1940) 8-15in (381mm)/45 Mod 35 (2 × 4), 9-6in (152mm)/55 Mod 36 DP (3 × 3), 12-3.9in (100mm)/45 Mod 31 AA (6 × 2), 8-37mm AA (4 × 2), 16-13.2mm AA (4 × 4), 3 aircraft |
| **Complement:** | 1670 (*Richelieu* in 1940), 2134 (*Jean Bart* as flagship) |

| Name | Builder | Laid down | Launched | Comp | Fate |
|---|---|---|---|---|---|
| RICHELIEU | Arsenal de Brest | 22.10.35 | 17.1.39 | July 1940 | Stricken 1959, BU 1964 |
| JEAN BART | A C de St-Nazaire-Penhoët | Jan 1939 | 6.3.40 | Jan 1949 | Stricken 1961 BU 1970 |
| CLEMENCEAU | Arsenal de Brest | 17.1.39 | 1943 | — | Hull sunk 27.8.44 |
| GASCOIGNE | A C de St-Nazaire-Penhoët | — | — | — | Cancelled |

*Jean Bart* at Toulon after 1961.
CPL

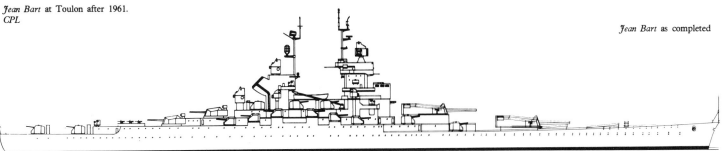

*Jean Bart* as completed

was built by A C de la Loire, St-Nazaire, and *Jean Bart*'s by F C de l'Atlantique.

*Richelieu* was 95 per cent complete when France surrendered, and was ordered to Dakar, where she was temporarily immobilised during the British attack on 8 July 1940. An attempt was made to disable propellers and steering gear by dropping depth charges from a motor boat, while an airborne torpedo hit right aft. However, she was still able to help repel the British and Free French attack in September 1940; in 1942 she joined the Allies and was sent to the USA for a major refit, emerging in October 1943 with radar added, aircraft and catapults removed, and the 37mm and 13.2mm AA replaced by 56–40mm (14×4) and 48–20mm (48×1). This increased displacement by 3000t, 500t of which was increased bunkerage. Range was 5500/2500/1800nm at 18/26/32kts and during postwar trials she reached 179,000shp = 32.5kts. *Richelieu* was employed with the British Eastern Fleet in 1944–45 and later off French Indo-China. After the war she remained largely unaltered, except for the removal of some

of the smaller AA weapons, until placed in reserve in 1956. She paid off in 1959 and was hulked at Brest as an accommodation ship.

*Jean Bart* was an estimated 77 per cent complete when France was overrun, but escaped to Casablanca in June 1940 under her own power. Only the forward 15in turret was mounted and it was late 1942 before this was in any condition to fire. At the time of the US invasion of North Africa *Jean Bart* also carried 8–90mm (4 × 2), 5–37mm (2 × 2, 1 × 1) and 22–13.2mm (4 × 2, 14 × 1) AA; during this attack the ship was badly damaged, being hit by three bombs from carrier aircraft and 5 16in shells from the battleship *Massachusetts* (only two of which exploded). The work of completion did not begin until 1946 at Brest, although various proposals for make-shift completion (with one main turret or as an aircraft carrier) were put forward during the later stages of the war. Completion was delayed because of postwar French economic difficulties and, but for the strength of public opinion, would probably have been abandoned. Sea trials began on 16.1.49 when she obtained 162,855shp = 31.84kts over 6

hours and 176,030shp = 32.13kts for 2 hours. The new AA armament was not installed until the winter of 1951–52. In May 1955 she was finally completed with 8–15in/45 (2 × 4), 9–6in (3 × 3), 24–3.9in AA (12 × 2), 28–57mm (14 × 2), 20–20mm (20 × 1). The 3.9in turrets were disposed symmetrically in four groups on either side of the superstructure. There were six of the new 57mm twin mountings amidships, with four abreast 'B' turret and a further four on the quarterdeck. Modifications were made to the turret mast, and the latest search and fire control radars fitted. To compensate for the increased topweight, *Jean Bart* was fitted with a tear-shaped anti-torpedo bulge which increased beam to 35.4m. She was present as a fire support ship at Suez in 1956, and subsequently served with the Mediterranean Fleet and as gunnery school tender. Paid off in January 1961, she was hulked at Toulon as accommodation ship for the gunnery school, with main battery in place but AA guns removed.

*Clemenceau*, like her sisters, was built in drydock and was only 10 per cent complete in June 1940. The incomplete hull, about 133m × 20m ×

10m deep (436ft × 66ft × 33ft), was floated out in 1943 and later bombed by Allied aircraft, on 27.8.44. The design incorporated some modifications to the secondary armament (12–6in) and AA guns, with aircraft facilities deleted.

*Gascoigne* was to have had the main armament turrets mounted one forward and one aft. She was never laid down. Two sisters were approved in April 1940 – although they may have been built to a new design – but were not begun.

# Germany

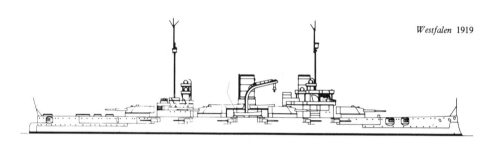

*Westfalen* 1919

The first German dreadnoughts, built under the 1906-7 programme (and that of 1907-8 for *Rheinland* and *Posen*), were flush-decked ships, easily distinguished by their goose-neck cranes. Freeboard at normal load was about 22ft forward, 17ft 9in midships and 19ft 6in aft with GM 7.65ft, and it was originally thought that bilge keels were not necessary. It was found however that their rolling was synchronous with the North Sea swell and bilge keels had to be fitted. *Nassau*, and particularly *Westfalen*, were not so satisfactory as the other two.

The heavy gun turrets were arranged fore and aft on the centreline with two on either beam, a peculiar distribution which gave a broadside of only 8 guns. The beam turret mountings were Drh LC/1906 in all ships as were the centreline mountings in *Nassau* and *Westfalen*, but the other two had Drh LC/1907 here: C/1906 was a short trunk mounting with fixed working chamber while C/1907 was of long trunk type. Both allowed 20° elevation. Magazines were above shell rooms except for the centreline turrets in *Nassau* and *Westfalen*. The 15cm was on the main deck, and 2-8.8in Flak L/45 eventually replaced the 8.8cm SKL/45 guns. The TT were located at bow and stern and on either beam forward and abaft the torpedo bulkhead.

The belt was 11.8in–11.5in between end barbettes for about 4ft along the lwl, tapering to 6.3in at the main deck and to 6.7in at the lower edge 63in below lwl. Forward it was 5.5in–3.1in and aft 4.7in–3.5in. The barbettes were 11in–7.9in reduced to 3.1in–2in behind the battery and belt, and the turrets had 11in faces, 8.7in sides, 10.3in rears and 3.5in–2.4in roofs. The armour deck was 1.5in with 2.3in slopes amidships, 2.2in forward and

3.1in–2.2in aft with the upper deck 1.2in–1in over the battery. The torpedo bulkhead ran between end barbettes and was 1.2in–0.8in.

There were 6 boiler and 3 engine rooms and 160 tons of tar oil were later carried for spraying on the coal in the furnaces. Boiler pressure was 235lb/in². Trials were prolonged, the commissioning dates being *Nassau* 1 October 1909, *Westfalen* 16 November 1909, *Rheinland* 30 April 1910, *Posen* 31 May 1910. On the mile all attained 20–20.2kts with 26,244–28,117ihp.

*Rheinland* ran aground at 15kts on rocks off Lagskär on 11 April 1918 and over 6000t, including belt armour and all guns, had to be removed before she could be got to Kiel; she was never repaired. *Westfalen* was torpedoed amidships by *E 23* on 19 August 1916 and took on 800t of water, but though bulkheads were sagging, she returned to harbour at 14kts.

## NASSAU class *battleships*

| | |
|---|---|
| **Displacement:** | 18,570t normal; 21,000t deep load |
| **Dimensions:** | 451ft 9in pp, 479ft 4in oa × 88ft 5in (*Nassau* 88ft 2in) × 26ft 6in mean, 29ft 3in mean deep load |
| | *137.7m, 146.1m × 26.9m × 8.08m, 8.9m* |
| **Machinery:** | 3-shaft 3-cyl VTE, 12 Schulz-Thornycroft boilers, 22,000ihp = 19.5kts. Coal 2950t. Range 8000nm/2200nm at 10kts/19kts |
| **Armour:** | Belt 300mm–80mm (11.8in–3.1in), bulkheads 210mm–90mm (8.3in–3.9in), battery 160mm (6.3in), barbettes 280mm–50mm (11in–2in), turrets 280mm–60mm (11in–2.4in), CT 300mm–80mm (11.8in–3.2in) |
| **Armament:** | 12-11in (280mm) SKL/45 (6 × 2), 12-5.9in (150mm) SKL/45, 16-3.5in (88mm) SKL/45, 6-17.7in (450mm) TT sub |
| **Complement:** | 1008 (1124–1139 at Jutland) |

| Name | Builder | Laid down | Launched | Comp | Fate |
|---|---|---|---|---|---|
| NASSAU | Wilhelmshaven N Yd | 22.7.07 | 7.3.08 | 3.5.10 | BU 1921 |
| WESTFALEN | Weser, Bremen | 12.8.07 | 1.7.08 | 3.5.10 | BU 1924 |
| RHEINLAND | Vulcan, Stettin | 1.6.07 | 26.9.08 | 21.9.10 | BU 1921 |
| POSEN | Germaniawerft, Kiel | 11.6.07 | 12.12.08 | 21.9.10 | BU 1922 |

*Posen* as completed.
CPL

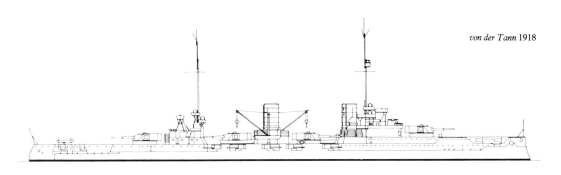

*von der Tann* 1918

This ship, the first German battle-cruiser and built under the 1907–8 programme, was a considerably better fighting ship than any of the 6 British 12in gun battlecruisers. There was a short forecastle extending to the foremast and at normal load freeboard was about 26½ft forward and 19ft amidships and aft. GM is given as 6.92ft and Frahm anti-rolling tanks were fitted during construction, but were later used to take 200 tons of extra coal, and bilge keels fitted instead. Fighting draught was less than deep load and was 28ft 11in (8.8m) with displacement 21,082 tons.

The main turrets were disposed fore and aft with 2 echelonned amidships, the latter being sufficiently far inboard

## VON DER TANN *battlecruiser*

| | |
|---|---|
| **Displacement:** | 19,064t normal; 21,700t deep load |
| **Dimensions:** | 563ft 4in oa × 87ft 3in × 26ft 6¾in mean, 29ft 8in mean at deep load |
| | *171.7m × 26.6m × 8.1m, 9.0m* |
| **Machinery:** | 4-shaft Parsons turbines, 18 Schulz-Thornycroft boilers, 43,600shp = 24.75kts. Coal 2760t + 200t in Frahm tanks. Range 4400nm at 14kts |
| **Armour:** | Belt 250mm–80mm (9.8in–3.1in), bulkheads 180mm–100mm (7.1in–3.9in), battery 150mm (5.9in), barbettes 230mm–30mm (9.1in–1.2in), turrets 230mm–60mm (9.1in–2.4in), CT 250mm–80mm (9.8in–3.1in) |
| **Armament:** | 8-11in (280mm) SKL/45 (4 × 2), 10-5.9in (150mm) SKL/45, 16-3.5in (88mm) SKL/45, 4-17.7in (450mm) TT sub |
| **Complement:** | 923 (1174 at Jutland) |

| Name | Builder | Laid down | Launched | Comp | Fate |
|---|---|---|---|---|---|
| VON DER TANN | Blohm & Voss, Hamburg | 25.3.08 | 20.3.09 | 20.2.11 | Scuttled 21.6.19 |

*von der Tann* as completed
CPL

to give a 125° arc on the opposite beam. The long trunk Drh LC/1907 mountings allowed 20° elevation and magazines were above shell rooms except in the after turret. The 15cm were in a main deck battery and the TT at bow, stern and on either broadside forward of the torpedo bulkhead. The 8.8cm SKL/45 guns were later removed and 2-8.8cm Flak L/45 added.

The main belt ran from the forward edge of the fore barbette to a little past the after one and was 9.8in for 35in above and 14in below lwl, tapering to 5.9in at the main deck and lower edge 63in below lwl. Forward to the bows it was 4.7in–3.9in and aft 3.9in–3.1in. The barbettes were 9.1in–6.7in above the hull armour but behind the battery and main belt were drastically reduced

to 1.2in while the turrets had 9.1in faces and rears, 7.1in sides and 3.5in–2.4in roofs. The armour deck was 1in behind the main belt with 2in slopes and 2in forward while aft it was 3.1in with 2in–1in slopes. The main deck was 1in over the belt outside the battery, the upper deck 1in over the battery and the forecastle deck 0.9in round the fore barbette. The torpedo bulkhead was 1.2in–1in and about 13ft inboard amidships, running for the same length as the main belt.

There were 10 boiler rooms and 4 engine rooms with the main high pressure turbines on the wing shafts in the 2 forward rooms and the main low pressure ones on the inner shafts in the 2 after rooms. Boiler pressure was 235lb/in², and about 200 tons tar oil was later carried for spraying on the

coal in the boiler furnaces. As usual the boilers were heavily forced on the mile and trial figures were 79,000shp = 27.4kts. She was commissioned for trials on 1 September 1910.

At Jutland she blew up *Indefatigable* in the first 14 or 15 minutes and was later hit by 2-15in and 2-13.5in shells which caused damage aft and put two turrets out of action while troubles in the other two caused the ship to be without any heavy guns for 1¼ hours. The *von der Tann* was raised at Scapa Flow on 7 December 1930 and broken up at Rosyth in 1931–34.

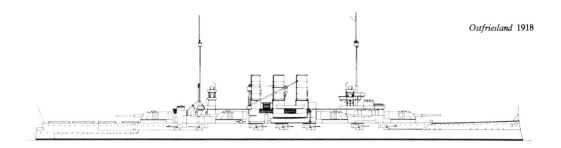

*Ostfriesland* 1918

This class, built under the 1908–09 programme (except for *Oldenburg* under that of 1909–10), was a considerable improvement on the *Nassau*. They were easily distinguished by the three funnels arranged close together, and were flush-decked with freeboard at normal load similar to the previous class; BM was 8.53ft.

The turrets were arranged as in *Nassau* with the guns in long trunk Drh LC/1908 mountings with 13½° elevation, increased later to 16°. Magazines were below shell rooms in all turrets. The 15cm battery was on the main deck, and the 8.8cm were eventually replaced by 2–8.8cm Flak L/45. TT were arranged as previously.

The armour belt was 11.8in between end barbettes for 35in above and 14in below lwl, tapering to 6.7in at the lower edge 63in below lwl and to 6.7in

## HELGOLAND class *battleships*

**Displacement:** 22,440t normal; 25,200t deep load
**Dimensions:** 548ft 7in oa × 93ft 6in × 26ft 11in mean, 26ft 6in mean deep load
*167.2m × 28.5m × 8.2m, 9.0m*
**Machinery:** 3-shaft 4-cyl VTE, 15 Schulz-Thornycroft boilers, 28,000ihp = 20.3kts. Coal 3150t. Range 1790nm at 10 kts
**Armour:** Belt 300mm–80mm (11.8in–3.1in), bulkheads 210mm–90mm (8.3in–3.5in), barbettes 300mm–60mm (11.8in–2.4in), turrets 300mm–70mm (11.8in–2.8in), CT 300mm–100mm (11.8in–3.9in)
**Armament:** 12-12in (305mm) SKL/50 (6 × 2), 14–5.9in (150mm) SKL/45, 14–3.5in (88mm) SKL/45, 6–19.7in (500mm) TT sub
**Complement:** 1113 (1284–1390 at Jutland)

| Name | Builder | Laid down | Launched | Comp | Fate |
|------|---------|-----------|----------|------|------|
| HELGOLAND | Howaldtswerke, Kiel | 24.12.08 | 25.9.09 | 19.12.11 | BU 1924 |
| OSTFRIESLAND | Wilhelmshaven N Yd | 19.10.08 | 30.9.09 | 15.9.11 | Target, sunk 21.7.21 |
| THÜRINGEN | Weser, Bremen | 7.11.08 | 27.11.09 | 10.9.11 | BU 1923 |
| OLDENBURG | Schichau, Danzig | 1.3.09 | 30.6.10 | 1.7.12 | BU 1921 |

*Helgoland* during the war.
*CPL*

at the main deck but to 9.8in in way of the wing barbettes. Forward there was 5.9in-3.1in and aft 5.1in-3.5in. The barbettes varied with exposure from 11.8in to 7.9in, the centreline ones being reduced to 4.7in-3.1in behind side armour while the wing barbettes were 3.9in-2.4in behind the battery armour and below this protected only by the 9.8in side. Turrets had 11.8in faces, 9.8in sides, 11.5in rears and 3.9in-2.8in roofs. The armour deck was 1.6in with 2.4in slopes amidships, 2.2in forward and 3.1in-2.2in aft while the upper deck over the battery and the main deck amidships outside the battery were 1.8in-1in. The torpedo bulkhead was 14¾ft inboard amidships and 1.2in-1.0in.

There were 9 boiler and 3 engine rooms; boiler pressure was 235lb/in² and c200 tons tar oil was later carried for spraying on the coal. *Helgoland* was commissioned for trials on 23 August 1911, *Ostfriesland* 1 August 1911, *Thüringen* 1 July 1911, *Oldenburg* 1 May 1912. On the mile 20.8kts-21.3kts was attained with 31,258ihp-35,500ihp, *Oldenburg* being the fastest.

The only serious war damage was to *Ostfriesland* on 1 June 1916 when she struck a mine below the starboard forward wing turret on 1 June 1916. She was able to steam at 15kts, reduced to 10 after the damage had been increased by a sharp turn in avoiding an imaginary submarine.

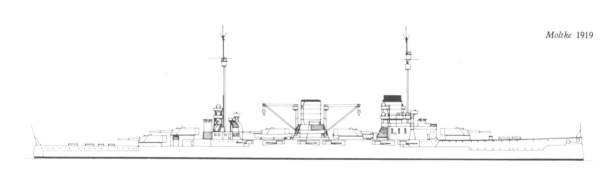

*Moltke* 1919

This class was a considerable improvement on the *von der Tann* and in addition to increased size, had a different hull form with greater amidships beam and finer ends. The *Moltke* was built under the 1908-9 programme and the *Goeben* under that for 1909-10. The forecastle deck ran to abaft the mainmast and freeboard at normal load was about 24ft forward and 14ft aft. GM was 9.87ft and it was originally intended to use Frahm anti-rolling tanks. Tandem rudders were fitted.

The main turrets were distributed as in *von der Tann* except that the after turret was replaced by a super-firing pair. The Drh LC/1908 mountings were similar to C/1907 but only 13½° elevation was allowed though this was increased to 16° in *Moltke* after Jutland and to 22½° in *Goeben* by the end of the war. All magazines were above shell rooms. The 15cm guns were in an upper deck battery and during the war were reduced to 10, and for a time to 9, in *Goeben*. By the end of 1916 the 3.5in SKL/45 had been replaced in both ships by 4-8.8cm Flak L/45. The TT were located at bow, stern and on either broadside forward of the torpedo bulkhead.

The main belt was 10.6in between the outer edges of the end barbettes and from 55in above to 14in below lwl. It was tapered to 5.1in at the lower edge 69in below lwl, while the upper part was a uniform 7.9in to the battery port sills or upper deck outside the battery. Forward the belt was 4.7in-3.9in and aft 3.9in. The barbettes were 9.1in-7.9in but the amidships ones were 3.1in behind the 5.9in battery armour, and all 1.2in behind the 7.9in upper belt. The turrets had 9.1in faces and rears, 7.1in sides and 3.5in-2.4in roofs, and the armour deck was 1in behind the main belt with 2in

## MOLTKE class *battlecruisers*

| | |
|---|---|
| **Displacement:** | 22,616t normal; 25,300t deep load |
| **Dimensions:** | 611ft 11in oa × 96ft 10in × 26ft 11in mean, 29ft 5½in mean at deep load<br>186.5m × 29.5m × 8.2m, 9.0m |
| **Machinery:** | 4-shaft Parsons turbines, 24 Schulz-Thornycroft boilers, 52,000shp = 25.5kts. Coal 3050t. Range 4120nm at 14kts |
| **Armour:** | Belt 270mm-100mm (10.6in-3.9in), bulkheads 200mm-100mm (7.9in-3.9in), battery 200mm-150mm (7.9in-5.9in), barbettes 230mm-30mm (9.1in-1.2in), turrets 230mm-60mm (9.1in-2.4in), CT 350mm-80mm (13.8in-3.1in). |
| **Armament:** | 10-11in (280mm) SKL/50 (5 × 2), 12-5.9in (150mm) SKL/45, 12-3.5in (88mm) SKL/45, 4-19.7in (500mm) TT sub |
| **Complement:** | 1053 (1355 at Jutland) |

| Name | Builder | Laid down | Launched | Comp | Fate |
|---|---|---|---|---|---|
| MOLTKE | Blohm & Voss, Hamburg | 7.12.08 | 7.4.10 | 31.3.12 | Scuttled 21.6.19 |
| GOEBEN | Blohm & Voss, Hamburg | 28.8.09 | 28.3.11 | 28.8.12 | BU 1971 |

slopes, 2in forward and 3.1in with 2in slopes aft. The forecastle deck was 1in over the battery and the upper deck 1in over the main belt outside the battery. The torpedo bulkhead was 2in-1.2in.

There were 12 boiler rooms and 4 engine rooms with main turbines arranged as in *von der Tann*; boiler pressure was also as in this ship, as was the later use of tar oil. On the mile *Moltke* attained 85,780shp = 28.4kts and *Goeben* 85,660shp = 28.0kts. The commissioning dates for trials were respectively 30 September 1911 and 2 July 1912.

In the 1914-18 War *Moltke*, undamaged at Dogger Bank and possibly never fired at, was torpedoed by *E 1* on 19 August 1915 but the hit was right forward and little damage was done. At Jutland she scored 9 hits on *Tiger* in the first 12 minutes and in spite of 4-15in hits and 1-13.5in near miss, was in good fighting order and able to do 25kts at the end of the day. On 24 April 1918 the starboard inner screw fell off and before the turbine could be stopped, the wheel of the engine turning gear disintegrated, wrecking the auxiliary condenser outlet and causing about 2000 tons of water to flood in with salting of all boilers. Emergency repairs enabled her to proceed under own power about 36 hours later, and she was then torpedoed in way of the port engine rooms by *E 42*. Flooding amounted to 1730 tons but no vital damage was caused. The *Moltke* was raised at Scapa Flow in 1927 and broken up in 1927-29.

The *Goeben* was in the Mediterranean in 1914, briefly shelled Philippeville (Algeria) on 3 August 1914 and was able to outrun the *Indomitable* and *Indefatigable* on 4 August. With the *Breslau*, she fired at the pursuing cruiser HMS *Gloucester* in the Ionian Sea on 6 August, entered the Dardanelles on the 10th, was nominally transferred to the Turkish flag as *Yavuz Sultan Selim* on the 16th (the German Admiral, officers and crew were retained; the ship was not *de facto* Turkish property until 1918). During the war, she operated with moderate success against the Russian Black Sea Fleet (for details of the ship's career after 1914, see under Turkey). She was laid up in 1948, decommissioned in 1960 and sold for BU in 1971.

*Goeben* as completed.
CPL

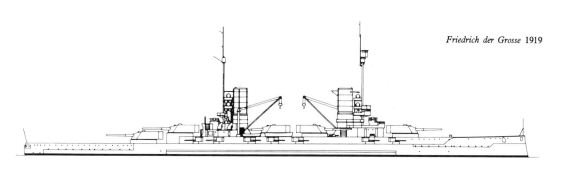

*Friedrich der Grosse* 1919

This class marked a break with previous dreadnoughts. The first two were built under the 1909–10 programme and the others under that of 1910–11. There was a forecastle deck extending to past the mainmast and the boiler rooms and funnels were widely spaced. Freeboard at normal load was about 23ft forward and 13ft aft, with GM 8.50ft.

The arrangement of the main turrets was altered to one forward, two echelonned amidships and two superfiring aft. A 10-gun broadside was practicable as the midships turrets had arcs of 120° on the opposite beam. The mountings were Drh LC/1909, generally similar to C/1908, and with 13½° elevation, later increased to 16°. Magazines in all were below shell rooms. The 15cm guns were in an upper deck battery and the 8.8cm SKL/45 were later removed and the Flak L/45 finally cut to 2. TT were arranged as previously except that there was no stern tube.

The side armour was much improved, the belt between end barbettes

## KAISER class *battleships*

| | |
|---|---|
| **Displacement:** | 24,330t normal; 27,400t deep load |
| **Dimensions:** | 565ft 7in oa × 95ft 2in × 27ft 3in mean, 30ft mean deep load |
| | *172.4m × 29.0m × 8.3m, 9.1m* |
| **Machinery:** | 3-shaft Parsons (*F d Grosse* AEG-Curtis, *K Albert* Schichau) turbines, 16 Schulz-Thornycroft boilers, 31,000shp = 21kts. Coal 3540t. Range 6000nm/4000nm at 12kts/19kts |
| | *P Luitpold* 2-shaft Parsons turbines, 1-shaft Germania diesel (never installed), 14 Schulz-Thornycroft boilers, 26,000shp + 12,000bhp = 22kts. Coal 3150t, diesel oil 395t. Range 7200nm at 12kts (2000nm at 12kts on diesel, as designed) |
| **Armour:** | Belt 350mm–80mm (13.8in–3.1in), bulkheads 300mm–130m (11.8in–5.1in), battery 170mm (6.7in), barbettes 300mm–80mm (11.8in–3.1in), turrets 300mm–80mm (11.8in–3.1in) CT 350mm–150mm (13.8in–5.9in) |
| **Armament:** | 10-12in (305mm) SKL/50 (5 × 2), 14-5.9in (150mm) SKL/45, 8-3.5in (88mm) SKL/45, 4-3.5in (88mm) Flak L/45, 5-19.7in (500mm) TT sub |
| **Complement:** | 1084 (1249-1278 at Jutland) |

| Name | Builder | Laid down | Launched | Comp | Fate |
|---|---|---|---|---|---|
| KAISER | Kiel N Yd | 12.09 | 22.3.11 | 7.12.12 | Scuttled 21.6.19 |
| FRIEDRICH DER GROSSE | Vulcan, Hamburg | 26.1.10 | 10.6.11 | 22.1.13 | Scuttled 21.6.19 |
| KAISERIN | Howaldtswerke, Kiel | 11.10 | 11.11.11 | 13.12.13 | Scuttled 21.6.19 |
| KÖNIG ALBERT | Schichau, Danzig | 17.7.10 | 27.4.12 | 8.11.13 | Scuttled 21.6.19 |
| PRINZREGENT LUITPOLD | Germaniawerft, Kiel | 1.11 | 17.2.12 | 6.12.13 | Scuttled 21.6.19 |

being 13.8in from the main deck 70in-72in above lwl to 14in below lwl, and tapering to 7.1in at 67in below lwl, with 7.9in between main and upper decks. Forward there was 7.1in-3.1in and aft 7.1in-5.1in with 5.9in-3.1in forward and 5.9in aft in *Kaiserin* and *Prinzregent Luitpold*. Barbettes were 11.8in-8.7in behind the battery and upper belt armour and to 3.1in behind the main belt, while the turrets had 11.8in faces, 9.8in sides, 11.5in rears and 4.3in-3.1in roofs. The armour deck was 1.2in amidships,

2.4in forward and 4.7in-2.4in aft while between end barbettes the upper deck was 1.2in-1.0in outside the battery and the forecastle deck 1.2in over the latter. The torpedo bulkhead was 1.6in with 2in in *Kaiserin* and *Prinzregent Luitpold*, and in all was continued as a 1.2in splinter bulkhead to the upper deck.

There were 10 boiler rooms and 3 sets of turbines in 6 engine rooms – except in *Prinzregent Luitpold* which had 2 sets in 4 – and boiler pressure and tar oil were as in *Helgoland*. Turbines and boilers were noted for giving

trouble in *Kaiserin*. Commissioning dates for trials were *Kaiser* 1 August 1912, *Friedrich der Grosse* 15 October 1912, *Kaiserin* 14 May 1913, *König Albert* 31 July 1913, *Prinzregent Luitpold* 19 August 1913. On the mile *Kaiser* was forced to 55,187shp = 23.4kts, while the other 3-shaft ships made 39,813shp-42,181shp = 22.1kts-22.4kts, and *Prinzregent Luitpold* without her diesel 38,751 shp = 21.7kts.

None of the class was seriously damaged in 1914-18. They were raised

for scrap at Scapa between 1929 and 1937.

*Kaiser* and *Kaiserin* (on left) at Kiel.
CPL

*Seydlitz* November 1918.
CPL

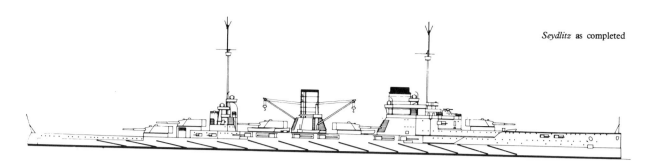

Built under the 1910–11 programme this ship was in some features an enlarged *Moltke* but the hull form was different and an additional weather deck was added from stem to foremast. Freeboard was 29–30ft forward at normal load and elsewhere slightly less than in *Moltke*. GM was 10.23ft and Frahm anti-rolling tanks were fitted but not so used. There were tandem rudders, the forward one being somewhat ineffective as in *Moltke*, and like all German battlecruisers, *Seydlitz* turned slowly and with considerable loss of speed. Full details of her design were obtained by the British but these appear to have had no influence whatsoever on future ships.

The main and secondary armament

## SEYDLITZ *battlecruiser*

| | |
|---|---|
| **Displacement:** | 24,594t normal, 28,100t deep load |
| **Dimensions:** | 657ft 11in oa × 93ft 6in × 26ft 11in mean, 30ft 3in mean at deep load |
| | *200.5m × 28.5m × 8.2m, 9.2m* |
| **Machinery:** | 4-shaft Parsons turbines, 27 Schulz-Thornycroft boilers, 63,000shp = 26.5kts. Coal 3540t. Range 4700nm at 14kts. |
| **Armour:** | Belt 300mm–100mm (11.8in–3.9in), bulkheads 220mm–100mm (8.7in–3.9in), battery 200mm–150mm (7.9in–5.9in), barbettes 230mm–30mm (9.1in–1.2in), turrets 250mm–70mm (9.8in–2.8in), CT 350mm–80mm (13.8in–3.1in) |
| **Armament:** | 10–11in (280mm) SKL/50 (5 × 2), 12–5.9in (150mm) SKL/45, 12–3.5in (88mm) SKL/45, 4–19.7in (500mm) TT sub |
| **Complement:** | 1068 (1425 at Jutland) |

| Name | Builder | Laid down | Launched | Comp | Fate |
|---|---|---|---|---|---|
| SEYDLITZ | Blohm & Voss, Hamburg | 4.2.11 | 30.3.12 | 17.8.13 | Scuttled 21.6.19 |

were arranged as in *Moltke* except that the fore turret was on the weather deck. The Drh LC/1910 mountings were generally similar to C/1908 and the initial 13½° elevation was increased to 16° before Jutland. All turret magazines were above the shell rooms. By Jutland the 8.8cm SKL/45 had been replaced by 2-8.8cm Flak L/45; TT were disposed as in previous battlecruisers.

The main belt was 11.8in between end barbettes from 55in above to 14in below lwl and was tapered to 5.9in at the lower edge 67in below lwl. Above it was tapered to 9.1in at the upper deck and to 7.9in at the battery port sills.

Forward the armour was 4.7in-3.9in and 3.9in aft. Barbettes were 9.1in-7.9in but the wing barbettes were reduced to 3.9in behind the battery and all to 1.2in where protected by the 11.8in-9.1in belt. The turrets had 9.8in faces, 7.9in sides, 8.3in rears and 3.9in-2.8in roofs. The armour deck was 1.2in amidships, 2in forward and 3.1in with 2in slopes aft, while the forecastle deck was 2.2in-1in over the battery and the upper deck 1in outside. The torpedo bulkhead ran between end barbettes and was 13ft 2in inboard amidships. It was 2in-1.2in and continued as a 1.2in splinter bulkhead to the upper deck.

There were 15 boiler and 4 engine rooms with the main turbines; boiler pressure and later use of tar oil were as in the previous ships. She was commissioned for trials on 22 May 1913 and on the mile attained 89,740shp = 28.13kts.

At the Dogger Bank *Seydlitz* was hit by 3-13.5in shells, one of which (from *Lion*) burst as it holed the 9.1in barbette of the stern turret, and armour fragments caused a fire which spread to the superfiring turret and ignited 62 complete (main and fore) charges. She was mined forward of the torpedo bulkhead on 24 April 1916 and at Jutland was hit by a torpedo from *Petard* or possibly *Turbulent*, and by 8-15in, 6-13.5in and 8-12in shells. The worst damage was from flooding above the armour deck forward, 47in below lwl, caused by 5-15in hits and aggravated by trying to steam too fast after the action of 31 May 1916. She was nearly lost, the flooding at its worst being calculated as 5329 tons with draughts of 46ft 1in forward and 24ft 4in aft and a list of 8° to port.

*Seydlitz* was raised at Scapa Flow for scrap in November 1928.

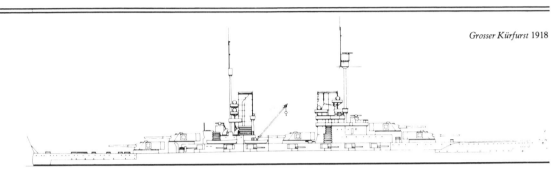

*Grosser Kürfürst* 1918

Below: *Markgraf* 1917.
CPL

These ships were essentially improved *Kaiser*s with a much better turret distribution. The first three were built under the 1911-12 programme and *Kronprinz* – renamed *Kronprinz Wilhelm* on 27 January 1918 – under that of 1912-13. The run of the forecastle deck and freeboard were similar but the funnels were not as far apart as in *Kaiser*. GM was 8.50ft and fighting draughts apparently varied from 29ft 0½in to 29ft 8¼in (8.85m-9.05m).

The turrets were all on the centre-line with superfiring pairs fore and aft and the fifth between the funnels at the same height as the after superfiring one. The mountings were Drh LC/1911, similar to C/1909 and with 13½° elevation, increased to 16°. Magazines were all below shell rooms. The 15cm battery was on the upper

## KÖNIG class *battleships*

| | |
|---|---|
| **Displacement:** | 25,390t normal; 29,200t deep load |
| **Dimensions:** | 575ft 6in oa × 96ft 9in × 27ft 3in mean, 30ft 6½in mean deep load |
| | *175.4m × 29.5m × 8.3m, 9.3m* |
| **Machinery:** | 3-shaft Parsons (*G Kurfürst* AEG-Vulcan, *Markgraf* Bergmann) turbines, 15 Schulz-Thornycroft boilers, 31,000shp = 21kts. Coal 3540t, oil 690t. Range 6800nm/4600nm at 12kts/19kts |
| **Armour:** | Belt 350mm-80mm (13.8in-3.1in), bulkheads 300mm-130mm (11.8in-5.1in), battery 170mm (6.7in), barbettes 300mm-80mm (11.8in-3.1in), turrets 300mm-80mm (11.8in-3.1in), CT 350mm-170mm (13.8in-6.7in) |
| **Armament:** | 10-12in (305mm) SKL/50 (5 × 2), 14-5.9in (150mm) SKL/45, 6-3.5in (88mm) SKL/45, 4-3.5in (88mm) Flak L/45, 5-19.7in (500mm) TT sub |
| **Complement:** | 1136 (1284-1315 at Jutland) |

| Name | Builder | Laid down | Launched | Comp | Fate |
|---|---|---|---|---|---|
| KÖNIG | Wilhelmshaven N Yd | 10.11 | 1.3.13 | 1.15 | Scuttled 21.6.19 |
| GROSSER KURFÜRST | Vulcan, Hamburg | 10.11 | 5.5.13 | 9.14 | Scuttled 21.6.19 |
| MARKGRAF | Weser, Bremen | 11.11 | 4.6.13 | 1.15 | Scuttled 21.6.19 |
| KRONPRINZ | Germaniawerft, Kiel | 5.12 | 21.2.14 | 2.15 | Scuttled 21.6.19 |

deck, and the 8.8cm SKL/45 were later removed and the Flak L/45 reduced to 2. TT were arranged as in *Kaiser*.

The armour was generally as in *Kaiser* but the belt forward was 7.9in-3.1in and 7.9in-5.1in aft. The upper deck amidships was 1.2in outside the battery and 0.8in as the battery floor, while the torpedo bulkhead was 2in and continued as a 1.2in splinter bulkhead to the upper deck.

There were 3 oil-fired and 12 coal-fired boilers, with the oil-fired in the 3 foremost boiler rooms, 6 coal-fired in the next 3 and another 6 in the 3 after boiler rooms. The 3 sets of turbines were in 6 engine rooms, and boiler pressure remained at 235lb/in².

Commissioning dates for trials were *König* 10 August 1914, *Grosser Kurfürst* 30 July 1914, *Markgraf* 1 October 1914, *Kronprinz* 8 November 1914, but the deep water mile at Neukrug could not be used and figures were 41,400shp–46,200shp = 21.0kts–21.3kts. In service they were faster than the *Kaiser* class, and *Grosser Kurfürst* was apparently considered the fastest and was said to have touched 24kts, though at Jutland she was outpaced by *König*.

*Grosser Kurfürst* and *Kronprinz* were both torpedoed by *J 1* on 5 November 1916, respectively right aft (jamming the port rudder) and under the bridge, but both maintained 17kts–19kts. In the Gulf of Riga operations *Grosser Kurfürst* was mined on 12 October 1917 and *Markgraf* on the 29th but the torpedo bulkhead limited flooding in both to 260-280 tons.

At Jutland *König* was hit by 1–15in and 9–13.5in shells, *Grosser Kurfürst* by 5–15in and 3–13.5in, and *Markgraf* by 3–15in, 1–13.5in and 1–12in. The worst damage to *König* was from a 13.5in CPC on the 7.1in extreme lower edge of the belt which burst about 7ft inboard sending many fragments through 6½ft of coal and the 2in torpedo bulkhead into a 5.9in ammunition room. Sea water flooding in limited the fire to 15 cartridges, but most of the 1630 tons reported after the battle was from this hit. In *Grosser Kürfurst* a 13.5in APC hit the 5.9in armour forward near the waterline and burst making a hole 51in × 35in. Almost the whole fore part of the ship except the torpedo flats and trimming tanks flooded up to the main deck increasing the draught forward by 5ft.

*Grosser Kurfürst* was raised at Scapa for scrap in 1936, but salvage rights on the others were not granted until 1962.

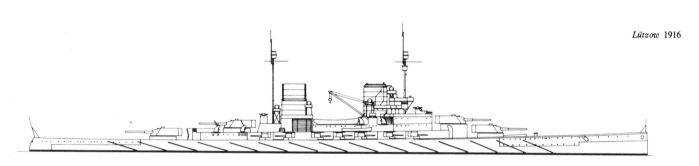

*Lützow* 1916

This class was a great improvement on *Seydlitz* and of markedly different design. They were flush-decked with a pronounced sheer giving freeboard at normal load of about 24ft forward and 15ft aft, and an extra deck known as the upper main deck, was worked in forward of the CT. *Derfflinger* was built under the 1911-12 programme and *Lützow* under that of 1912-13. GM is given as 8.53ft and they were accounted excellent seaboats though the casemates were wet. Tandem rudders were fitted and *Derfflinger* had Frahm anti-rolling tanks but they were apparently not used. A heavy tripod foremast was added to her after Jutland.

The 30.5cm turrets were arranged in superfiring pairs fore and aft, the latter being separated by the length of the after engine rooms. The Drh LC/1912 mountings allowed 13½° elevation, increased to 16° after Jutland. Magazines were below shell rooms except, for reasons of space, in the sternmost turret and this turret also differed in that the shell hoists were not broken at the working chamber. The 15cm were in an upper deck battery and the 8.8cm SKL/45 were later removed in *Derfflinger*, both ships having 8–8.8cm Flak L/45 at Jutland later reduced to 4 in *Derfflinger*. The TT were arranged as in previous battlecruisers.

The main belt ran from the fore barbette to a little past the after one, and was 11.8in from 55in above to 14in below lwl tapering to 5.9in at the lower edge 67in below lwl and to 9.1in at the

## DERFFLINGER class *battlecruisers*

**Displacement:** 26,180t normal (*Lützow* 26,318t); 30,700t deep load
**Dimensions:** 690ft 3in oa × 95ft 2in × 27ft 3in mean, 31ft mean at deep load
210.4m × 29.0m × 8.3m, 9.5m
**Machinery:** 4-shaft Parsons turbines, 18 Schulz-Thornycroft boilers, 63,000shp = 26.5kts. Coal 3640t, oil 985t. Range 5600nm at 14kts
**Armour:** Belt 300mm-100mm (11.8in-3.9in), bulkheads 250mm-100mm (9.8in-3.9in), battery 150mm (5.9in), barbettes 260mm-30mm (10.2in-1.2in), turrets 270mm-80mm (10.6in-3.1in), CT 350mm-80mm (13.8in-3.1in)
**Armament:** 8-12in (305mm) SKL/50 (4 × 2), 12-5.9in (150mm) SKL/45, 4-3.5in (88mm) SKL/45, 4-19.7in (500mm) TT sub (*Lützow* 14-5.9in, no 3.5in, 4-23.6in (600mm) TT sub)
**Complement:** 1112 (1391 at Jutland)

| Name | Builder | Laid down | Launched | Comp | Fate |
|------|---------|-----------|----------|------|------|
| DERFFLINGER | Blohm & Voss, Hamburg | 1.12 | 1.7.13 | 11.14 | Scuttled 21.6.19 |
| LÜTZOW | Schichau, Danzig | 5.12 | 29.11.13 | 3.16 | Sunk 1.6.16 |

upper deck. Forward there was 4.7in-3.9in and 3.9in aft. The barbettes were 10.2in with the two superfiring ones reduced to 3.9in behind the battery armour and all to 2.4in behind the main belt with the two forward ones further reduced to 1.2in behind the upper main deck. The turrets had 10.6in faces and rears, 8.7in sides and 4.3in-3.1in roofs. The armour deck was 1.2in amidships, 2in forward and 3.1in-2in aft, and the upper deck 1.2in-0.8in outside the battery which had a 2in-1in roof. The torpedo bulkhead ran for the length of the main belt and was 1.8in, continuing to the upper deck as a 1.2in splinter bulkhead.

The boilers were double-ended and there were 12 boiler rooms with the 4 oil-fired boilers in the forward 4. Pressure was still 235lb/in² and oil fuel sprays were later provided for the coal-fired furnaces. The main turbines were arranged in 4 engine rooms as previously. *Derfflinger* was commissioned for trials on 1 September 1914 and *Lützow* on 8 August 1915, but the latter had serious turbine troubles and did not join the fleet until the end of the following March. At Jutland her gunnery was of the highest quality but her watertight integrity was far below normal German standards. The usual deep water mile at Neukrug was considered unsafe in war and the 115ft deep Belt mile was used. At 30ft 6in (9.3m) *Derfflinger* attained 76,600shp = 25.8kts, and *Lützow* at about 29ft 6in (9m) 80,990shp = 26.4kts equivalent to 28.0kts and 28.3kts in deep water at normal load.

At the Dogger Bank *Derfflinger* was hit by 3–13.5in shells with little damage but at Jutland, where she blew up the *Queen Mary* in 11 salvos, she was hit by 10–15in, 1–13.5in and 10–12in shells. Both after turrets were put out of action with serious cartridge fires by 15in shells from *Revenge*, while other 15in hits had earlier caused flooding forward. At the end of the battle 3350 tons of flood water were in her, but 1020 tons of this was in the flooded after turret magazines and 206 tons in the wings to correct a 2° list.

She was raised at Scapa in 1934 for scrap.

*Derfflinger* 1918.

*CPL*

At Jutland *Lützow* was hit by at least 24 heavy shells, believed to be 4-15in, 12-13.5in and 8-12in. The worst damage was from 2-12in from *Invinc-* *ible* which burst below water in or near the broadside torpedo flat and with other shells caused flooding that became uncontrollable, and when the water line forward had reached the upper edge of 'B' barbette, she was sunk in 2 minutes by a torpedo from *G 38*. Her own gunnery was excellent and she blew up *Invincible* and probably *Defence*.

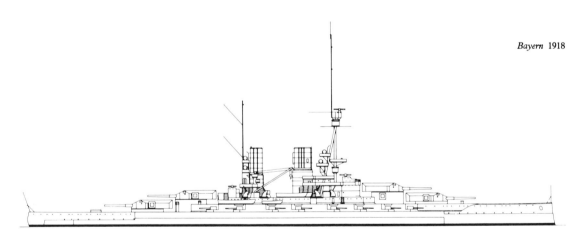

*Bayern* 1918

In this class the main armament was increased from 12in to 15in without any intervening 13.8in (35cm) as was to have been the case in battlecruisers. Both ships were built under the 1913-14 programme. The forecastle deck extended to the after superfiring turret and freeboard at normal load was 23ft 8in forward and 15ft 1in aft. The funnels were not widely separated and both ships had a tripod foremost with a small mainmast close abaft the after funnel, though initially *Bayern* had none. GM was 8.4ft at 27ft 8in and mean fighting draught 29ft 10in (9.09m). When examined in Britain it was thought that *Baden* was more than 12in over her designed draught at normal load.

The turrets were in superfiring pairs fore and aft and the Drh LC 1913

## BAYERN class *battleships*

| | |
|---|---|
| **Displacement:** | 28,074t normal; 31,690t deep load |
| **Dimensions:** | 589ft 10in oa × 98ft 5in × 27ft 8in mean, 30ft 9in mean deep load |
| | *179.8m × 30.0m × 8.4m, 9.4m* |
| **Machinery:** | 3-shaft Parsons turbines, 14 Schulz-Thornycroft boilers, 48,000shp = 21kts. Coal 3350t, oil 610t. Range 5000nm/2390nm at 13kts/21.5kts |
| **Armour:** | Belt 350mm-120mm (13.8in-4.7in), bulkheads 300mm-140mm (11.8in-5.5in), battery 170mm (6.7in), barbettes 350mm-25mm (13.8in-1in), turrets 350mm-100mm (13.8in-3.9in), CT 350mm-170mm (13.8in-6.7in) |
| **Armament:** | 8-15in (380mm) SKL/45 (4 × 2), 16-5.9in (150mm) SKL/45, 8-3.5in (88mm) Flak L/45, 5-23.6in (600mm) TT sub |
| **Complement:** | 1187-1271 |

| Name | Builder | Laid down | Launched | Comp | Fate |
|---|---|---|---|---|---|
| BAYERN | Howaldtswerke, Kiel | 1.14 | 18.2.15 | 30.6.16 | Scuttled 21.6.19 |
| BADEN | Schichau, Danzig | 20.12.13 | 30.10.15 | 2.17 | Target, sunk 16.8.21 |

mountings allowed 16° elevation, later increased to 20° in *Bayern*. There was a 26.9ft rangefinder in each turret. The magazines were all above the shell rooms with crowns formed by the armour deck. The 15cm battery was on the upper deck and the 8 Flak guns were never carried, the number varying from 2 to 4. The TT were arranged as in *Kaiser*, but after *Bayern* was mined the 2 forward broadside tubes were removed in both ships.

The main 13.8in belt ran from 70in above lwl to 14in below between end barbettes, tapering to 6.7in at the lower edge 67in below lwl. Between main and upper decks it was 9.8in. Forward the armour was 7.9in–5.9in ending 50ft from the bows and aft 7.9in–4.7in. The barbettes were 13.8in–9.8in reduced to 6.7in behind the battery armour, 7.9in–3.1in behind the 9.8in side and 4.5in–1in behind the 13.8in. The turrets had 13.8in faces, 9.8in sides, 11.5in rears and 7.9in–3.9in roofs. Decks, torpedo and splinter bulkheads were as in *König* except that the forecastle deck was 1.6in near the centreline amidships and the battery floor 1.0in.

There were 3 oil-fired and 11 coal-fired boilers in 9 boiler rooms with the oil-fired in the 3 foremost. Oil fuel sprays could be used in the coal furnaces. The 3 sets of turbines were in 6 engine rooms, and boiler pressure was still 235lb/in². *Bayern* was commissioned for trials on 18 March 1916 and *Baden* on 19 October 1916. On the Belt mile they both recorded 22.0kts with 55,967 and 56,275shp respectively.

*Bayern* was mined on 12 October 1917 during the Gulf of Riga operations, near the forward torpedo flat beyond the torpedo bulkhead, and flooding was serious, involving the bow torpedo flat and increasing draught forward to 36ft. Temporary patching ran into difficulties and she did not reach Kiel for 19 days. *Bayern* was raised at Scapa for scrap in September 1934 and broken up at Rosyth.

*Bayern* after being mined in October 1917.

*CPL*

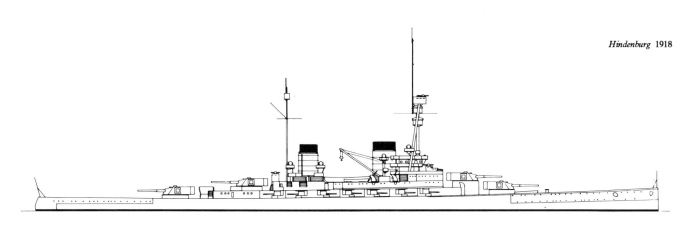

*Hindenburg* 1918

This ship, built under the 1913–14 programme, was generally similar to the *Derfflinger* class and only the differences are noted. The additional length was mainly due to finer stern lines and a tripod foremast was fitted before completion. She could be distinguished from *Derfflinger* by having shallower funnel caps and the tripod legs less spread.

The armament was arranged as in the previous class but the 30.5cm mountings were Drh LC/1913 allowing 16° elevation and the 10ft turret rangefinders were replaced by 25½ft. In all 4 turrets the magazines were above the shell rooms and the shell

## HINDENBURG *battlecruiser*

| | |
|---|---|
| **Displacement:** | 26,513t normal; 31,000t deep load |
| **Dimensions:** | 698ft 2in oa × 95ft 2in × 27ft 3in mean, 30ft 11¼in mean at deep load |
| | *212.8m × 29.0m × 8.3m, 9.4m* |
| **Machinery:** | 4-shaft Parsons turbines, 18 Schulz-Thornycroft boilers, 72,000shp = 27.5kts. Coal 3640t, oil 1180t. Range 6800nm at 14kts |
| **Armour:** | As *Derfflinger* class |
| **Armament:** | 8–12in (305mm) SKL/50 (4 × 2), 14–5.9in (150mm) SKL/45, 4–3.5in (88mm) Flak L/45, 4–23.6in (600mm) TT sub |
| **Complement:** | 1182 |

| Name | Builder | Laid down | Launched | Comp | Fate |
|---|---|---|---|---|---|
| HINDENBURG | Wilhelmshaven N Yd | 30.6.13 | 1.8.15 | 25.10.17 | Scuttled 21.6.19 |

*Hindenburg* November 1918.
*CPL*

hoists were not broken at the working chamber though the cartridge hoists were. It was possible to load the forward and aft superfiring turret shell hoists from depot rooms on the upper main and main (armour) decks respectively.

The main belt tapered to 8.7in at the upper deck, and forward there was 4.7in to 54ft from the bows and then 1.2in plating. Aft the side armour ended 24ft from the stern instead of 15ft. The sloping front roof of the turrets was increased to 5.9in.

The boiler rooms were rearranged with the 4 oil-fired boilers in two groups, one forward and the other separated by 4 coal-fired rooms. The *Hindenberg* was commissioned for trials on 10 May 1917 and attained 95,777shp = 26.6kts at 29ft 6in (9m) on the Belt mile, equivalent to 28.5kts at normal displacement in deep water. She was raised at Scapa for scrap on 22 July 1930 and was still of sufficient interest to be examined in some detail by the Royal Corps of Naval Constructors.

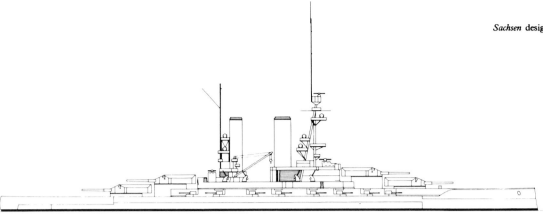

These ships were slightly lengthened *Bayerns*, *Sachsen* being built under the 1914–15 programme and *Württemberg* under War Estimates, and would have been similar in appearance except for higher funnels in *Sachsen*.

The designed armament was unchanged except that the 38cm mountings were Drh LC/1914 with 20° elevation, and TT would certainly have been reduced to 3. The forward submerged torpedo-tube was being completely fitted at the armistice, in spite of *Bayern's* experience in the Gulf of Riga. Armour was also as in *Bayern* with a few exceptions. *Sachsen* had a structure protecting the top of the diesel engine for about halfway between armour and main decks. This was 7.9in–5.5.in with 3.1in roof, and both ships are shown with all barbettes 1.6in behind the 13.8in belt, and with the armour deck 2in over some areas amidships. By 1918, improvements in protection, for example extra deck armour against long range plunging gunfire, might have

## SACHSEN class *battleships*

| | |
|---|---|
| **Displacement:** | 28,345 normal (*Württemberg* 28,247)t; 31,987t deep load (*Württemburg* 31,700t) |
| **Dimensions:** | 598ft 5in oa × 98ft 5in × 27ft 8in mean, 30ft 9in mean deep load |
| | *182.4m × 30.0m × 8.4m, 9.4m* |
| **Machinery:** | *Sachsen* 2-shaft Parsons turbines, 1-shaft MAN diesel, 9 Schulz-Thornycroft boilers, 31,800shp + 12,000bhp = 21.5kts. Coal 2660t, oil 1280t |
| | *Württemberg* 3-shaft AEG-Vulcan turbines, 12 Schulz-Thornycroft boilers, 48,000shp = 22kts. Coal 3050t, oil 890t |
| **Armour:** | Belt 350mm–120mm (13.8in–4.7in), bulkheads 300mm–140mm (11.8in–5.5in), battery 170mm (6.7in), barbettes 350mm–40mm (13.8in–1.6in), turrets 350mm–100mm (13.8in–3.9in), CT 350mm–170mm (13.8in–6.7in) |
| **Armament:** | 8–15in (380mm) SKL/45 (4 × 2), 16–5.9in (150mm) SKL/45, 8–3.5in (88mm) Flak L/45, 5–23.6in (600mm) TT sub |
| **Complement:** | 1165 (*Württemberg* 1196) |

| Name | Builder | Laid down | Launched | Comp | Fate |
|---|---|---|---|---|---|
| SACHSEN | Germaniawerft, Kiel | 7.4.14 | 21.11.16 | – | BU 1921 |
| WÜRTTEMBERG | Vulcan, Hamburg | 4.1.15 | 20.6.17 | – | BU 1921 |

been expected from war experience; however, postwar British inspection of this class and of *Baden* showed no signs that such modifications were even contemplated.

In *Sachsen* the centre shaft was to be diesel-powered and the two outer steam with 3 oil- and 6 coal-fired boilers and 2 sets of turbines in 4 engine rooms, while in *Württemberg*

there were 3 oil- and 9 coal-fired boilers with 3 sets of turbines in 6 engine rooms. Range was to be 2000nm at 12kts on diesel alone.

These ships would have differed from previous battlecruisers in having a full length forecastle deck and a return was made to twin instead of tandem rudders. They would have been handsome ships with tripod foremasts and 2 funnels. *Mackensen* was laid down under the 1914–15 programme, *Ersatz Freya* under the War Estimates and the others were ordered in April 1915. It was originally hoped to complete them from the summer of 1917 to the autumn of 1918, and their 35cm guns would have made them formidable antagonists. *Ersatz Freya* was to have been named *Prinz Eitel Friedrich*; *Ersatz A*, later known as *Ersatz Friedrich Carl*, was to have been named *Fürst Bismarck*.

The main armament was arranged as in *Hindenburg* and the Drh LC/1914 mountings allowed 20° elevation, while the 15cm were in a long

## MACKENSEN class *battlecruisers*

| | |
|---|---|
| **Displacement:** | 30,500t normal, *c*35,500t–36,000t deep load |
| **Dimensions:** | 731ft 8in oa × 99ft 9in × 27ft 6¾in mean |
| | *223.0m × 30.4m × 8.4m* |
| **Machinery:** | 4-shaft Parsons turbines, geared cruising (*Ersatz A* hydraulic drive main turbines), 32 Schulz-Thornycroft boilers, 90,000shp = 28kts. Coal 3940t, oil 1970t. Range 8000nm at 14kts |
| **Armour:** | Belt 300mm–100mm (11.8in–3.9in), bulkheads 250mm–100mm (9.8in–3.9in), battery 150mm (5.9in), barbettes 290mm–90mm (11.4in–3.9in), turrets 320mm–110mm (12.6in–4.3in), (*Graf Spee* 300mm–100mm (11.8in–3.9in)), CT 350mm–100mm (13.8in–3.9in) |
| **Armament:** | 8–13.8in (350mm) SKL/45 (4 × 2), 12–5.9in (150mm) SKL/45, 8–3.5in (88mm) Flak L/45, 5–23.6in (600mm) TT sub |
| **Complement:** | 1186 |

| Name | Builder | Laid down | Launched | Comp | Fate |
|---|---|---|---|---|---|
| MACKENSEN | Blohm & Voss, Hamburg | 30.1.15 | 21.4.17 | – | BU 1923–24 |
| ERSATZ FREYA | Blohm & Voss, Hamburg | 1.5.15 | 13.3.20 to clear slip | – | BU 1920–22 |
| GRAF SPEE | Schichau, Danzig | 30.11.15 | 15.9.17 | – | BU 1921–23 |
| ERSATZ A | Wilhelmshaven N Yd | 3.11.15 | – | – | BU on slip 1922 |

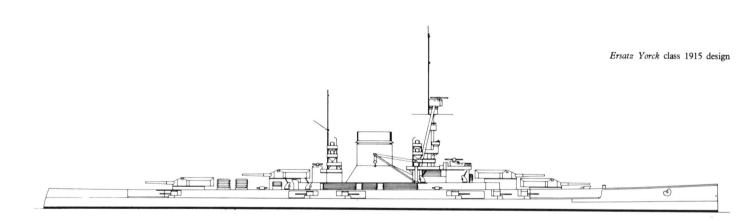

*Mackensen* class 1913 design

upper deck battery extending from the forward turret to the after superfiring one. The 5 TT would have been arranged with one in the bows and two on either broadside forward and aft of the torpedo bulkhead.

The 11.8in main belt ran from 10ft forward of the fore turret to 10ft abaft the after one and tapered to 5.9in at the lower edge and 9.4in at the upper deck. Foward and aft the armour stopped short of the ends and was respectively 4.7in and 3.9in. The

barbettes were reduced to 4.7in (*Ersatz A* 5.9in) behind the battery armour and to 3.5in behind the main belt, while the turrets had 12.6in faces, 7.9in sides, 8.6in rears, 7.1in–4.3in roofs except that in *Graf Spee* the figures were 11.8in, 7.9in, 8.3in, 5.9in–3.9in. The armour deck did not extend outboard of the torpedo bulkhead amidships where it was 2.4–1.2in with 2in forward and 4.3in–3.1in aft. The upper deck was 1in over the main belt and the fore-

castle deck 2in–1in over the battery. The torpedo bulkhead was 2in increased to 2.4in by the turrets, and continued as a 1.2in splinter bulkhead to the upper deck. Subdivision was to the same extent as in earlier battle-cruisers, but main bulkheads were intact below the lower protective deck. A centre-line bulkhead was built through all the machinery spaces, an unsatisfactory feature and potentially dangerous in the event of a damaged main side compartment.

The boilers comprised 24 single-ended coal-fired and 8 double-ended oil-fired and were smaller than in the previous ships. Leak pumps were increased to 8 from 5 in *Hindenburg*.

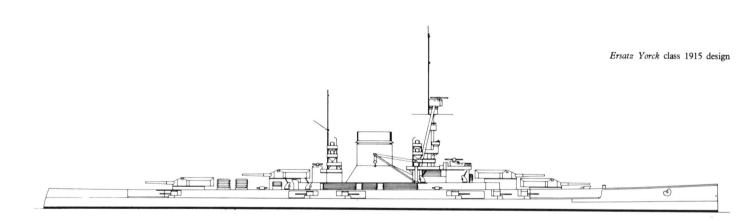

*Ersatz Yorck* class 1915 design

Originally ordered in April 1915 as units of the *Mackensen* class, the design was altered in January 1917 in an attempt to produce a battlecruiser with 8-38cm guns using machinery already ordered. Appearance would have been quite distinct with the uptakes trunked into a single large funnel.

The main armament was arranged as in *Mackensen* but the upper deck 15cm battery was lengthened to 413ft with 6 guns from 'A' barbette to the CT, 4 by the mainmast and 2 by the aftermost barbette. The bow TT was retained with one on either beam aft of the boiler rooms and thus within the area of the torpedo bulkhead.

Armour was generally as in *Mackensen* but the main belt tapered to 9.4in–7.9in at the upper deck and the barbettes were reduced to 7.1in behind the battery and to 4.7in–3.5in behind the belt. The turrets were to have 11.8in faces, 9.8in sides, 11.5in rears and 9.8in–5.9in roofs, while the

## ERSATZ YORCK class *battlecruisers*

| | |
|---|---|
| **Displacement:** | 33,000t normal, c38,000t–38,500t deep load |
| **Dimensions:** | 747ft 5in oa × 99ft 9in × 28ft 6½in mean |
| | *227.8m × 30.4m × 8.7m* |
| **Machinery:** | 4-shaft Parsons turbines, hydraulic drive, geared cruising (*Ersatz Scharnhorst* direct drive main turbines), 32 Schulz-Thornycroft boilers, 90,000shp = 27.25kts. Coal 3940t, oil 1970t. Range 8000nm at 14kts |
| **Armour:** | Belt 300mm–100mm (11.8in–3.9in), bulkheads 250mm–100mm (9.8in–3.9in), battery 150mm (5.9in), barbettes 300mm–90mm (11.8in–3.5in), turrets 300mm–150mm (11.8in–5.9in), CT 350mm–100mm (13.8in–3.9in) |
| **Armament:** | 8-15in (380mm) SKL/45 (4 × 2), 12-5.9in (150mm) SKL/45, 8-3.5in (88mm) or 4.1in (105mm) Flak L/45, 3-23.6in (600mm) or 27.6in (700mm) TT sub |
| **Complement:** | 1227 |

| Name | Builder | Laid down | Launched | Comp | Fate |
|---|---|---|---|---|---|
| ERSATZ YORCK | Vulcan, Hamburg | 7.16 | – | – | Building stopped |
| ERSATZ GNEISENAU | Germaniawerft, Kiel | – | – | – | – |
| ERSATZ SCHARNHORST | Blohm & Voss, Hamburg | – | – | – | – |

armour deck was 3.9in–2.8in aft and the forecastle deck 2in–0.8in.

Construction of *Ersatz Yorck* was

halted after 1000–1100 tons of steel had been assembled.

This design, dated 2 October 1917, was selected from a number of fast battleship and battlecruiser designs for construction on 11 September 1918, though by this time there was no chance of them ever being built. Outlines show a single trunked funnel with tripod foremast and a forecastle extending to the after superfiring barbette.

The turrets were arranged with superfiring pairs fore and aft, the latter being widely separated by engine rooms. The 15cm were in an upper deck battery. There was a single bow TT and one on either beam abaft the boiler rooms and thus within the torpedo bulkhead, though these would probably have been moved to an above water position behind the forward side armour.

The 13.8in belt armour extended from a little forward of the fore barbette to a little abaft the after one, and from 77in above lwl to 14in below. It

## L 20α design *battleships*

| | |
|---|---|
| **Displacement:** | c43,800t normal; c48,700t deep load |
| **Dimensions:** | 781ft lwl × 110ft × 29ft 6in mean, c32ft 6in mean deep load |
| | *238.0m × 33.5m × 9.0m, c9.9m* |
| **Machinery:** | 4-shaft turbines, 22 Schulz-Thornycroft boilers, 100,000shp = 26kts. Coal 2950t, oil 1970t |
| **Armour:** | Belt 350mm-130mm (13.8-5.1in), bulkheads 250mm-60mm (9.8in-2.4in), battery 170mm (6.7in), barbettes 350-100mm (13.8in-3.9in), turrets 350mm-150mm (13.8-5.9in), CT 350mm-150mm (13.8in-5.9in) |
| **Armament:** | 8-16.5in (420mm) SKL/45 (4 × 2), 12-5.9in (150mm) SKL/45, 8-3.5in (88mm) or 4.1in (105mm) Flak L/45, 3-23.6in (600mm) or 27.6in (700mm) TT sub |
| **Complement:** | ? |

tapered to 6.7in at the lower edge 67in below lwl, and was 9.8in between the main and upper decks. Forward the armour was 9.8in with 5.9in lower edge not extending to the stem, and aft 11.8in with 5.1in lower edge. Barbettes are shown as 13.8in reduced to 9.8in behind the battery, 9.8in-5.9in behind the 9.8in side and 5.9in-3.9in behind the 13.8in. Turrets

had 13.8in faces, 9.8in sides, 11.8in rears and 9.8in-5.9in roofs. The armour deck was 2.4in-2in amidships, 2in forward and 4.7in-2in aft, with a 1.6in-0.8in forecastle deck over the battery, apparently 0.8in on most of the upper deck and on the main deck aft. The torpedo bulkhead was 2.4in-2in continued as a 1.2in splinter bulkhead to the upper deck.

There were to be 6 oil-fired and 16 coal-fired boilers but it is not clear whether there were 2 or 4 sets of turbines. They would obviously have been very powerful ships but the decks were thin as was the belt lower edge, and armour of 9.8in or less would have been vulnerable to later 15in shells.

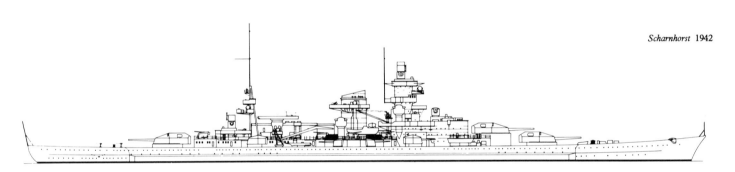

*Scharnhorst 1942*

Much more than any other capital ship of any other navy, the two units of the *Scharnhorst* class were a compromise of political, military and technical requirements. Hitler's original conception was a ship possessing the same armament and speed as the 'pocket-battleships' but having a displacement of 19,000 tons, the increase being taken up by superior protection; the *Kriegsmarine*'s viewpoint was that such a vessel, carrying only six 280mm guns, would be an ill-balanced design – at the very least a third triple turret was required, even though this would raise the displacement figure to 26,000 tons. Hitler rejected this idea because he did not want to draw criticism from Great Britain by breaking the Versailles Treaty; he did not appear to realise that the construction of an 'unsinkable' commerce raider such as he had advocated would provoke Britain much more than the construction of a relatively straightforward battlecruiser which, with a main calibre of only 280mm, would be inferior to all the British battleships in commission in 1934. The Navy's arguments were, however, reluctantly accepted, and the ships were designed with three triple turrets; the German naval programme, published after the

## SCHARNHORST class *battleships*

| | |
|---|---|
| **Displacement:** | 31,850t standard; 38,900t deep load |
| **Dimensions:** | 741ft 5in wl, 753ft 11in oa × 98ft 5in × 27ft, 32ft 6in max |
| | *226.0m, 229.8m × 30.0m × 8.2m, 9.9m* |
| **Machinery:** | 3-shaft Brown-Boveri (*Gneisenau* Germania) geared turbines, 12 Wagner boilers, 165,000shp = 32kts |
| **Armour:** | Belt 350mm-170mm (13.8in-6.7in), torpedo bulkhead 45mm (1.8in), deck 50mm (2in), armoured deck 50mm (2in), slope 105mm (4.1in), main turrets 360mm-150mm (14.2in-5.9in), secondary turrets 140mm-50mm (5.5in-2in), gunshields 50mm (2in), CT 350mm-100mm (13.8in-3.9in) |
| **Armament:** | 9-11in (280mm)/54.5 C28 (3 × 3), 12-5.9in (150mm)/55 C28 (4 × 2, 4 × 1), 14-4.1in (105mm)/65 C33 (7 × 2), 16-37mm/83 C33 (8 × 2), 8-20mm C30, 3-4 aircraft |
| **Complement:** | 1669-1840 |

| Name | Builder | Laid down | Launched | Comp | Fate |
|---|---|---|---|---|---|
| SCHARNHORST | Wilhelmshaven D Yd | 16.5.35 | 30.6.36 | 7.1.39 | Sunk 26.12.43 |
| GNEISENAU | Deutsche Werke, Kiel | 3.5.35 | 8.12.36 | 21.5.38 | Scuttled 28.3.45 |

Anglo-German Naval Agreement of 1935, therefore contained 'two *Panzerschiffe* of 26,000 tons with 280mm guns'. The *Kriegsmarine* regarded the vessels as a reply to the French *Dunkerque* class.

The Anglo-German Naval Agreement allowed a maximum calibre of 16in, and Hitler soon had second thoughts, ordering the ships to be equipped with 380mm (15in) guns; but as the 280mm triple turret was readily available and the development

of a new 15in turret would take some years, he agreed that the two vessels should have 11in weapons initially because he urgently needed capital ships for his political ideas. The ships would be upgunned at the earliest possible opportunity. The 380mm twin turret was later to be used for the *Bismarck* class – which was therefore tied to this mounting as other navies were settling on 16in as the ideal battleship calibre.

In the winter of 1938-39, each ship

was refitted with a clipper bow, increasing overall length to 770ft 8in (234.9m). Two catapults were originally fitted, but that on 'C' turret was removed in 1938-39, when *Scharnhorst* received a new tripod mainmast. Close-range armament was increased during the war, *Scharnhorst* receiving an additional 24-20mm C38 and *Gneisenau* 12-20mm C38. *Scharnhorst* was also later fitted with 6-533mm torpedo tubes (2 × 3) removed from the light cruiser *Nürnberg*.

Scharnhorst April 1939.

Plans to upgun both ships were still alive at the beginning of World War II. When *Gneisenau* was badly damaged following an RAF raid in Kiel during the night of 26/27 November 1942 it was decided to reconstruct the ship to take 380mm guns, with length oa increased to about 245.0m (803ft 10in) and standard displacement to ca35,000t. This plan was, however, abandoned in 1943 and she remained idle without her bow section forward of 'A' turret. The main armament was used for coastal batteries: three 280mm guns were installed near the Hook of Holland and the other six in Norway; the 150mm secondary armament was used, in at least one instance, as a railway gun, complete with turret. Later in the war the ship was towed to Gotenhafen (Gdynia) where she was scuttled as a harbour blockship in 1945. The wreck was broken up *in situ* by a Polish company from 1947 to 1951. *Scharnhorst* was sunk 26.12.43 (during an attempt to intercept convoy JW-55B) by the battleship *Duke of York*, the cruisers *Belfast*, *Sheffield*, *Jamaica* and *Norfolk*, and destroyers, receiving an estimated 13 hits from 14in shells and 14 or 15 from 21in torpedoes.

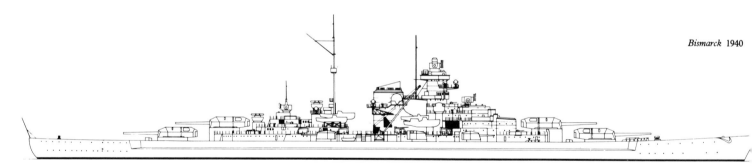

*Bismarck* 1940

Although the two ships of the *Bismarck* class are regarded by many as representing the epitome of German battleship design and construction, they were a political compromise in so far as Hitler did not want to provoke the British, with whom he had concluded an agreement in 1935. At this time, France was regarded as the potential enemy on the continent, and one whose navy needed to be balanced by battleship construction.

*Bismarck* and *Tirpitz*, the first genuine German battleships laid down since World War I, exhibited many features of the last battleship design of the Imperial Navy, the *Baden* class. The armour arrangement followed closely that of *Baden*, with thicker horizontal and somewhat

## BISMARCK class *battleships*

| | |
|---|---|
| **Displacement:** | 41,700t (*Tirpitz* 42,900t) standard; 50,900t (*Tirpitz* 52,600t) deep load |
| **Dimensions:** | 792ft 4in wl, 813ft 8in oa × 118ft 1in × 28ft 6in, 34ft 9in max |
| | *241.5m, 248.0m × 36.0m × 8.7m, 10.6m* |
| **Machinery:** | 3-shaft Blohm & Voss (*Tirpitz* Brown-Boveri) geared turbines, 12 Wagner boilers, 138,000shp = 29kts |
| **Armour:** | Belt 320mm–270mm (12.6in–10.6in), deck 50mm (2in), armoured deck 120mm–80mm (4.7in–3.1in), slopes 100mm (3.9in), torpedo bulkhead 45mm (1.8in), main turrets 360mm–180mm (14.2in–7.1in), secondary turrets 100mm–40mm (3.9in–1.6in), CT 350mm–60mm (13.8in–2.4in) |
| **Armament:** | 8–15in (380mm)/47 C34 (4 × 2), 12–5.9in (150mm)/55 C28 (6 × 2), 16–4.1in (105mm)/65 C32 (8 × 2), 16–37mm/83 C30 8 × 2), 12–20mm C30, 4–6 aircraft |
| **Complement:** | 2092 (*Tirpitz* 2608) |

| Name | Builder | Laid down | Launched | Comp | Fate |
|---|---|---|---|---|---|
| BISMARCK | Blohm & Voss, Hamburg | 1.7.36 | 14.2.39 | 24.8.40 | Sunk 27.5.41 |
| TIRPITZ | Wilhemshaven N Yd | 20.10.36 | 1.4.39 | 25.2.41 | Sunk 12.11.44 |

*Tirpitz* 1942

Above and below: *Bismarck* in Grimstadfjord, May 1941. *CPL*

thinner vertical protection. Internal sub-division was extensive, although the major compartments were larger than those of *Baden* to obviate the problem of cramped conditions, especially in the boiler rooms. The main armament generally complied with accepted international practice in calibre and number, and in characteristics the weapons were very similar to contemporary Italian and French 15in naval guns. Speed and radius of action were inferior to those of the preceding *Scharnhorst* class.

The extremely broad beam of 118ft was adopted for reasons of stability: as a result, the ships were steady gun platforms even in heavy seas. One of the outstanding features was the optical rangefinder equipment. However, *Tirpitz*'s original radar was never updated and she retained her two *Seetakt* sets until the end.

The class were built to Tirpitz's request for the best possible internal protection and stability rather than too heavy an armament. The official displacement figure of 35,000 tons came from calculations arising out of the Anglo-German Naval Agreement: the real figures were a military secret and not until the war was over did it become known for certain that the official figure had been exceeded by so wide a margin. Dimensions as furnished officially under the Agreement were length and beam as in the table, and draught 26ft, figures that

aroused instant suspicion in London as being utterly impracticable for a 35,000t ship.

Both vessels were sunk by the British. *Bismarck* was hunted down and sunk by British battleships on 27.5.41 during her first commerce raiding sortie, after her rudder had been jammed by an airborne torpedo from one of *Ark Royal*'s Swordfish. Numerous 14in and 16in hits from *King George V* and *Rodney* rapidly put the main armament and fire control system out of action, reducing the topsides to a shambles; the order to fire scuttling charges was given, but before these could take effect *Bismarck* was torpedoed on both sides by the cruiser *Dorsetshire*. *Tirpitz* played an

important role as part of the 'fleet in being' in Norway. From 1942 she carried 6-533mm torpedo tubes in triple mountings (removed from the cruiser *Leipzig*), and from that date her AA armament was steadily increased up to 40-20mm C38 in single and quadruple mountings. Damaged by limpet mines from midget submarines, and by Fleet Air Arm and RAF bombs, she was finally sunk by RAF Lancasters while moored off Haakoy Island near Tromso. Three direct hits from 12,000lb (5443kg) bombs and several near misses caused massive explosions, and the ship capsized; the wreck was BU 1948-57.

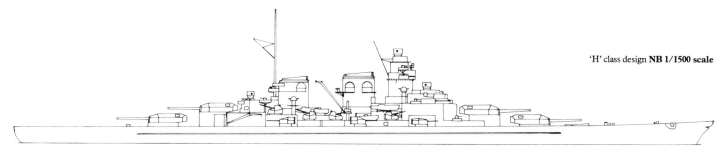

When Hitler adopted the 'Z-Plan' on 1 January 1939, the six units of the 'H' class were to be the heart of this ambitious programme. Not only would these huge battleships provide tough opposition for British capital ships, they would also serve as a useful 'fleet in being' and act as a valuable political instrument. Hitler wanted this battleship fleet to be completed within six years, and so a number of unprecedented steps had to be taken: the naval building programme was accorded top priority over *Luftwaffe* and Army requirements; full responsibility for the whole programme was given to a single person, Rear-Admiral Werner Fuchs, who was to have great powers of authority; and Blohm und Voss was chosen to have overall responsibility for the design, construction, orders for materials and personnel requirements concerning all six ships.

The 'H' class was designed to the same general principles as the preceding *Bismarck* class. The two weak points of the design might have been the torpedo tubes and the aircraft arrangements. Underwater torpedo tubes were stipulated – the first time since World War I that such an obsolete feature was incorporated. The catapult was sited directly under the gun barrels of 'D' turrets and would probably have given rise to serious problems in any engagement.

Owing to the outbreak of war the 'Z-Plan' was cancelled, and work on both 'H' and 'J' ceased on 10 October 1939. 1200t of material for 'H' had been assembled, and 3500t more were under construction; 'J' was less advanced. Contracts for the next pair were cancelled in 1940, and for 'M' and 'N' on 10 October 1939. 'H' and 'J' were later scrapped on slip to provide materials and man-power for the

submarine building programme. Only a few of the 406mm guns were manufactured. Three formed the famous *Batterie Lindemann* at Cap Blanc Nez, and four were installed in concrete bunkers at Trondesnes securing the Vestfjord leading to Narvik.

Further designs derived from the 'H' class led to the 'H42', 'H43' and 'H44' studies, very large projects with deep load displacements of 98,000t, 120,000t and 141,500t respectively. These must be considered as purely paper studies, the results of keeping a large design team in being for the major part of the war. The truly colossal 'H44' project had proposed dimensions 345.1m wl × 51.5m × 13.5m max (1132ft 3in × 169ft × 44ft 4in) and a main armament of 8–508mm (20in) guns. Combined diesels and turbines were to develop 270,000hp for 30.1kts max.

## 'H' class *battleships*

**Displacement:** 52,607t standard; 62,497t deep load
**Dimensions:** 872ft wl, 911ft 5in oa × 122ft × 33ft 6in
*265.8m, 277.8m × 37.2m × 10.2m*
**Machinery:** 3-shafts, 12 MAN double-acting 2-stroke 9cyl diesels, 165,000bhp = 30kts
**Armour:** Belt 300mm–180mm (11.8in–7.1in), deck 80mm–50mm (3.1in–2in), armoured deck 120mm–100mm (4.7in–3.9in), torpedo bulkhead 45mm (1.8in), armoured bulkhead 220mm (8.7in), main turrets 385mm–130mm (15.2in–5.1in), secondary turrets 100mm–40mm (3.9in–1.6in), CT 390mm (15.4in)
**Armament:** 8–16in (406mm)/47 (8 × 2), 12–5.9in (150mm)/55 C28 (6 × 2), 16–4.1in (105mm)/65 C33 (8 × 2), 16–37mm/83 C33 (8 × 2), 24–20mm C38 (6 × 4), 6–21in (533mm) TT sub, 4 aircraft
**Complement:** 2600 (estimate)

| Name | Builder | Laid down | Launched | Comp | Fate |
|------|---------|-----------|----------|------|------|
| 'H' | Blohm & Voss, Hamburg | 15.7.39 | – | – | BU 1939 |
| 'J' | A G Weser Bremen | 15.8.39 | – | – | BU 1939 |
| 'K' | Deutsche Werke, Kiel | – | – | – | – |
| 'L' | Wilhelmshaven D Yd | – | – | – | – |
| 'M' | Blohm & Voss, Hamburg | – | – | – | – |
| 'N' | A G Weser, Bremen | – | – | – | – |

The 'Riskflotte' – the pre-World War I German High Seas Fleet at Kiel. *CPL*

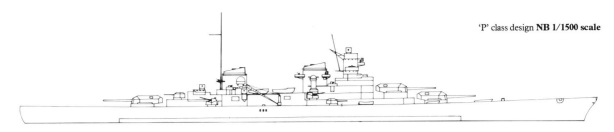

Designs for these three battlecruisers started in 1937, in parallel to designs for an improved 'pocket-battleship' which was later rejected. The class were incorporated into the 'Z-Plan' in 1939, the same year it was planned to lay them down. The ships were designed to act as long-range merchant raiders (action radius 14,000nm at 19kts) that would have forced Great Britain to give each of her convoys strong battleship escort. Because of the outbreak of war the keels were never laid; in fact only 'Q' was ordered, on 8 August 1939.

## 'P' class *battlecruisers*

| | |
|---|---|
| **Displacement:** | 30,500t standard; 35,720t deep load |
| **Dimensions:** | 807ft wl, 841ft 6in oa × 98ft 5in × 31ft 6in, 34ft 6in max |
| | *246.0m, 256.5m × 30.0m × 9.6m, 11.2m* |
| **Machinery:** | 3-shafts, 8 MAN double-acting 2-stroke 24cyl diesels (outer shafts) plus 1 Brown-Boveri geared turbine, 4 Wagner boilers (central shaft), 116,000bhp = 27kts (outer shafts only), 176,000hp = 33.4kts (all three) |
| **Armour:** | Belt 180mm–100mm (7.1in–3.9in), torpedo bulkhead 45mm (1.8in), deck 50mm (2in), armoured deck 80mm (3.1in), main turrets 210mm–50mm (8.2in–2in), secondary turrets 140mm (5.5in), CT 200mm–60mm (7.9in-2.4in) |
| **Armament:** | 6-15in (380mm)/47 C34 (3×2), 6-5.9in (150mm)/48 (3×2), 8-4.1in (105mm)/65 C33 (4×2), 8-37mm/83 C33 (4 × 2), 20-20mm C38, 6-21in TT (533mm) TT aw, 4 aircraft |
| **Complement:** | 1965 |

| Name | Builder | Laid down | Launched | Comp | Fate |
|---|---|---|---|---|---|
| 'O' | Deutsche Werke, Kiel | – | – | – | – |
| 'P' | Wilhemshaven | – | – | – | – |
| 'Q' | Germaniawerft, Kiel | – | – | – | – |

# Great Britain

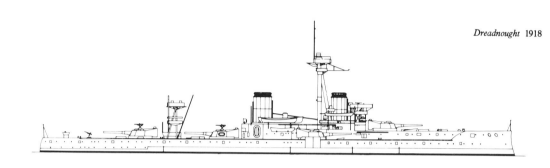

*Dreadnought* 1918

Although the broad outlines of the design history of HMS *Dreadnought* are too well known to require more than a brief summary, certain points about her are not common knowledge. She was a logical step in British battleship design rather than a sudden departure inspired by the fertile brain of Admiral Sir John Fisher. Deadman and Narbeth, the Constructors who worked on the *King Edward VII* design had pressed for a heavier armament then, and had proposed an all-12in gun armament for the *Lord Nelson* class. Although most historians claim that General Cuniberti's article in *Jane's Fighting Ships'* 1903 edition inspired the concept, it can had had little effect on the outcome as both the Gunnery Branch and the DNC's department had already reach the conclusion that a simplified one-calbire armament made sense; gunnery ranges were increasing to the point where 6in, 9.2in and 12in shell splashes could not be distinguished from one another. In 1904 the US Navy's designers started work on a ship with four twin 12in turrets and no secondary gun bigger than 3in, for exactly the same reasons, and experience in the Russo-Japanese War would very soon convince the Japanese to go the same way.

Fisher himself does not seem to have grasped the potential for long-range gunnery; what impressed him most about the sketch designs put before him was the economy of maintenance of a ship driven by steam turbines and carrying only one outfit of spares and ammunition. With a programme of increased expenditure planned Fisher was bound to be swayed by the argument that 30 *Dreadnought*s would cost the same as 29 *Lord Nelson*s to run. What was in many ways a much more

## DREADNOUGHT *battleship*

| | |
|---|---|
| **Displacement:** | 18,110t load; 21,845t deep load |
| **Dimensions:** | 490ft pp, 527ft oa × 82ft × 31ft deep load |
| | *149.4m, 160.6m × 25.0m × 9.4m* |
| **Machinery:** | 4-shaft Parsons turbines, 18 Babcock & Wilcox boilers, 23,000shp = 21kts. Coal 2900t, oil 1120t. Range 6620nm at 10kts |
| **Armour:** | Belt 11in–4in (279mm–102mm), barbettes, turret faces and CT 11in (279mm), decks 3in–1.5in (76mm–38mm) |
| **Armament:** | 10–12in (305mm)/45 Mk X (5 × 2), 24/27 (from 1916 10)-12pdr (76mm) 18cwt, 5 (from 1916 4-)18in (457mm) TT sub (4 beam, 1 stern) |
| **Complement:** | 695–773 |

| Name | Builder | Laid down | Launched | Comp | Fate |
|---|---|---|---|---|---|
| DREADNOUGHT | Portsmouth DYd | 2.10.05 | 10.2.06 | 12.06 | Sold for BU 9.5.21 |

revolutionary and risky step was the proposal by the Engineer-in-Chief, Sir John Durston, to adopt 4-shaft Parsons turbines. With the backing of the DNC, Sir Philip Watts, the Parsons turbine won the day, despite the fact that the first RN destroyers with turbines had only gone to sea four years earlier, the first turbine-driven cruiser was not yet at sea, and the first large commercial turbine-driven ship had not even been laid down.

The high-ranking (and high-powered) Committee on Design first met on 3 January 1905 and reached the stage of making its final report only seven weeks later, a remarkably short time for such a complex series of decisions. In fact this haste, plus the lack of good professional engineering knowledge of weapons may have contributed to the mistake which were made. Three distinguished captains agreed to site the tripod mast with its all-important fire control platform immediately abaft the forward funnel,

where it would inevitably be smoked out at high speed. This was done by merely to provide a convenient method of handling the boats, and taken with some recorded remarks by the Committee, confirms that neither Fisher nor his appointees had entirely grasped the implications of long-range gunnery. The same gunnery experts opted for an inconvenient layout of the five 12in turrets, with two wing turrets which had limited arcs of fire. A more serious weakness was the omission of the upper strake of 8in armour in previous designs. This was probably done to keep the displacement down, for political reasons, but it meant that at deep load (21,845t) with 2900t of coal on board the draught would rise to 31ft. At this draught the 11in belt was completely submerged, and the ship would be protected only by a 4ft strake of 8in armour. It was a failing of three designs which followed the *Dreadnought*, and was contrary to the wishes of the DNC.

When the ship appeared in 1906 her revolutionary appearance stifled such criticisms, however, and most commentators were at a loss to understand how a ship of such heavy armament and freeboard had been achieved on only a small increase in displacement over her predecessors. Herein lay the secret of the design, for the steam turbine machinery was about 300t lighter than reciprocating engines of the same power. Furthermore, the greater weight would have meant bigger engine rooms, and the true saving in weight was probably nearer 1000t. The construction then contributed their part by designing an efficient hull-form to meet the unusually high speed of 21kts, using tank models at Haslar to achieve the best form.

The weight of hull structure and fittings was strictly controlled, and the steady reduction in weights which had been going on for a decade or more was maintained. For example, the hull

*Dreadnought* 1907. CPL

weight was no greater than the *Majestic* (1894) despite an overall increase of 3000t. The newer model of 12in turret and turntable introduced in the *King Edward VII* also helped to keep weight down. The intention was to build the ship in a very short time, and so the hull structure was designed for simplicity, without losing the rigidity necessary to withstand the shock of eight-gun broadsides. Part of this 'streamlining' was the adoption of standard plates in various sizes and thicknesses. These plates were ordered well in advance. The unpierced bulkheads and separate pumping and flooding arrangements used in the *Lord Nelson*s were repeated in order to speed construction, although their value in reducing vulnerability was also recognised.

The building of HMS *Dreadnought* in 14 months (for publicity purposes a basin trial after 12 months was treated as completion) set a record which has never been equalled, and although Fisher's drive helped to enthuse everyone connected with the project, most of the credit must go to the staff of Portsmouth Dockyard. The yard was already the most efficient in the country, having built the *Majestic* in 22 months and averaging only 31 months

for battleships built between 1894 and 1904. Once authority was given to divert four 12in turrets from the *Lord Nelson* and *Agamemnon* the way was clear. The keel was laid on 2 October 1905, and the official start of trials was 3 October 1906, although the ship could not be called complete for another two months.

Sea trials were very satisfactory, as the high forecastle stayed dry and the full section amidships helped to damp the roll. Above all, the risk taken with the Parsons turbine more than justified itself as vibration was much reduced. Imitation is the most sincere form of flattery, and in all foreign navies work

on 'dreadnoughts' started immediately. She gave her name to a new breed of battleship, and epitomised the naval arms race between Great Britain and Germany.

The ship's light secondary armament was subject to a number of changes during the trials period, but eventually settled in 1907: 10–12pdrs in pairs on the turret roofs and another 14 in the superstructure. She underwent very little modification during the war, apart from getting lower topmasts in 1915, and in later 1916 receiving the standard enlarged fire control position, searchlight control positions, and the removal of

torpedo nets, etc.

She was flagship 4th Battle Squadron, Home Fleet in August 1914 and went to Scapa Flow. While engaged on a sweep in the North Sea on 18 March 1915 she rammed and sank *U 29* (K/Lt Otto Weddigen), making her the only battleship to have sunk a submarine. She received a major refit early in 1916, and in May 1916 became flagship, 3rd BS (*King Edward VII* class) stationed at Sheerness, thus missing Jutland. On sale list March 1920.

*Dreadnought* about 1917.
*CPL*

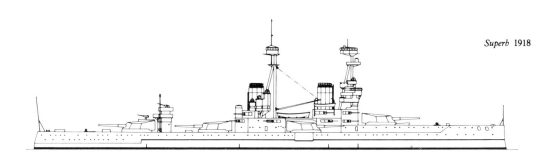

*Superb* 1918

## BELLEROPHON class *battleships*

| | |
|---|---|
| **Displacement:** | 18,800t load; 22,102t deep load |
| **Dimensions:** | 490ft pp, 526ft oa × 82ft 6in × 27ft 3in mean |
| | *149.4m, 160.3m × 25.2m × 8.3m* |
| **Machinery:** | 4-shaft Parsons turbines, 18 Babcock & Wilcox or Yarrow boilers, 23,000shp = 20¾kts. Coal 2648t, oil 842t, patent fuel 170t. Range 5720nm at 10kts. |
| **Armour:** | Belt 10in–5in (254mm–127mm), bulkheads 8in (203mm), barbettes 9in–5in (229mm–127mm), turret faces 11in (279mm), CT 11in–8in (279mm–203mm), decks 4in–0.5in (102mm–13mm) |
| **Armament:** | 10–12in (305mm)/45 Mk X (5 × 2), 16–4in (102mm)/50 QF, 4–3pdr (47mm) saluting, 3–18in (457mm) TT sub (2 beam, 1 stern) |
| **Complement:** | 732 |

The first class of battleships to follow the *Dreadnought* were virtually repeats of the design, with the same propulsion but some minor improvements. The tripod foremast was moved forward of the fore funnel, but a second tripod and spotting position was equally likely to be smoked out, as it was placed immediately forward of the second funnel. The puny armament of 12pdr (3in) guns were replaced by 4in QF, an altogether more credible defence against destroyer attack. Although the main armour belt was slightly thinner, overall protection was improved by the inclusion for the first time of a torpedo bulkhead, an inner longitudinal bulkhead designed to localise a torpedo hit.

The tall twin tripods gave the ships a more balanced profile than the *Dreadnought* but war service quickly showed the uselessness of the after fire control position and the exposed platforms for the 4in guns. Topmasts were reduced in height in 1915 because of new, more powerful radio

| Name | Builder | Laid down | Launched | Comp | Fate |
|---|---|---|---|---|---|
| BELLEROPHON | Portsmouth DYd | 3.12.06 | 27.7.07 | 2.09 | Sold for BU 8.11.21 |
| SUPERB | Elswick | 6.2.07 | 7.11.07 | 5.09 | Sold for BU 12.12.23 |
| TEMERAIRE | Devonport DYd | 1.1.07 | 24.8.07 | 5.09 | Sold for BU 7.12.21 |

equipment, and in 1916 all 4in were removed from the turret roofs. New double-decked positions were provided in the superstructure, where they had good arcs of fire. In 1917 a 4in AA gun was added on the

quarterdeck and a 3in on the after superstructure (in *Superb* the 4in AA gun was on the after 12in turret). Torpedo nets were removed, along with the stern TT, enclosed searchlight platforms were added, and a

clinker screen (funnel cap) was added to the fore funnel. The torpedo nets had been removed in 1915, at the same time that the after fire control position had been eliminated. By 1918 all three had been equipped to operate aircraft from platforms on 'A' and 'Y' turrets, a Sopwith Pup fighter and a 1½-Strutter reconnaissance machine. Although they suffered from the same weaknesses as the *Dreadnought* they were built rapidly to maintain the lead, and were successful ships which remained in front-line service until 1918.

All joined the Grand Fleet in 1914 and saw action at Jutland, 31 May 1916. *Superb* and *Temeraire* went to the Mediterranean in 1918, the former leading the Allied Fleet through the Dardanelles in November 1918. *Bellerophon* and *Superb* became turret drillships in 1919 after paying off, and were stricken in 1920. *Superb* was used as a target before being sold for BU. *Temeraire* was Cadets' sea-going TS from 1919 until put up for sale in late 1921.

*Bellerophon* as completed.                                                                   *CPL*

*Vanguard* as completed.                                                                   *CPL*

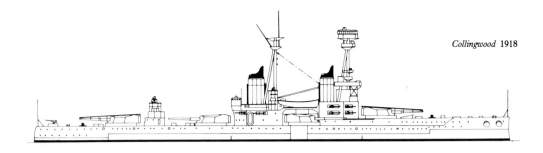

## ST VINCENT class *battleships*

| | |
|---|---|
| **Displacement:** | 19,560t load; 23,030t deep load |
| **Dimensions:** | 500ft pp, 536ft oa × 84ft × 27ft 11in |
| | *152.4m, 163.4m × 25.6m × 8.5m* |
| **Machinery:** | 4-shaft Parsons turbines, 18 Babcock & Wilcox or Yarrow boilers, 24,500shp = 21kts. Coal 2800t, oil 940t, patent fuel 190t. Range 6900nm at 10kts |
| **Armour:** | Belt 10in–7in (254mm–178mm), bulkheads 8in–4in (203mm–102mm), barbettes 9in–5in (229mm–127mm), turret faces 11in (279mm), CT 11in–8in (279mm–203mm), decks 3in–0.75in (76mm–19mm) |
| **Armament:** | 10–12in (305mm)/50 Mk XI (5 × 2), 20–4in (102mm)/50 QF, 4–3pdr (47mm) saluting, 3–18in (457mm) TT sub (2 beam, 1 stern) |
| **Complement:** | 718 |

| Name | Builder | Laid down | Launched | Comp | Fate |
|---|---|---|---|---|---|
| COLLINGWOOD | Devonport DYd | 3.2.07 | 7.11.08 | 4.10 | Sold for BU 12.12.22 |
| ST VINCENT | Portsmouth DYd | 30.12.07 | 10.9.08 | 5.09 | Sold for BU 1.12.21 |
| VANGUARD | Vickers, Barrow | 2.4.08 | 22.2.09 | 2.10 | Sunk 9.7.17 |

The next class of battleships followed the lines of the *Bellerophons*, largely to speed construction, but a new model of 12in gun was adopted. Horsepower was increased slightly to offset the rise in displacement caused by greater length (for longer guns) and a slight increase in beam and draught. The 50cal Mk XI gun was not a success as its high muzzle velocity shortened barrel life and reduced accuracy at long range. As in the *Bellerophons* the after fire control position was all but useless because of smoke interference.

Modifications before 1914 were restricted to lowering the topmasts and removing 2–4in guns from the roof of 'A' turret. By 1916 all three had lost their torpedo nets and in 1916–17 the fore funnel had been given a clinker screen (*Collingwood* had a clinker screen on the after funnel as well), the stern TT had been removed and a single 4in AA gun had replaced the 2–3in AA installed in 1915–16. *Collingwood* was also fitted with aircraft platforms and operated the standard Pup and 1½-Strutter aircraft in 1918. Both *St Vincent* and *Collingwood* had their bridgework and control tops enlarged, and the superstructure was built up, with 4in guns mounted on two levels. Searchlights were regrouped as well, being mounted in 'coffee pot' towers.

All joined the Grand Fleet in August 1914 and fought at Jutland, without casualties. *Vanguard* blew up at anchor in Scapa Flow on 9 July 1917, due to faulty ammunition (804 killed). The survivors became gunnery TS after the armistice until paid off late in 1919. Both were BU to comply with Washington Treaty.

Since the 1890s the armoured cruiser had risen in size and gunpower until it outstripped many 2nd and 3rd class battleships. The Royal Navy in particular built a series of enormously expensive cruisers, and in the last years before the advent of the *Dreadnought*, each class of battleship had its corresponding 'homologue': the *Minotaur* design, for example, had many of the *Lord Nelson* features. It was thus entirely logical that in 1902 Admiral Fisher should discuss with W H Gard the design of a new armoured cruiser to be built in parallel with the new battleship. As first conceived it would have 6in armour, 2 twin 9.2in turrets and 6 twin 7.5in turrets; speed would be 25kts with turbines developing 35,000shp. The Admiralty built the *Minotaur* class instead, but they were too slow by Fisher's standards.

The Russo-Japanese War gave

*Invincible* 1910.
CPL

54 · ALL THE WORLD'S BATTLESHIPS

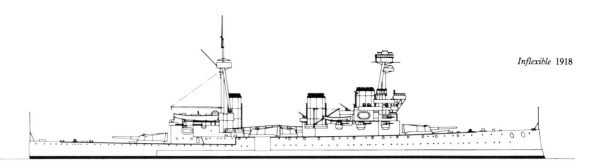

fresh impetus to plans for a new armoured cruiser, especially as armoured cruisers had apparently proved capable of fighting battleships without suffering unduly. The appalling inefficiency and tactical ineptitude of the Russian Baltic Fleet was conveniently overlooked, and Fisher was not alone in thinking that speed offered sufficient protection against heavy shells. The Committee on Designs, as soon as it had finished with the *Dreadnought* design, turned to discussion of a specification for an armoured cruiser equivalent of the *Dreadnought*, having her 12in guns, the 6in armour of the *Minotaur* but the unheard-of speed of 25kts.

The design which emerged bore a strong resemblance to the most recent armoured cruisers, rather than to the *Dreadnought*, although clearly some of her features were repeated. With a much longer hull needed to accommodate the extra boilers and machinery it was possible to have the midships 12in turrets slightly *en echelon*, but the broadside was only six guns; the off-side turret had a cross-deck firing angle of about 30 deg, but could be used only if the near-side turret were disabled. The forecastle deck was carried aft for two-thirds of

## INVINCIBLE class *battlecruisers*

| | |
|---|---|
| **Displacement:** | 17,373t average load; 20,078t average deep load |
| **Dimensions:** | 530ft pp, 567ft oa × 78ft 6in × 26ft 2in mean |
| | *161.5m, 172.8m × 23.9m × 8.0m* |
| **Machinery:** | 4-shaft Parsons turbines, 31 Babcock & Wilcox or Yarrow boilers, 41,000shp = 25½kts. Coal 3085t, oil 710t–725t. Range 3090nm at 10kts |
| **Armour:** | Belt 6in–4in (152mm–102mm), bulkheads 7in–6in (178mm–152mm), barbettes 7in–2in (178mm–51mm), turret faces 7in (178mm), CT 10in–6in (254mm–152mm), decks 2.5in–0.75in (64mm–19mm) |
| **Armament:** | 8-12in (305mm)/45 Mk X (4 × 2), 16-4in (102mm)/45 Mk III QF, 7 Maxim MGs, 5-18in (457mm) TT sub (4 beam, 1 stern) |
| **Complement:** | 784 |

| Name | Builder | Laid down | Launched | Comp | Fate |
|---|---|---|---|---|---|
| INDOMITABLE | Fairfield | 1.3.06 | 16.3.07 | 6.08 | Sold 1922 |
| INFLEXIBLE | Clydebank | 5.2.06 | 26.6.07 | 10.08 | Sold 1922 |
| INVINCIBLE | Elswick | 2.4.06 | 13.4.07 | 3.09 | Sunk 31.5.16 |

the lengths, giving high command to the midships turrets, and 4in QF Mk III guns replaced the 12pdr (3in) guns of the *Dreadnought*.

The main drawings and detailed work were complete by 22 June 1905 and the first of class was laid down the following February. Although there was no question of emulating the building-time of the *Dreadnought* all three took little more than 26–32

months to build, a creditable time for large and novel ships. They were driven by no fewer than ten turbines, two HP and two LP ahead turbines, two HP and two LP astern sets and two HP cruising sets, with steam provided by 31 boilers. *Indomitable* reached a record speed of 25.3kts with 43,700shp over a period of three days, and all three were economical steamers. Like the *Dreadnought*, their

twin balanced rudders made them handy ships with a small tactical diameter. They were capable of 25½kts at load draught and 24.6kts at deep load, while the average radius of action at 23kts was 2300 miles (rising to nearly 3100nm if oil fuel were used).

The *Invincible* class was later condemned as a badly conceived and poorly executed design. This, however, is a harsh judgement on the men who carried out Fisher's instructions. They produced a logical successor to the previous classes of armoured cruisers, with all-round improvements in speed, gunpower and range, and no sacrifice in protection. The trials were an outstanding success, showing that the ships met all specifications. If there is a valid criticisms of the design, it is the expense of the ships, for they cost nearly 50 per cent more than the *Minotaur* class.

The *Invincible* had been fitted with electrically driven 12in turrets, 'A' and 'Y' to Vickers' design and 'P' and 'Q' to Armstrongs' design. These installations did not prove a great success as the rate of 'creep' was too slow and uneven, and although conversion to hydraulic power was planned to take place in October 1912–May 1913 it did not happen until March 1914.

What was wrong with the *Invincible* class was their role. The validity of the armoured cruiser was already in doubt, and what the Royal Navy really needed was a cruiser capable of working with the Fleet. By giving the *Invincible* 12in guns instead of 9.2in or 10in the error was compounded, for she would inevitably be regarded as equivalent to a battleship. The introduction of the

term 'battlecruiser' in 1912 was proof of this, and the term 'capital ship' was then used to cover both battleships and battlecruisers. It was asking a lot of any admiral to leave out of his battle line any ship armed with 12in guns, and it was only a matter of time before a battlecruiser's thin armour was exposed to a weight of shellfire it was never intended to face.

As completed all three ships had short funnels, following Fisher's insistence on reducing the silhouette to a minimum, but in 1910 *Indomitable* had her fore funnel raised, followed by *Inflexible* a year later. *Invincible* did not follow suit until January 1915. From 1911 the 4in guns on turret roofs were fitted with canvas spray screens, and from August 1914 they underwent a variety of minor alterations. These included removal of torpedo nets, fitting of various rangefinder baffles on masts, addition of a 3in AA gun (at the after end of the shelter deck) and enlarging of the control platforms aloft. After Jutland the two survivors were given additional armour on the turret roofs and 1in armour was added over the crowns of the magazines. By 1918 both had a Sopwith Pup and a 1½-Strutter, with flying-off platforms on 'P' and 'Q' turrets.

All three served in the Home Fleet and Mediterranean between completion and 1914. *Inflexible* and *Indomitable* with the rest of the Mediterranean Fleet hunted the *Goeben* and *Breslau* in August 1914. *Indomitable* with *Indefatigable* bombarded the outer Dardanelles forts on 3 November 1914. *Invincible* and *Inflexible* were ordered to the Falklands 4 November 1914, leaving Devonport on the 11th and arriving at Port Stanley on 7 December 1914 (*Invincible* flagship of Admiral Sturdee). The following day they destroyed Vice-Admiral von Spee's armoured cruisers *Scharnhorst* and *Gneisenau* (*Invincible* fired 512 12in shells, and was hit by 22 8.3in and 5.9in shells, 2 below the waterline, disabling 1 4in gun and flooding a coal bunker, *Inflexible* fired 661 12in shells and was hit 3 times, with insignificant damage). On her return, *Inflexible* was sent to Mediterranean, and relieved *Indefatigable* as flagship of C-in-C. Bombarded outer Dardanelles forts, on 19 February and 15 March 1915, and during the attack on the 18th put two 14in guns out of action. Suffered superficial damage from Turkish gunfire, but was seriously damaged by a mine of 18 March, suffering flooding

forward. Towed to Malta and repaired by May 1915 but then returned to Rosyth, where she joined her sisters in the 3rd BCS. On 24 January 1915 *Indomitable* took part in the Battle of the Dogger Bank, when she opened fire at 16,250yds (she was the slowest of the class and still had 2crh shells). Fired 134 12in shells at *Blücher* at ranges down to 6000yds, as well as 2 12in at a Zeppelin airship, and in spite of machinery problems reached 25kts. She towed the crippled flagship *Lion* back to Rosyth. All detached to Scapa Flow in May 1916, for gunnery exercises and to replace the 5th BS in the Grand Fleet. At Jutland *Invincible* flew the flag of Rear-Admiral the Hon Horace Hood, and engaged light cruisers of the German 2nd Scouting Group at 10,000yds. Although her fire disabled the *Wiesbaden* and *Pillau* and then inflicted two serious hits on the battlecruiser *Lützow*, her target and the *Derfflinger* scored five hits on her. The last shell blew the roof off 'Q' turret and set fire to the cordite propellant. The flash quickly reached the magazine and the *Invincible* was blown in half by a massive explosion. All but 3 of her complement were lost, including the Admiral. *Indomitable* hit *Derfflinger* three times and *Seydlitz*

once during the deployment phase, and later scored a hit on the pre-dreadnought *Pommern*.

Altogether she fired 175 12in shells and, like *Inflexible*, was undamaged. Both ships reduced to reserve early in 1919 and paid off in March 1920.

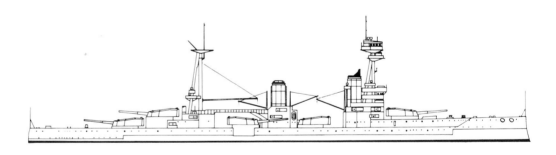

British designers were aware that the disposition of guns in the *Dreadnought* and her successors was far from ideal, particularly in the light of developments abroad. The latest ships, the *St Vincent*s, could only fire 8 guns on the broadside, whereas the American *Delaware* class and the Argentine *Moreno* class, for example, could fire 10 and 12 guns respectively. The solution chosen for the first ship of the 1908 Programme was far from satisfactory, but it was a step in the right direction. The wing turrets were staggered to give a limited degree of cross-deck firing, and to avoid too long a hull, 'X' turret was raised a deck level over 'Y', as in American ships. Cross-deck firing proved of limited value as it strained the hull, but the new layout did at least permit 10 guns to be fired on the broadside. Unfortunately, not all other theoretical advantages were feasible; axial firing from the wing turrets caused unacceptable damage to

## NEPTUNE *battleship*

| | |
|---|---|
| **Displacement:** | 19,680t load; 22,720t deep load |
| **Dimensions:** | 510ft pp, 546ft oa × 85ft × 28ft 6in max<br>*155.4m, 166.4m × 25.9m × 8.7m* |
| **Machinery:** | 4-shaft Parsons steam turbines, 18 Yarrow boilers, 25,000shp = 21kts. Coal 2710t, oil 790t. Range 6330nm at 10kts. |
| **Armour:** | Belt 10in–2.5in (254mm–64mm), bulkheads 8in–4in (203mm–102mm), barbettes 9in–5in (229mm–127mm), turret faces 11in (279mm), CT 11in (279mm), decks 3in–0.75in (76mm–19mm) |
| **Armament:** | 10-12in (305mm)/50 Mk XI (5 × 2), 16-4in (102mm)/50 Mk VII, 4-3pdr (47mm), 3-18in (457mm) TT (2 beam, 1 stern) |
| **Complement:** | 759 |

| Name | Builder | Laid down | Launched | Comp | Fate |
|---|---|---|---|---|---|
| NEPTUNE | Portsmouth DYd | 19.1.09 | 30.9.09 | 1.11 | Sold for BU 9.22 |

the superstructure, and the superimposed turret could not fire directly aft because blast concussed the gunlayers in 'Y' turret. The exposed positions for the 4in guns on turret roofs were abandoned, and the

secondary guns were mounted in the superstructure. To keep the arcs for the 12in guns clear the boats were carried on a prominent 'flying bridge', but it was soon recognised that these were likely to be destroyed by gunfire,

with the inevitable consequence that the wreckage would foul the guns below. For the first time cruising turbines were provided, to cut coal consumption at slow and medium speed. She was the fastest British

*Neptune* as completed.
CPL

battleship to date, making 22.7kts on trials and sustaining 21¾kts for 8 hours.

In 1912 her fore funnel was raised, and in 1913 twin searchlights were grouped on the forward super-structure. Shortly after the outbreak of war the forward flying bridge was removed, and in 1916 the twin searchlights were replaced by singles. At the same time a funnel cap or clinker screen was added to the fore funnel and the after fire control platform was re-moved. It had been found that the 4in guns were exposed, and the upper positions were enclosed by light steel structures. The stern TT was removed c1915.

She was flagship of the Home Fleet from May 1911 to May 1912, and joined the Grand Fleet in August 1914. Fought at Jutland, suffering no casualties, and paid off into Reserve 1919.

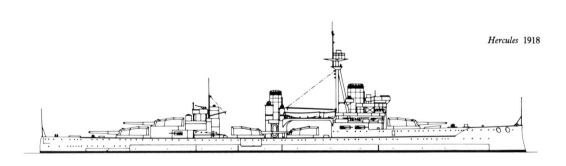

*Hercules* 1918

## COLOSSUS class *battleships*

| | |
|---|---|
| **Displacement:** | 20,255t load; 23,050t deep load |
| **Dimensions:** | 510ft pp, 546ft oa × 85ft × 28ft 9in max |
| | *155.4m, 166.4m × 25.9m × 8.8m* |
| **Machinery:** | 4-shaft Parsons steam turbines, 18 Babcock & Wilcox (*Hercules* Yarrow) boilers, 25,000shp = 21kts. Coal 2900t, oil 800t. Range 6680nm at 10kts. |
| **Armour:** | Belt 11in-7in (279mm-178mm), bulkheads 10in-4in (254mm-102mm), barbettes 11in-4in (279mm-102mm), turret faces 11in (279mm), CT 11in (279mm), decks 4in-1.75in (102mm-44mm) |
| **Armament:** | 10-12in (305mm)/50 Mk XI (5 × 2), 16-4in (102mm)/50 Mk VII, 4-3pdr (47mm), 3-21in (533mm) TT sub (2 beam, 1 stern) |
| **Complement:** | 755 |

| Name | Builder | Laid down | Launched | Comp | Fate |
|---|---|---|---|---|---|
| COLOSSUS | Scotts | 8.7.09 | 9.4.10 | 7.11 | Sold for BU 7.28 |
| HERCULES | Palmers | 30.7.09 | 10.5.10 | 8.11 | Sold for BU 11.21 |

In 1908 a 'panic' started over allegations that Germany was laying down dreadnoughts in secret, to over-take the Royal Navy. Reports sug-gested that by the spring of 1912 there would be 21 German and 21 British dreadnoughts each, and the public debate become violently partisan. Ironically the Admiralty figures were contested most fiercely by Winston Churchill, then President of the Board of Trade. The Conservative opposition and the Navy League adopted as their slogan 'We Want Eight and We Won't Wait', de-manding that the four capital ships proposed for 1909 should be increased to eight. The figures provided by naval intelligence and various informants who had visited Germany were incorrect, but they gave the Admiralty an excuse to ask for six ships. In fact this figure restored cuts imposed by the Liberal government. The Cabinet finally gave in to public agitation, and voted for all eight ships: two battle-ships similar to the *Neptune* and six much larger 13.5in-gunned ships.

The first two battleships were half-sisters to the *Neptune*, but with numerous minor changes. The layout of main armament was unchanged, but to save weight the arrangement of siting the tripod mast abaft the fore funnel was reintroduced. The midships 'P' and 'Q' turrets were closer together, permitting a longer forward superstructure and a better concentration of secondary guns. The 21in Hardcastle 'heater' torpedo also

*Colossus* 1913.

replaced the 18in, necessitating larger torpedo rooms below the waterline. It was vital to keep displacement down to avoid submerging the belt any further, and great efforts were made to improve protection on the gun positions and along the waterline. Unfortunately the designers were asked to do all this on the same length and beam as the *Neptune*, so the additional 1in armour on the belt and 2in on the barbettes

could only result in thinner plating elsewhere. This was the last attempt to keep displacement down to an artificial limit, but the subsequent increase in size was accompanied by a big jump in gun calibre, which largely used up the additional margin created.

In 1912 the fore funnel was raised in both ships to keep smoke away from the bridge. The principal visual difference between the two ships was

in the 4in gun battery: *Hercules* had shields to her light guns, while her sister had open ports with dropping lids. In 1915–16 both ships lost their torpedo nets and in 1917 the after flying deck was removed; other standard wartime charges were made during this period. Three 4in were replaced by one 4in AA and one 3in AA.

Both fought at Jutland, where *Colossus* was the only Grand Fleet

battleship hit (two hits, five casualties). *Hercules* carried the Allied Naval Commission to Kiel in November 1918. *Colossus* served in 1919–20 as a Cadets' TS at Devonport, being painted in Victorian black, white and buff livery. She was stricken in 1920 but not sold for BU until July 1928.

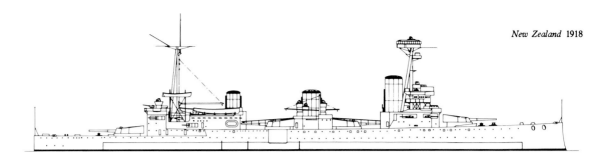

The second ship of the 1908 Programme was to be a battlecruiser equivalent of the *Neptune*, but instead of taking the opportunity to remedy the weaknesses of the *Invincibles* they were virtually repeats of the design. The only excuse for building such a ship would be to speed up construction, but there was no justification for repeating the design when the Dominions of Australia and New Zealand voted money for their own capital ships. HMAS *Australia* was to become the flagship of the new Royal Australian Navy, but the *New Zealand* was presented to the RN on completion. For some reason the design was credited with much greater fighting power than the ship possessed – presumably the result of official 'leaks' inspired by Admiral Fisher. To

## INDEFATIGABLE class *battlecruisers*

| | |
|---|---|
| **Displacement:** | 18,500t (*Indefatigable* 18,470t) load; 22, 110t (*Indefatigable* 22,080t) deep load |
| **Dimensions:** | 555ft pp, 590ft oa × 80ft × 26ft 6in mean |
| | *169.2m, 179.8m × 24.4m × 8.1m* |
| **Machinery:** | 4-shaft Parsons turbines, 32 Babcock & Wilcox boilers, 44,000shp (*Indefatigable* 43,000shp) = 25kts. Coal 3170t, oil 840t (*Indefatigable* 3340/870t). Range 6330nm at 10kts |
| **Armour:** | Belt 6in–4in (152mm–102mm), bulkheads 4in (102mm), barbettes 7in–3in (178mm–76mm), turret faces 7in (178mm), CT 10in (254mm), decks 2.5in–1in (64mm–25mm) |
| **Armament:** | 8–12in (305mm)/45 Mk X (4 × 2), 16–4in (102mm)/50 Mk VII, 4–3pdr (47mm), 3–18in (457mm) TT sub (2 beam, 1 stern) |
| **Complement:** | 800 |

| Name | Builder | Laid down | Launched | Comp | Fate |
|---|---|---|---|---|---|
| INDEFATIGABLE | Devonport DYd | 23.2.09 | 28.10.09 | 4.11 | Sunk 31.5.16 |
| AUSTRALIA (RAN) | John Brown | 23.6.10 | 25.10.11 | 6.13 | Scuttled 12.4.24 |
| NEW ZEALAND | Fairfield | 20.6.10 | 1.7.11 | 11.12 | Sold for BU 19.12.22 |

this day most reference books credit the ship with Mk XI 50cal 12in guns, whereas photos indicate the same Mk X turrets as the *Invincible* (a fact confirmed by official drawings and other primary sources). Even the normally well-informed Fred T Jane greatly exaggerated the scale of armour (8in belt, 3in decks and 10in on turrets) and claimed a speed of 29–30kts. In fact she was simply a repeat *Invincible* lengthened both to permit both 'P' and 'Q' turrets to fire on the broadside, but unlike the original, displaced 1000t less than her battleship equivalent, HMS *Neptune*, Some attempt was made to improve the armouring in the *Australia* and *New Zealand* by deleting the thin armour at bow and stern and thickening the belt abreast of 'A' and 'X' turrets to 5in. There was also an increase of 1000shp, with the result that they had less difficulty in exceeding the designed speed of 25kts. *Indefatigable* barely reached 25 kts on trials, but by forcing the boilers she recorded 26.89kts with over 55,000shp. The other two exceeded 26kts on trials, and during the Dogger Bank HMS *New Zealand* is credited with developing 65,000shp.

The smoke nuisance was becoming evident by the time the *Indefatigable* was designed, and so she was given a tall fore funnel. In spite of the gap between the third funnel and the fire control position on the after tripod it still proved unusable and during the war was dismantled. In October 1914

*New Zealand* had 1–3in/20cwt. Mk I and 1–6pdr (57mm) Hotchkiss AA guns added on the after superstructure; *Indefatigable* and *Australia* each received 1–3in/20cwt Mk I AA gun in March 1915. After Jutland the two survivors were given 1in deck armour between 'P' and 'Q' barbettes and on the main deck in the wake of all four barbettes. They also received all the standard modifications to searchlights, range clocks and deflection scales, as well as enlarged fire control positions and bridgework (director platforms for the main armament had been added to the foremast in 1915–16 in all three ships). The stern 18in TT was removed from all three ships c1915. In June 1917 *Australia* was given an additional AA gun, a 4in Mk VII on a 60° mounting, and at about the same time *New Zealand* was modified in similar manner, losing her 6pdr AA gun. In 1918 both ships were fitted with aircraft platforms on 'P' and 'Q' turrets, to operate a Sopwith Camel fighter and a 1½-Strutter spotter, and on 4 April 1918 *Australia* successfully flew off the first 1½-Strutter from 'Q' turret. In February 1919 *New Zealand*'s 3in AA gun was replaced by 2–2pdr pompons, and 4–4in secondary guns were removed (a fifth had been removed in 1917). *Australia* had both AA guns replaced by 2–4in QF Mk V on 80° mountings in January 1920.

*Indefatigable* was transferred from the Home Fleet to the Mediterranean in 1913, and in August 1914 took part

in the hunt for the *Goeben* and *Breslau*. Bombarded Cape Helles, 4 November 1914 and returned to the Grand Fleet in February 1915. Was sunk by 11in shellfire from the *von der Tann* during the first phase of Jutland, 31 May 1916. Two shells apparently caused an explosion in 'X' magazine and she staggered out of line, sinking by the stern; then another salvo hit on the foredeck, causing a much more severe explosion which destroyed her.

*Australia* went out to Australia on completion, and became the flagship of the RAN. She was flagship of a combined Australian and New Zealand force assembled in the Pacific to prevent any incursion by von Spee's squadron. After the Falklands battle she joined in the search for Spee's supply ships and then joined the Grand Fleet, missing Jutland as she had been damaged in collision with *New Zealand* in April 1916. Returned to Australia as flagship in 1919. Was declared surplus to tonnage under the Washington Disarmament Treaty in 1922 and was ceremonially scuttled off Sydney Heads on 12 April 1924.

*New Zealand* made a world cruise of the Dominions between February and December 1913, and joined the Grand Fleet in August 1914. At the Battle of the Dogger Bank she fired 147 12in shells, without any known result. She became Beatty's temporary flagship when the *Lion* was put out of action during the battle. In collision with the *Australia* on 22 April 1916 but repaired

in time for Battle of Jutland. Hit by an 11in shell on 'X' turret but without serious damage or casualties; she fired more shells than any other dreadnought (420 12in) but scored only four hits. In 1919 she carried Admiral Jellicoe on his tour of the Dominions, but was one of the ships listed for disposal under the Washington Treaty and was sold in December 1922.

*Orion* 1918.
*CPL*

---

## ORION class *battleships*

| | |
|---|---|
| **Displacement:** | 22,200t load; 25,870t deep load |
| **Dimensions:** | 545ft pp, 581ft oa × 88ft 6in × 24ft 11in mean |
| | *166.1m, 177.1m × 27.0m × 7.6m* |
| **Machinery:** | 4-shaft Parsons turbines, 18 Babcock & Wilcox (*Monarch* Yarrow) boilers, 27,000shp = 21kts. Coal 3300t, oil 800t. Range 6730nm at 10kts |
| **Armour:** | Belt 12in–8in (305mm–203mm), bulkheads 10in–3in (254mm–76mm), barbettes 10in–3in (254mm–76mm), turret faces 11in (279mm), CT 11in (279mm), decks 4in–1in (102mm–25mm) |
| **Armament:** | 10–13.5in (343mm)/45 Mk V (5 × 2), 16–4in (102mm)/50 BL Mk VII, 4–3pdr (47mm), 3–21in TT sub (2 beam, 1 stern) |
| **Complement:** | 752 |

| Name | Builder | Laid down | Launched | Comp | Fate |
|---|---|---|---|---|---|
| CONQUEROR | Beardmore | 5.4.10 | 1.5.11 | 11.12 | Sold for BU 12.22 |
| MONARCH | Armstrong | 1.4.10 | 30.3.11 | 3.12 | Sunk as target 20.1.25 |
| ORION | Portsmouth DYd | 29.11.09 | 20.8.10 | 1.12 | Sold for BU 12.22 |
| THUNDERER | Thames IW | 13.4.10 | 1.2.11 | 6.12 | Sold for BU 12.26 |

Under the 1909 Programme four much larger battleships and one battlecruiser were approved. Dissatisfaction with the 50cal 12in gun led the Director of Naval Ordnance to press for a return to the 13.5in calibre last seen in the Naval Defence Act battleships. The increase in calibre not only gave greater range and much greater hitting power (at least 300lb greater shell weight) but improved shooting. By keeping the muzzle velocity down the designers were able to eliminate much of the tendency of the shell to 'wobble' in flight, improving accuracy at extreme range, and there was the additional benefit of reduced barrel wear. For comparatively small increases in weight and size the 13.5in/45cal gun offered a significant advantage over the German 12in and other foreign navies' guns. The provision of a heavier shell (1400lb instead of 1250lb) further improved the ballistics of the gun, and with 20° elevation (as against 15° previously) it had no difficulty in ranging out to 24,000yds. There were other improvements in design, and clearly the new battleships benefitted from a slight relaxation in the tempo of battleship building. The cumbersome layouts seen in the early dreadnoughts gave way to an all-centreline

disposition, with superimposed turrets forward and aft (although the Admiralty's insistence on sighting hoods at the forward end of the turret caused unbearable blast effect on personnel in the lower turret, and so limited them to broadside arcs). Side

armour was extended up to the main deck, thus curing a major weakness of all the early dreadnoughts, and splinter protection was given to the boats. There was an inexplicable weakness in the layout: the tripod mast was stepped between the funnels, as it had

been in the *Dreadnought*, *Colossus* and *Hercules*. The problem of smoke interference with fire control was well known, and the only reason that can be found in the same one as before – it provided a convenient position to place the booms for handling the boats.

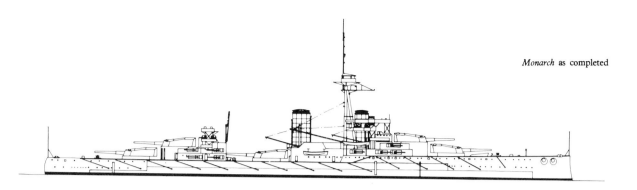

However the majestic profile of the *Orion* class emphasized their impressive armament, and their design proved a good basis for a further five classes.

A weak point of the later British dreadnoughts was their lack of beam. As compared with German dreadnoughts there was insufficient beam to provide the scale of underwater protection found in German ships, and it is interesting to find that the DNC's staff did consider adding beam in order to improve subdivision against torpedo hits. If the original *Dreadnought* length: beam ratio had been preserved

the *Orions* would have had 91ft as against the 88½ft given to them. An increase was vetoed by the Naval Staff, who wished to restrict metacentric height and thereby improved the ship as a gunnery platform. Another factor was the need to keep speed at 21kts. Beam was only permitted to increase to the point where it provided initial stiffness and preserved the correct metacentric height.

*Thunderer* was the second ship to be fitted with the Scott director system, which permitted the guns to be fired from the central fire control position, placed high on the tripod mast. When

she fired in competition with the *Orion* in 1912 she scored six times as many hits as the *Orion* – both ships had started firing at the same time. All four ships received the usual wartime alterations: topmasts reduced and torpedo nets removed in 1915, fire control platforms extended and extra plating over magazines after Jutland and aeroplane platforms in 1917 (*Thunderer* had runways on 'B' and 'X' turrets, the rest had platforms on 'B' only). The original bridgework around the fore funnel proved totally inadequate, and by 1918 had been considerably extended. Fortunately the

fore funnel served only a third of the boilers, so heat and smoke caused less trouble than in the earlier dreadnoughts.

All joined the Grand Fleet in August 1914, and fought at Jutland, sustaining no damage or casualties. Retained in the post-war Fleet, but discarded to comply with the Washington Treaty. *Monarch* was used for experimental tests and then expended as a fleet target for planes, cruisers and battleships, 20 January 1925, being sunk by deliberate fire from *Revenge*. *Thunderer* became Cadets' TS 1922–26.

*Princess Royal* preparing for trials,
August 1912.

The battlecruiser equivalents of the *Orion* class reflected their improvements in armament, with 13.5in guns on the centreline. They were 6kts faster, and to achieve that the shp was increased by over 150 per cent, but in spite of an increase of 4000t in displacement they had grave weaknesses. Instead of eliminating the midships 13.5in turret the after superimposed mounting was deleted, giving a cumbersome arrangement of magazine and shellroom between two groups of boilers, and restricted arcs of fire for 'Q' turret. The tripod mast was sited abaft the fore funnel, but whereas the *Orion* class had only 6 boilers served by that funnel, in the *Lion*s there were 14 boilers. The worst error, however, was to provide armour protection only against 11in shellfire, and only in

## LION class *battlecruisers*

| | |
|---|---|
| **Displacement:** | 26,270t load; 29,680t deep load |
| **Dimensions:** | 660ft pp, 700ft × 88ft 6in × 27ft 8in mean |
| | *201.2m, 213.4m × 27.0m × 8.4m* |
| **Machinery:** | 4-shaft Parsons turbines, 42 Yarrow boilers, 70,000shp = 27kts. Coal 3500t, oil 1135t. Range 5610m at 10kts |
| **Armour:** | Belt 9in–4in (229mm–102mm), bulkheads 4in (102mm), barbettes 9in–3in (229mm–76mm), turret faces 9in (229mm), CT 10in (254mm), decks 2.5in–1in (64mm–25mm) |
| **Armament:** | 8–13.5in (343mm)/45 Mk V (4 × 2), 16–4in (102mm)/50 Mk VII, 4–3pdr (47mm), 2–21in (533mm) TT sub (beam) |
| **Complement:** | 997 |

| Name | Builder | Laid down | Launched | Comp | Fate |
|---|---|---|---|---|---|
| LION | Devonport DYd | 29.9.09 | 6.8.10 | 5.12 | Sold for BU 31.1.24 |
| PRINCESS ROYAL | Vickers | 2.5.10 | 24.4.11 | 11.12 | Sold for BU 12.22 |

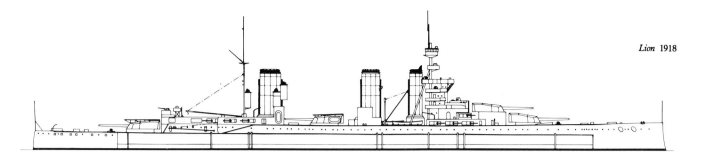

limited areas. The vast hull was totally vulnerable to 12in shells, and in some areas the side armour could be pierced by 11in as well. The worst deficiencies were masked by a policy of official lying about the armour protection (leaks to the Press suggested a 'battleship scale' and the term 'capital ship' was coined, suggesting that they were fast battleships). But the problems with smoke could not be disguised; on her preliminary trials the *Lion*'s tripod became so hot that personnel could not leave the fire control platform. On the initiative of the new First Lord, Churchill, both the *Lion* and the incomplete *Princess Royal* were altered at a cost of £60,000. Official leaks also greatly exaggerated the speed of the class, *Princess Royal* being credited with 33½kts mean (34.7kts maximum) and *Lion* was credited with having exceeded 31kts. The truth is that neither ship was capable of 28kts except by forcing the machinery. Even when the *Princess Royal* was ordered to go for maximum power over the Polperro Mile in 1913 the staggering total of 96,240shp only yielded 28.06kts, and the strain on her machinery meant that she was ever after the 'lame duck' of the battlecruiser force.

The war service of the *Lion* and the 'Splendid Cats' kept them in the forefront of the action, and their reputation did not suffer until the near-loss of the *Lion* and the disaster to the *Queen Mary* at Jutland. Thanks to adroit

manipulation of the Press they were regarded with affection by the public but they must surely be ton-for-ton the least satisfactory ships built for the RN in modern times. The faults of the original battlecruiser could be forgiven for lack of experience with new tactics and technology, but the *Lion*s were expensive second-rate ships.

Only *Lion* had the fore funnel ahead of the tripod, until taken in hand in February 1912. Both ships commissioned with light pole masts, but these were soon stiffened by light struts. In 1915 these gave way to proper tripod legs (fabricated locally at Scapa Flow) as the masthead control platforms were enlarged. Nets were removed, searchlight platforms enclosed and other standard alterations were carried out as the War progressed. In 1918 both ships had aircraft platforms on 'Q' and 'X' turrets.

The secondary and anti-aircraft armament changed frequently:

*Lion*
*Post-August 1914:* 1–3pdr saluting gun lost overboard in gale.
*October 1914:* 6pdr Hotchkiss AA added.
*January 1915:* 3in/20cwt AA Mk I added.
*April 1915:* 2–3pdr removed.
*July 1915:* 6pdr AA replaced by second 3in/20cwt AA.
*August 1915:* last 3pdr removed.
*April 1917:* 1–3in/20cwt AA received from *Princess Royal* (replacement), 1–4in/50 removed from port side aft,

put on 60° mounting and given to *Princess Royal*.
*May–June 1919:* 4–3pdr saluting guns added.

*Princess Royal*
*October 1914:* 6pdr Hotchkiss AA added.
*January 1915:* 3in/20cwt AA Mk I added.
*April 1915:* 2–3pdr removed.
*April 1917:* 1–4in/50 removed from starboard aft, put on 60° AA mounting and remounted with gun from *Lion*, 2–3in/20cwt AA removed.
*May–June 1919:* 4–3pdrs added, 4in/50 AA replaced by 2–3in/20cwt AA Mk I and 2–2pdr AA Mk II (removed March 1922).

The effect of these modifications was to increase *Lion*'s deep load displacement to 30,945t.

In January 1913 *Lion* hoisted flag of 1st Battle Cruiser Squadron (Rear-Admiral Beatty). Joined Grand Fleet in August 1914 and took part in Heligoland Bight action against German light forces. At the Dogger Bank on 24 January 1915 she fired 243 shells, but scored only one hit on the *Blücher*, one on the *Derfflinger* and two on the *Seydlitz*, at a range of about 16,000yds. She was hit by 16 11in and 12in shells, and one 8.3in, suffering serious damage. The port engine room was flooded and eventually the starboard turbines stopped as well, and she had to be towed home by *Indomitable*. She was temporarily repaired at Rosyth, with more per-

manent repairs completed by Palmers before returning to service as flagship of the newly constituted Battle Cruiser Force (BCF). At Jutland she suffered much more serious damage, being hit by 13 12in shells from the *Lützow*. The most damaging hit started a fire in 'Q' turret which was only stopped from blowing up the magazine by the presence of mind of a fatally wounded Marine Officer, who gave the order to flood the magazine. On her return to Rosyth, 'Q' turret had to be removed for repairs, and she went to sea from 20 July to 23 September 1916 without it. Paid off under Washington Treaty and sold for BU in 1924.

*Princess Royal* fought at Heligoland Bight, 28 August 1914. Sent to West Indies during hunt for von Spee's squadron. In action at Dogger Bank but without damage or casualties. At Jutland was hit by eight 12in and one 11in from *Derfflinger*, *Markgraf* and *Posen*, suffering 22 killed and 81 wounded. Numerous fires were started and two legs of the tripod foremast were badly hit, but the ship remained operational. Returned to Rosyth on 21 July 1916 after repairs. Sold for BU in December 1922 to comply with Washington Treaty; resold and not BU until 1926.

*Lion* as completed.

*Centurion* as a target ship, 1935.
*CPL*

The four battleships of the 1910 Programme were to have been repeat *Orion*s but fortunately the lessons from the *Lion*'s trials were available and the design was altered to a pole foremast stepped ahead of the fore funnel. It was widely felt that the 4in secondary guns should have been replaced by 6in, in the light of the growing threat from torpedo-boats and destroyers, but that would have meant an extra 2000t at a time when the Liberal Government was trying to reduce naval expenditure. However the increase in dimensions did permit a slight improvement in deck armour. With their tall, flat-sided funnels the *King George V* class were handsome ships. The lead ship and the *Centurion* were completed with a light pole foremast but the last pair were completed for director firing and had to have struts halfway up the mast. *Centurion* was then altered in similar fashion but *King George V* merely received stiffening flanges. She was finally given a full tripod in 1918. The three survivors received the full set of wartime modifications: removal of nets, searchlights enclosed in towers, enlarged bridgework etc, and were fitted to carry aircraft in 1918. Although the 13.5in Mk V gun was repeated in the new ships it was modified to fire a 1400lb shell, which further improved its long-range shooting. From 1915 2–4in AA guns

## KING GEORGE V class *battleships*

**Displacement:** 23,000t load; 25,700t deep load
**Dimensions:** 555ft pp, 597ft 6in oa × 89ft × 28ft 8in mean
*169.2m, 182.1m × 27.1m × 8.7m*
**Machinery:** 4-shaft Parsons turbines, 18 Babcock & Wilcox (*Audacious, Centurion* Yarrow) boilers, 31,000shp = 21kts. Coal 2870t–3150t, oil 800t. Range 6730nm at 10kts
**Armour:** Belt 12in–8in (305mm–203mm), bulkheads 10in–4in (254mm–102mm), barbettes 10in–3in (254mm–76mm), turret faces 11in (279mm), decks 4in–1in (102mm–25mm)
**Armament:** 10–13.5in (343mm)/45 Mk V (5 × 2), 16–4in (102mm)/50 BL Mk VII, 4–3pdr (47mm), 3–21in (533mm) TT sub (2 beam, 1 stern)
**Complement:** 782

| Name | Builder | Laid down | Launched | Comp | Fate |
|------|---------|-----------|----------|------|------|
| KING GEORGE V (ex-*Royal George*) | Portsmouth DYd | 16.1.11 | 9.10.11 | 11.12 | Sold for BU 12.26 |
| CENTURION | Devonport DYd | 16.1.11 | 18.11.11 | 5.13 | Target ship 1927. Scuttled 9.6.44 |
| AUDACIOUS | Cammell Laird | 2.11 | 14.9.12 | 10.13 | Mined 27.10.14 |
| AJAX | Scotts | 27.2.11 | 21.3.12 | 3.13 | Sold for BU 9.11.26 |

were added on the quarterdeck, while 2–4in/50 BL on either side below the forecastle deck abreast of 'A' and 'B' turrets were removed when found to be unworkable in heavy weather. Wartime additions increased the deep load displacements to 26,595–26,740 tons.

All served with Grand Fleet from August 1914. *Audacious* sank after striking mines laid off Lough Swilly on 27 October 1914. In fact damage was comparatively light but progressive flooding outside the armoured citadel made her unmanageable as the weather worsened, and she foundered before she could be towed to safety. Others fought at Jutland. *Ajax* and *Centurion* served in the Black Sea in 1919, and returned from the Mediterranean in 1924. *King George V* was gunnery TS from 1923 to 1926. All discarded 1926 under terms of Washington Treaty, to offset completion of *Nelson* and *Rodney*.

*Centurion* converted to radio-controlled target ship to replace *Agamemnon*, and used for guns up to 8in calibre until April 1941 at Plymouth. Converted to resemble the new *Anson* and sailed to India in 1942, then reduced to static AA battery in Suez Canal until 1944. Finally sunk as blockship for 'Mulberry' harbour off Normandy on 9 June 1944.

Although often listed as a third *Lion*, the battlecruiser ordered under the 1910 Programme was a half-sister with many internal improvements later extended in the *Tiger*. These included higher power, 1400lb shells for the main armament and a different arrangement of the 4in belt armour. However, apart from having round funnels and a single-decked 4in gun battery she appeared identical. Her battleship equivalents were the *King George V* class. On trials she made 28.1kts with 83,000shp. The heavier shells improved the accuracy of the guns but in spite of the great range of

## QUEEN MARY *battlecruiser*

**Displacement:** 26,770t load; 31,650t deep load
**Dimensions:** 660ft pp, 703ft 6in oa × 89ft × 28ft mean
*201.2m, 214.4m × 27.1m × 8.5m*
**Machinery:** 4-shaft Parsons turbines, 42 Yarrow boilers, 75,000shp = 27½kts. Coal 3600t, oil 1170t. Range 5610nm at 10kts
**Armour:** As *Lion* class (see notes)
**Armament:** As *Lion* class
**Complement:** 997

| Name | Builder | Laid down | Launched | Comp | Fate |
|------|---------|-----------|----------|------|------|
| QUEEN MARY | Palmers | 6.3.11 | 20.3.12 | 8.13 | Sunk 31.5.16 |

the 13.5in Mk V, sights only allowed for a maximum elevation of 15°. This was not rectified in the Grand Fleet and the battlecruisers until 1916, when super-elevation 6° prisms were fitted to the central sight in each turret (*Queen Mary* had been fitted before Jutland). Director control for the main armament was fitted in December 1915. Alterations to the ship included the addition of struts halfway up the pole foremast, lowering of topmasts, enlargement of masthead control positions and bridgework, but torpedo nets were still carried at Jutland. The 4–3pdr Hotchkiss saluting guns were

removed early in 1915, and in October 1914 she had received 1-3in/20cwt AA Mk I and a 6pdr Hotchkiss AA.

Her completion was delayed by industrial trouble and she did not finally commission until September 1913, when she joined 1st Cruiser Squadron (1st Battle Cruiser Squadron from January 1914). Joined Grand Fleet in August 1914 and was in action at Heligoland Bight on 28 August 1914. She was refitting during the Dogger Bank battle but rejoined 1st BCS shortly after. At Jutland she came

under fire from *Derfflinger*. She had fired about 150 shells, and had scored 4 hits on the *Seydlitz*, when she was hit on 'Q' turret above the right-hand gun. That hit put the gun out of action but as the left-hand gun carried on firing the damage had not seriously harmed the ship. Then two more 12in shells hit, one in the vicinity of 'A' and 'B' turrets, and the other on 'Q'. Almost immediately 'A' and 'B' magazines exploded, destroying the forward part of the ship as far as the foremast. As the shattered hull listed to port a further

explosion sent the remains to the bottom, only 38 minutes after the start of the battle. Hardly any survivors were found, and 1266 men lost their lives. The exact cause of loss cannot be identified, for at 14,400yds her armour was vulnerable to shells plunging at 12°. However the near-disaster in the *Lion* showed that the poor quality of British cordite and the lack of flash-tight doors made it all too easy for damage in the turret, barbette or working chamber to generate a flash which could detonate the magazine.

*Queen Mary* 1916

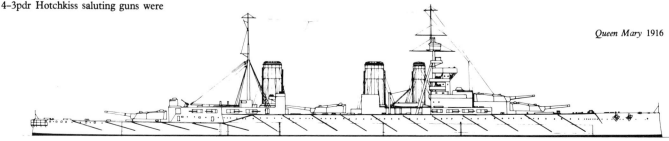

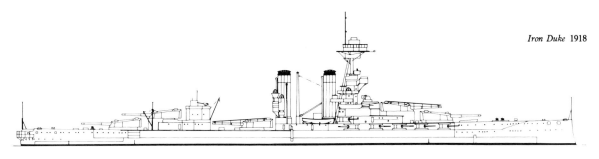

*Iron Duke* 1918

Growing pressure from the Fleet finally forced the Board of Admiralty to reintroduce the 6in secondary gun in the 1911 Programme battleships. The introduction of the 21in heater torpedo had given the torpedo more range, and it was clear to all but the most obstinate supporters of 'all-big-gun' theories that the 4in gun was no longer adequate. The fact that Fisher had retired from the post of First Sea Lord in 1910 also cleared the way for a less dogmatic approach to the problem. The 1911 battleships were generally similar to the *King George V* class, but 25ft longer and slightly beamier and deeper, the extra length being necessary to preserve buoyancy against the heavier weight of the 6in battery, both forward and aft. The extra length

*Iron Duke* as a gunnery training ship about 1938.
*CPL*

## IRON DUKE class *battleships*

**Displacement:** 25,000t load; 29,560t deep load
**Dimensions:** 580ft pp, 622ft 9in oa × 90ft × 29ft 6in mean
*176.8m, 189.8m × 27.4m × 9.0m*
**Machinery:** 4-shaft Parsons turbines, 18 Babcock & Wilcox or Yarrow boilers, 29,000shp = 21¼kts. Coal 3250t, oil 1050t. Range 7780nm at 10kts
**Armour:** Belt 12in–4in (305mm–102mm), bulkheads 8in–1.5in (203mm–38mm), barbettes 10in–3in (254mm–76mm), turret faces 11in (279mm), decks 2.5in–1in (64mm–25mm)
**Armament:** 10–13.5in (343mm)/45 Mk V (5 × 2), 12–6in (152mm)/45 BL Mk VII, 2–3in (76mm)/20cwt AA Mk I, 4–3pdr (47mm), 4–21in (533mm) TT sub (beam)
**Complement:** 995–1022(war)

| Name | Builder | Laid down | Launched | Comp | Fate |
|---|---|---|---|---|---|
| IRON DUKE | Portsmouth DYd | 12.1.12 | 12.10.12 | 3.14 | Gunnery TS 1931. Sold for BU 2.3.46 |
| MARLBOROUGH | Devonport DYd | 25.1.12 | 24.10.12 | 6.14 | Sold for BU 27.6.32 |
| BENBOW | Beardmore | 30.5.12 | 12.11.13 | 10.14 | Sold for BU 3.31 |
| EMPEROR OF INDIA (ex-*Delhi*) | Vickers | 31.5.12 | 27.11.13 | 11.14 | Sunk as target 1.9.31 |

forward also moved the secondary guns further aft to reduce interference in bad weather. By the time the design was finalised the need for a big director and fire control top was recognised, and so the ships were given a heavy tripod foremast, but the funnels were much thinner than before, giving the *Iron Dukes* a distinctive look. They were the first ships to have AA guns, as 2-12pdr guns were mounted on the after superstructure, for use against airships.

*Iron Duke* ran her trials late in 1913 with torpedo nets but these were removed before she commissioned, and they were never installed in the rest of the class. The stern TT was finally dropped in this class but the siting of the aftermost 6in guns – right aft under the quarterdeck – showed little appreciation of what could happen in rough weather. The purpose of the after pair of 6in guns was to fire at torpedo-boats silhouetted against the setting sun, but in practice the ports were washed out in anything short of flat calm. They and the forward guns were in revolving shields, which could be closed by hinged plates, but these proved too fragile and were constantly washed away. During the winter of 1914–15 it was found necessary to unship them completely and water

then entered freely, finding its way below into messdecks and working spaces. Aboard the *Iron Duke* a cure, was devised: dwarf walls at the rear of the gun battery and india-rubber joints between the revolving shield and the fixed plating of the embrasure. This worked well and was applied to the battery guns in the *Tiger* and the *Queen Elizabeth* class. The after 6in positions were totally useless and were removed early in the war. The embrasures were plated over and a new unarmoured embrasure was provided amidships above the original battery, port and starboard. After Jutland, in addition to the usual improvements to searchlights and fire control they received 820t of extra protection, 1in–2in on decks around the barbettes and some thickening of magazine bulkheads. Wartime additions increased the deep load displacement to 30,380 tons.

As the only British dreadnought to be torpedoed the *Marlborough* provided interesting data. She was hit amidship and had a 70ft × 20ft hole blown in her side plating. At that point, abreast the boiler rooms, she was protected by coal bunkers, as the 1in–1½in torpedo bulkhead only protected the magazines and engine rooms. In spite of that she kept station at 17kts, and was only forced to cease

fire when her list to starboard prevented her guns from bearing. A day later, while making her way to the Humber, her draught had increased to 39ft and she could make only 10kts but she reached harbour.

Three of the class were scrapped to comply with the Washington Treaty, but *Iron Duke* was retained in 'demilitarised' state as a TS. This included removal of 'B' and 'Y' turrets as well as the belt armour, and sufficient boilers made inoperable to reduce speed to 18kts.

All served in Grand Fleet, from August 1914 or after working up, *Iron Duke* being flagship of C-in-C until

November 1916. Fought at Jutland, where *Marlborough* was torpedoed (repaired on Tyne in three months) and others sustained no casualties. To Mediterranean 1919, until 1926, then Atlantic Fleet until 1929. *Iron Duke* paid off 1929 for disarming and conversion to TS. Served with Home Fleet at Scapa Flow as depot ship 1939–45, but her remaining 13.5in and 6in guns were removed for use in shore defences. Badly damaged by near miss bombs on 17 October 1939 but repaired. Others paid off for disposal 1929; *Emperor of India*, sunk as gunnery target in 1931, was raised and sold 6 February 1932 for BU.

*Emperor of India* as completed. *CPL*

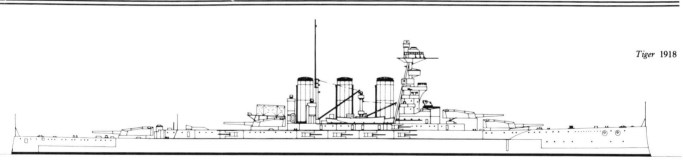

*Tiger* 1918

It was becoming clear that British battlecruisers were an expensive and dubious investment, and under the 1911–12 Estimates there was provision for only one, an improved *Queen Mary*. Considerable attention was paid to correcting some of the obvious defects of the earlier ships, notably the layout of main armament and the provision of a good secondary armament. Unfortunately the quest for ever-higher speed led to an increase in power to 85,000shp with an overload limit of 108,000shp to boost speed from 28kts to 30kts. The folly of such a design criterion became evident on trials late in 1914; at 91,103shp the *Tiger* reached 28.38kts but 104,635shp pushed this up only to 29.07kts. As she burned about 1245t of fuel daily at 59,500shp, a huge increase in bunker capacity was necessary simply to give her an endurance comparable to the *Lion* class. If the Naval Staff had been content with the same machinery, or if the Engineer-in-Chief had been allowed to use small-tube boilers there might have been sufficient margin to give this fine ship the scale of pro-

## TIGER *battlecruiser*

| | |
|---|---|
| **Displacement:** | 28,430t load; 35,710t deep load |
| **Dimensions:** | 660ft pp, 704ft oa × 90ft 6in × 28ft 6in mean |
| | *201.2m, 214.6m × 27.6m ×8.7m* |
| **Machinery:** | 4-shaft Brown-Curtis turbines, 39 Babcock & Wilcox boilers, 85,000shp = 28kts. Coal 2450t, oil 2450t. Range *c*4650nm at 10kts |
| **Armour:** | Belt 9in–3in (229mm–76mm), bulkheads 4in–2in (102mm–51mm), barbettes 9in–1in (229mm–25mm), turret faces 9in (229mm), CT 10in (254mm), decks 3in–1in (76mm–25mm) |
| **Armament:** | 8-13.5in (343mm)/45 Mk V (4 × 2), 12-6in (152mm)/45 BL Mk VII, 2-3in (76mm)/20cwt AA Mk I, 4-3pdr (47mm) saluting, 4-21in (533mm) TT sub (beam) |
| **Complement:** | 1121 |

| Name | Builder | Laid down | Launched | Comp | Fate |
|---|---|---|---|---|---|
| TIGER | John Brown | 20.6.12 | 15.12.13 | 10.14 | Sold for BU 7.3.32 |

tection she deserved. As things turned out she did not pay the worst penalty, but she was just as vulnerable to enemy shellfire as her half-sister *Queen Mary*.

The rearrangement of 'Q' turret transformed the appearance of the ship, and the combination of a heavy tripod and three round, equally-spaced funnels made an extremely

handsome profile. Although often claimed to be the result of the Japanese battlecruiser *Kongo*'s influence there is no evidence of this in Admiralty records. The details of *Tiger* had been settled before the *Kongo*'s design was complete, and what is more likely is that Vickers' chief designer was given details of the new ship's layout, so that

he could incorporate them in the Japanese design. The secondary armament was very similar to the *Iron Duke* but instead of the useless pair of 6in guns right aft an additional embrasure was provided a deck above the main deck battery, at its forward end. Like other 13.5in-gunned ships HMS *Tiger* was fitted with 6° prisms in 1916 to permit her to use the full range of the guns. She was completed with 2–3in/20cwt AA guns and kept these until 1923, when they were replaced by 4–4in QF Mk V (reduced by 2 in November 1924). In January 1925 she was rearmed with 4–3in/20cwt AA Mk I. In March 1929 these were once again replaced by 4–4in QF Mk V (4 × 1), and in March–September 1928 a pair of 2pdr Mk II pompoms were carried. In March 1915 two of her 3pdr saluting guns were removed but they were replaced in May 1919. Apart from an aircraft platform on 'Q' turret

she remained virtually unaltered, but in 1918 the fore topmast was moved to the derrick post between No 2 and No 3 funnel, destroying her elegant profile. In 1929 fuel was reduced to 300 tons coal and 3300 tons oil.

She was completed in October 1914 and joined the Grand Fleet on 6 November 1914 for service with 1st Battle Cruiser Squadron. At the Battle of the Dogger Bank on 24 January 1915 she was hit by six shells and suffered 10 killed and 11 wounded. One 11in hit 'Q' turret and splinters jammed the training gear and put the

turret out of action. She was repaired by 8 February 1915. At Jutland she fired 303 heavy shells and scored 3 hits, but in return she was hit 15 times by heavy shell, killing 24 and wounding 46. Although 'Q' turret and 'X' barbette were holed there was no ammunition explosion. Repairs at Rosyth lasted from 3 June to 1 July 1916, and she rejoined the BCF. From 1919 to 1922 she served in the Atlantic Fleet BCS and from 1924 to 1929 served as sea-going gunnery TS. Replaced *Hood* in BCS 1929–31 and paid off on 30 March 1931 at Devonport.

*Tiger* January 1915.
CPL

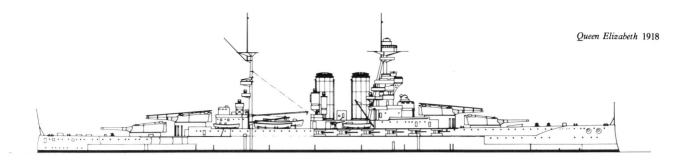

*Queen Elizabeth* 1918

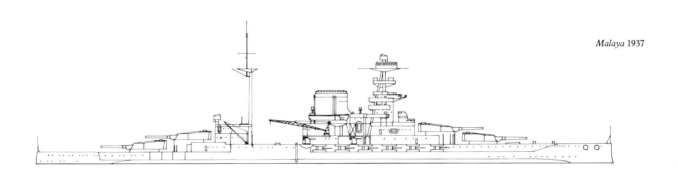

*Malaya* 1937

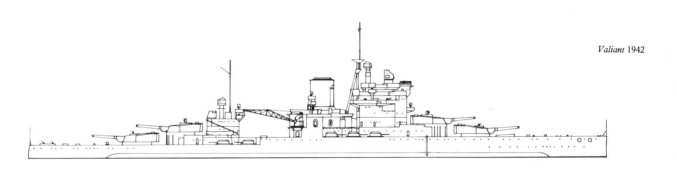

*Valiant* 1942

Under the 1912 Programme three battleships and a battlecruiser were planned. Originally intended to be improved *Iron Dukes*, growing unease about rumours that Germany was planning an increase in calibre plus the certainty that Japanese and American dreadnoughts were being armed with 14in guns, suggested that the new ships should be up-gunned. The gunmakers, the Elswick Ordnance Company, assured the Admiralty that a 15in gun, firing a 1920lb shell, was feasible. Because no 15in gun had yet been made it would be necessary to start the ships with no certainty that the new gun would be successful, but the Director of Naval Ordnance had no doubts at all. The only concession which Elswick could make was to hurry one gun 4 months ahead of the others, to allow proof-firing and the preparation of range tables in time for the lead ship. In the event DNO's confidence was more than justified as the 15in/42cal Mk I proved even more accurate than the 13.5in Mk V, with

## QUEEN ELIZABETH class *battleships*

| | |
|---|---|
| **Displacement:** | 27,500t normal; 31,500t deep load |
| **Dimensions:** | 600ft pp, 645ft 9in oa × 90ft 6in × 28ft 9in mean |
| | *182.9m 196.8m × 27.6m × 8.8m* |
| **Machinery:** | 4-shaft Parsons turbines (*Barham* and *Valiant* Brown-Curtis), 24 Babcock & Wilcox (*Barham* and *Valiant* Yarrow) boilers, 56,000shp = 23kts. Oil 3400t. Range c4500nm at 10kts |
| **Armour:** | Belt 13in–6in (331mm–152mm), bulkheads 6in–4in (152mm–102mm), barbettes 10in–4in (254mm–102mm), turret faces 13in (331mm), CT 11in (279mm), decks 3in–1in (76mm–25mm) |
| **Armament:** | 8-15in (381mm)/42 Mk I (4 × 2), 14 (*Queen Elizabeth* 16)-6in (152mm)/45 Mk XII, 2-3in (76mm)/20cwt AA Mk I, 4-3pdr (47mm) saluting, 4-21in (533mm) TT sub (beam) |
| **Complement:** | 925-951 |

| Name | Builder | Laid down | Launched | Comp | Fate |
|---|---|---|---|---|---|
| QUEEN ELIZABETH | Portsmouth DYd | 21.10.12 | 16.10.13 | 1.15 | Sold for BU 19.3.48 |
| WARSPITE | Devonport DYd | 31.10.12 | 26.11.13 | 3.15 | Sold for Bu 12.7.46 |
| VALIANT | Fairfield | 31.1.13 | 4.11.14 | 2.16 | Sold for BU 19.3.48 |
| BARHAM | John Brown | 24.2.13 | 31.10.14 | 10.15 | Sunk 25.11.41 |
| MALAYA | Armstrong | 20.10.13 | 18.3.15 | 2.16 | Sold for BU 20.2.48 |
| AGINCOURT | Portsmouth DYd | — | — | | Cancelled 26.8.14 |

the same long barrel-life. What was more important was its greater hitting power and range, which promised to give the Royal Navy a comfortable margin for a few years.

New designs were hurriedly prepared, initially for a five-turret, 21kt ship similar to the *Iron Duke* in layout. It was soon realised, however, that a reduction of one turret would still give a broadside of more than 15,000lb, as against 14,000lb in the *Iron Duke*. The space thus saved could be used for additional boilers to give a speed of 24–25kts. War College studies had shown that a fast wing to the battlefleet would be far more effective than a force of battlecruisers. To achieve 25kts on 27,000t would be impossible if the ship were to be coal-fired, but the greater thermal efficiency of oil would solve the problem and at the same time reduce weight. The only practical objection was, of course, that oil fuel was imported from the Middle East whereas anthracite coal was available in Britain. After considerable thought the First Lord of the Admiralty, Churchill, made the momentous decision to buy shares in the Persian oil companies, and thus secure access to the oilfields. Now that a fast wing to the battlefleet was possible there was

*Malaya* about 1920.
CPL

*Warspite* July 1931.
CPL

little point in keeping the battlecruiser in the 1912 Programme, and in its place a fourth fast battleship was ordered to create a complete Fast Division. Then the Federated Malay States offered to pay for a fifth unit, and to commemorate the gift she was named *Malaya*. A sixth unit, *Agincourt*, was ordered under the 1914 Programme but as she had not been laid down the order was cancelled shortly

after the outbreak of war. It should be mentioned that the failure in 1913 of the Canadian Naval Aid Bill, which proposed the building of three *Queen Elizabeth*s at Canada's expense, ruled out the ultimate goal of a fast wing of eight ships.

Although a great step forward, the *Queen Elizabeth* design attempted too much on the displacement, and they were not as good as they might have been. All five were seriously overweight when built (33,500t–34,000t) and the refusal yet again to sanction small-tube boilers made 25kts impossible to achieve. It should be noted that the designed speed was 23kts, and 25kts was only intended to be reached at the overload rating of 72,000shp. In practice they were good for nearly 24kts at 71,000–76,000shp.

*Queen Elizabeth* was the only one to have the full outfit of 16-16in Mk XII guns, but the four guns under the quarterdeck suffered as badly as the same guns did in the *Iron Duke*. They were hurriedly removed and a single gun in a shield was resited port and starboard above the battery amidships, the remaining four ships being completed this way. As in the *Iron Dukes* the forward guns in the battery suffered severely in a seaway and the battery was modified in similar fashion, with dwarf walls inside the battery and india-rubber sealing joints to stop water finding its way between the revolving shield and the embrasure. In 1916 2-6in guns were replaced by 3in/20cwt AA Mk I guns. Like other dreadnoughts they were modified after Jutland, with range clocks and deflector scales, searchlights in towers and additional deck armour around the barbettes. *Queen Elizabeth* was the only one with a sternwalk but this was removed late in 1915 or early in 1916. *Barham* had a searchlight platform on the forebridge from completion until 1917, when it was replaced by a rangefinder. In 1915–16 *Warspite* and *Barham* had large rangefinder baffles fitted between the funnels and on the mainmast in an attempt to defeat German rangefinders but this futile addition was removed from both ships in 1917–18. In 1918 all five were fitted with aircraft platforms on 'B' and 'X' turrets. The *Queen Elizabeth* class were extremely handsome ships and a considerable improvement over previous British battleships in protection. At Jutland the presence of four of them saved Beatty's battlecruisers from a severe mauling. In view of some of the criticisms of British gunnery in that battle it is interesting to note that the Germans were astounded by the accuracy of *Valiant*'s shooting, and noted that it demonstrated how far ahead British fire control was over German equipment. The deep load displacement after wartime modifications was between 33,530t (*Malaya*) and 34,050t (*Queen Elizabeth*).

*Queen Elizabeth* was sent to the Mediterranean in February 1915 for service in the Dardanelles. She fired against the Narrows forts and in support of the landings from 25 February to 14 May 1915, a total of 86 15in and 71 16in shells. Lack of 15in shell limited her value in shore bombardment and the Admiralty had also issued firm orders that her guns were not worn out. She returned to join the Grand Fleet in May 1915. Under refit at Jutland, and became Fleet Flagship from February 1917. The other four, as the 5th BS, were heavily engaged at Jutland. *Barham* fired 337 shells and was hit six times. She suffered severely from two hits but continued in action. Under repair 1 June–5 July 1916. *Malaya* suffered slight damage and completed repairs by 4 July, *Valiant* sustained no damage, but *Warspite* was heavily damaged, suffering at least 15 11in and 12in hits and 5 5.9in hits. One pierced her 7½in upper belt, wrecking the port feed tank and causing the engine room to flood. Her helm jammed at a crucial moment in the action, causing her to turn circles under fire from the head of the German battle line but she managed to limp clear. She had to be detached because her speed was dropping, and made her own way back to Rosyth. Under repair 1 June–22 July 1916.

All served in the Atlantic Fleet from 1919 or 1920 to 1924, and thereafter in the Mediterranean Fleet. By late 1926 all had 4-4in QF Mk V AA (4 × 1) replacing 2-3in, and they also underwent large refits and partial modernisations as follows: *Warspite* 1924–26, *Queen Elizabeth* 1926–27, *Malaya* 1927–29, *Valiant* 1929–30, *Barham* 1930–33. The funnels were trunked into one and bulges fitted, increasing beam to 104ft (31.7m) with deep load displacement 35,060–35,710 tons (excluding 815 tons water protection) in the first four and speed 23.5kts. In *Barham* the middle deck was increased to 5in on the flat over magazines, and the 6in casemates enclosed by 1.5in rear walls, so that deep load displacement was 35,970 tons or 36,785 tons with water protection. A single 8-barrelled pompom was added to *Valiant* and two to *Barham*, both ships having a catapult installed and 2 TT removed. The other three ships had 2TT removed in 1930–31, while *Valiant* had a second 8-barrelled pompom in 1936 and *Queen Elizabeth* two in 1935. In 1938 *Barham* had the remaining 2 TT removed and the 4in guns replaced by 8-4in QF Mk XVI (4 × 2), whilst in April 1940 a further 16-2pdr pompoms (2 × 8) were added. *Barham* sank in about 5 minutes from 3 torpedoes fired by *U331* off Sollum, in the Mediterranean, but on a previous occasion had withstood a single torpedo.

All except *Barham* underwent second reconstructions. *Malaya* was taken in hand at Devonport between October 1934 and December 1936.

The middle deck was increased to 5in over magazines and to 3.5in over engine rooms, and the CT was replaced by a smaller one with 5in max. The AA armament was now 8-4in QF Mk XVI (4 × 2), 16-2pdr pompoms (2 × 8), the last 2 TT were removed and a cross-deck catapult added with hangars for two aircraft. The catapult was removed and the hangars converted to other uses in late 1942 when 16-2pdr pompoms (2 × 8) were added, followed by 4–4in QF Mk XVI (2 × 2) in January 1943. In September 1943 the 12-6in guns and the battery armour were removed, 2in plating being fitted over the ports. By mid-1944, 45-20mm Oerlikons were mounted and deep load displacement had risen to 37,710 tons including water protection. Paid off early in 1945, and sold for BU in 1948.

*Warspite*'s second reconstruction, at Portsmouth from March 1934 to March 1937, was more radical, data becoming: displacement 36,450t deep load including 815t water in protection compartments, dimensions unchanged except draught 33ft 1in (10.1m) mean at deep load; machinery: 4-shaft Parsons geared turbines, 6 Admiralty 3-drum boilers, 80,000shp = 23.5kts, 3501 tons oil; armour: changed as follows – battery 2in, CT 3in–2in, middle deck 5in over magazines, 3.5in over engine and boiler rooms, main deck 3.125in over forward belt; armament: 8–15in/42 Mk 1 (4 × 2, 30 deg elevation), 8–4in QF Mk XVI AA (4 × 2), 32-2pdr pompoms (4 × 8). There was a cross-deck catapult and hangars for 2 aircraft, but the aircraft equipment was removed in 1943. *Warspite* was hit by a FX1400 guided AP bomb on 16.9.43 and near missed by another, and was never fully repaired although patched up as a bombardment ship with 6 usable 15in, no 6in, 8-4in AA, 40 pompoms (5 × 8) and 35-20mm. She was again patched up after a ground mine explosion on 13.6.44 but speed was reduced to 15.5kts. Paid off into reserve finally in February 1945 and sold for BU in July 1946. She left Portsmouth in tow for Faslane, but broke her tow and ran aground in Prussia Cove, Cornwall, on 23 April 1947; salvage and scrapping took another nine years.

*Valiant*'s reconstruction at Devonport from March 1937 to November 1939 and *Queen Elizabeth*'s at Portsmouth from August 1937 to December 1940 with a further month at Rosyth, were the most complete of any of the class (*Barham* and probably *Malaya* were scheduled for similar rebuildings, but war intervened), and resulted in the following new data; displacement 36,513 tons deep load including 815 tons water protection (*Valiant*, 1939), 38,450 tons (*Queen Elizabeth*, 1944); dimensions were unchanged except draught 32ft 10in (10.0m) mean at deep load (*Valiant*, 1939), 34ft 6in (10.5m) (*Queen Elizabeth*, 1944); machinery: 4-shaft Parsons geared

turbines, 8 Admiralty 3-drum boilers, 80,000shp = 23.5kts, *Valiant* 3393, *Queen Elizabeth* 3366 tons oil; armour: changed as follows, HA mountings 2in–1in, CT 3in–2in, middle deck 5in over magazines, 3.5in over engine and boiler rooms, main deck 3.25in–2.75in over forward belt; armament: 8–15in/42 Mk 1 (4 × 2, 30 deg elevation), 20–4.5in/45 QF Mk I or III (10 × 2), 32-2pdr pompoms (4 × 8). *Valiant* was completed with a pole mainmast, and did not receive a tripod until 1945; *Queen Elizabeth* was completed with a tripod. Aircraft equipment, removed in 1943, was as *Warspite*. *Queen Elizabeth*'s close-range AA armament was increased by at least 54-20mm Oerlikons and *Valiant* at one time had 47, while in 1946 the latter had 56-2pdr pompoms (7 × 8). Both ships were crippled by 'human torpedoes' at Alexandria on 19.12.41 and *Queen Elizabeth*, which had by far the worse damage, was out of service until June 1943. *Valiant* was again seriously damaged by the collapse of a floating dock at Trincomalee on 8.8.44. Paid off in August and July 1945 respectively and sold for BU in 1948.

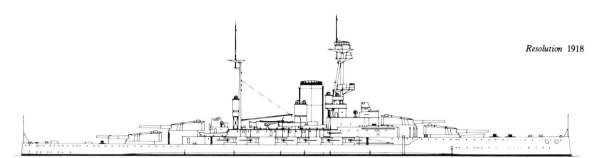

Admiralty papers of the 1914–18 period always refer to the 1913 Programme battleships as the *Revenge* class, although the general public knew them as the *Royal Sovereign* class, the name given in 1913.

They were a cheaper design than the *Queen Elizabeth*s, with a speed of only 21½kts, and were to revert to coal and oil fuel, but in other respects resembled the previous class. During the design stage the aftermost 6in guns were suppressed and a weatherdeck 6in gun was substituted, as in the *Tiger*. In January 1915 the design was altered to oil fuel only and shp was increased from 31,000 to 40,000 to increase speed from 21½kts to 23kts. Fuel stowage changed from 3000t coal/1500t oil to 3400t oil but the change did little to increase endurance as load tonnage had gone up from 25,500t to 28,000t. Eight ships were planned but on 26 August 1914 work stopped on all new capital ships. The new First Sea Lord, Admiral Fisher, succeeded in getting contracts for two suspended, with a view to redesigning them as battlecruisers (see *Renown* class).

## ROYAL SOVEREIGN class *battleship*

| | |
|---|---|
| **Displacement:** | 28,000t load; 31,000t deep load |
| **Dimensions:** | 580ft pp, 624ft 3in oa × 88ft 6in × 28ft 6in load |
| | *176.8m, 190.3m × 27.0m × 8.7m* |
| **Machinery:** | 4-shaft Parsons turbines, 18 Babcock & Wilcox or Yarrow boilers, 40,000shp = 23kts. Oil 3400t. Range 4200nm at 10kts |
| **Armour:** | Belt 13in–1in (331mm–25mm), bulkheads 6in–4in (152mm–102mm), barbettes 10in–4in (254mm–102mm), turret faces 13in (331mm), CT 11in (279mm), decks 2in–1in (51mm–25mm) |
| **Armament:** | 8–15in (381mm)/42 Mk I (4 × 2), 14–6in (152mm)/45 BL Mk XII, 2–3in (76mm)/20 cwt AA Mk I, 4–3pdr (47mm), 4–21in (533mm) TT sub (beam) |
| **Complement:** | 908–997 |

| Name | Builder | Laid down | Launched | Comp | Fate |
|---|---|---|---|---|---|
| RAMILLIES | Beardmore | 12.11.13 | 12.9.16 | 9.17 | Sold for BU 20.3.48 |
| RESOLUTION | Palmers | 29.11.13 | 14.1.15 | 12.16 | Sold for BU 5.5.48 |
| REVENGE (ex-*Renown*) | Vickers | 22.12.13 | 29.5.15 | 3.16 | Sold for BU 9.48 |
| ROYAL OAK | Devonport DYd | 15.1.14 | 17.11.14 | 5.16 | Torpedoed 14.10.39 |
| ROYAL SOVEREIGN | Portsmouth DYd | 15.1.14 | 29.4.15 | 5.16 | Sold for BU 5.4.49 |
| RENOWN | Palmers | — | — | — | Suspended 26.8.14 |
| REPULSE | John Brown | — | — | — | Suspended 26.8.14 |
| RESISTANCE | Devonport DYd | — | — | — | Cancelled 26.8.14 |

*Royal Soveriegn* as the Soviet *Arkangelsk* being handed back at Portsmouth 1949. *CPL*

Resolution 1924.
CPL

Although smaller than the *Queen Elizabeth*s the armour was better disposed, with the protective deck moved up to main deck level. Another improvement was to move the 6in guns further aft, and to ensure that the after pair of guns on either side bore aft. However they were still too close to the waterline, and this was the last class to have main deck batteries of this type. In March 1915 permission was given to fit anti-torpedo 'bulges' to the incomplete *Ramillies*. These were 7ft wide structures attached to the midships portion of the hull and faired into the lines to reduce drag. They were filled with compartments packed with steel tubes, oil fuel, water or air, and their purpose was to provide a bursting space for a torpedo warhead before it could inflict crippling damage on the main hull. The 'bulge' extended from the forward torpedo room to the after one and weighed some 2500t, including 773t of tubes (intended to offer resistance to the crushing effect of an explosion) and 194t of wood. The *Revenge* class were good gun platforms but tended to heel excessively when turning. The 'bulging' of *Ramillies* had the effect of reversing the original stability requirements, by increasing the beam and raising the metacentre. This gave the ship greater initial stability and improved the trim. However it did have the effect of making her roll too much, and after the war experiments were carried out to find an improved form of bulge. *Revenge* was fitted with bulges October 1917-February 1918, followed by

*Resolution* in late 1917–May 1918 and *Royal Sovereign* in 1920. The expected loss of speed did not occur, and the 'bulged' ships showed much less resistance at speed. On trials *Revenge*, without 'bulges' and displacing 30,750t, made 21.9kts with 42,650shp, whereas *Ramillies* at 33,000t made 21.5kts with 42,383shp.

Unlike the earlier dreadnoughts, which had twin balanced rudders, the new ships were given a single large rudder with a small auxiliary rudder ahead of it, on the centreline as well. This idea was intended to reduce vulnerability of the rudders to damage, to reduce resistance and to improve emergency hand-setting (hand-gear was connected only to the small rudder). In practice, however, the small rudder proved of very little use and it was later removed. The ships were completed with all the latest improvements, including director control for the 6in as well as the main armament, although secondary directors were not actually fitted until March–April 1917 (in *Ramillies* as late as June 1918). In common with all dreadnoughts their pumping, flooding and draining arrangements were extended and improved to cope with underwater damage. Extra 1in HT plating was fitted on the main deck over the magazines and on the transverse torpedo bulkheads, and flash-tight scuttles were provided for both 15in and 6in ammunition handling systems. All ships received aircraft platforms on 'B' and 'X' turrets in 1918, and they received the usual

searchlight towers, range clocks and deflection scales between 1916 and 1918. All joined the Grand Fleet on completion, *Revenge* and *Royal Oak* in time to fight at Jutland (no damage or casualties, *Revenge* fired both 3in AA and 15in at Zeppelins during later stages of action). *Ramillies* damaged her rudder at launch and was towed with great difficulty to Cammell Laird for repair.

The effect of wartime modifications was to increase deep load displacement to between 31,250t (*Royal Oak*) and 36,140t (*Ramillies*).

Post-1918 modifications to this class were not as extensive as to the *Queen Elizabeth*s. *Royal Oak* was refitted in late 1922–24 and bulged, altering beam and deep load draught to 102ft 1in × 31ft 6in mean (21.1m × 9.6m) at 33,240 tons. The bulge was of a new deep type, extending above the waterline and nearly reaching the 6in battery amidships. *Ramillies* was fitted with similar deep bulges in place of the original type in 1927. *Royal Oak* was again refitted in 1934–36 when the main deck was increased to 5in over magazines and 3½in over engine rooms. In the rest of the class the bulges were lightened by removing crushing tubes and wood and cement filling, and in 1942 the main deck over magazines was increased by 2in in *Royal Sovereign, Resolution* and *Ramillies*. The AA armament had been altered to 4–4in QF Mk V (4 × 1) in all by late 1928 and the 2 forecastle deck 6in removed. In 1931–38 *Resolution* had 5–4in AA with an experimental

twin mounting, but all were re-armed with 8–4in QF Mk XVI (4 × 2) in 1936–39. The elevation of *Resolution*'s forward 15in guns was increased to 30 deg in 1941–42. The four surviving ships had 4–6in removed in 1942–43. *Revenge* had one 8-barrelled pompom in December 1931, and by the outbreak of war all had two, while two 4-barrelled mountings were added in 1941–42 and up to 42 Oerlikons were mounted in 1944–45. The TT were reduced to 2 in 1931–34 and removed in 1938–39 except in *Royal Oak*, where they were replaced by 4 TT (above water) in 1934–36. A catapult was fitted to all except *Revenge*, but only *Resolution* retained one after 1939. Deep load displacements eventually reached 33,560-35,390 tons. *Royal Oak* was sunk by three torpedoes from *U47* in Scapa Flow, but *Resolution* and *Ramillies* each survived one, from a French submarine and a Japanese midget submarine respectively.

The inter-war period was spent in Fleet service in home waters and the Mediterranean. All saw service in Second World War, during which *Royal Oak* was sunk. Three units were sold for BU in 1948, but *Royal Sovereign* was transferred to Soviet Navy on 30 May 1944 and renamed *Arkhangelsk*. Returned 9 February 1949 and sold for BU.

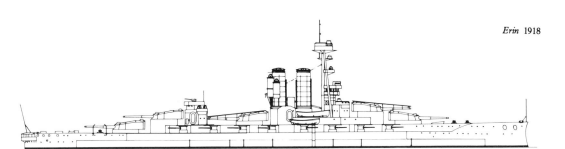

## ERIN *battleship*

| | |
|---|---|
| **Displacement:** | 22,780t load; 25,250t deep load |
| **Dimensions:** | 525ft pp, 559ft 6in oa × 91ft 7in × 28ft 5in mean |
| | *160.0m, 170.5m × 27.9m × 8.7m* |
| **Machinery:** | 4-shaft Parsons turbines, 15 Babcock & Wilcox boilers, 26,500shp = 21kts. Coal 2120t, oil 710t. Range 5300nm at 10kts |
| **Armour:** | Belt 12in–4in (305mm–102mm), bulkheads 8in–4in (203mm–102mm), barbettes 10in–3in 254mm–76mm), turret faces 11in (279mm), deck 3in–1.5in (76mm–38mm) |
| **Armament:** | 10–13.5in (343mm)/45 Mk V (5 × 2), 16–6in (152mm)/50 Mk XI, 6–6pdr (57mm), 2–3in (76mm)/20cwt AA Mk I, 4–21in (533mm) TT sub (beam) |
| **Complement:** | 1070 |

| Name | Builder | Laid down | Launched | Comp | Fate |
|---|---|---|---|---|---|
| ERIN (ex-*Reshadieh*) | Vickers | 1.8.11 | 3.9.13 | 8.14 | Sold for BU 12.22 |

When war broke out in August 1914 two battleships had nearly been completed for Turkey, and they were seized by order of the First Lord of the Admiralty, Winston Churchill. The first of these, the *Reshadieh* (ex-*Reshad V*) had been one of a pair ordered in 1911, but the *Reshad-i-Hamiss* was cancelled in 1912 and replaced by a purchase from Brazil (see below). The design was by Vickers' designer Thurston but was based on the *King George V*, with some features of the *Iron Duke*s. The hull was shorter and beamier, and the midships 'Q' 13.5in turret was a deck higher, which made for better shooting in a seaway, and the battery was marginally better arranged than in her British contemporaries. The short hull made for a tight turning circle. Although on paper nearly as good as the *Iron Duke*s on 2000t less, the *Erin* displayed the usual trade-off of qualities in private shipyard designs. The armour belt was shallower than the *King George V*'s; with 1130t less coal she also had considerably less endurance, but this was adequate for

North Sea operations, so did not reduce her effectiveness. Her appearance was unusual, with a pair of narrow funnels close together and a single tripod foremast with the legs trailing forward. She also had a 'plough' or 'cleaver' bow which was beginning to displace the more traditional ram type; this feature enhanced her looks and improved seakeeping. In 1917 she was given the standard modifications to fire control and searchlights, and in 1918 she was given aircraft platforms on 'B' and 'Q' turrets.

HMS *Erin* joined the 2nd Battle Squadron, Grand Fleet in September 1914; fought at Jutland and suffered no casualties. In 1919 became flagship, Nore Reserve until sold for BU in 1922 to comply with Washington Treaty.

*Erin* 1915. CPL

This unusual battleship was laid down for Brazil as the *Rio de Janeiro*, but in July 1912 the Brazilian Government began to look for a buyer for her (for design history, see under Brazil). Turkey, smarting from her defeat in the Balkan War, bought her for £2,725,000 early in 1914 and renamed her *Sultan Osman I*. The ship was almost complete as war approached and had been docked at Devonport, but Churchill ordered that she should be delayed until war was certain. As Turkey was friendly to Germany the ship was seized and incorporated into the RN as HMS *Agincourt*, giving her three owners in less than a year. She was also the

*Agincourt* 1915.
*CPL*

## AGINCOURT *battleship*

| | |
|---|---|
| **Displacement:** | 27,500t load; 30,250t deep load |
| **Dimensions:** | 632ft pp, 671ft 6in oa × 89ft × 27ft mean<br>*192.6m, 204.7m × 27.1m × 8.2m* |
| **Machinery:** | 4-shaft Parsons geared turbines, 22 Babcock & Wilcox boilers, 34,000shp = 22kts. Coal 3200t, oil 620t. Range *c*4500nm at 10kts |
| **Armour:** | Belt 9in–4in (229mm–102mm), bulkheads 8in–4in (203mm–102mm), barbettes 9in–3in (229mm–76mm), turret faces 12in (305mm), CT 12in (305mm), decks 2.5in–1in (64mm–25mm) |
| **Armament:** | 14–12in (305mm)/45 Mk XIII (7 × 2), 20–6in (152mm)/50 Mk XI, 10–3in (76mm)/45 QF, 2–3in (76mm)/20cwt AA Mk I, 3–21in (533mm) TT sub (2 beam, 1 stern) |
| **Complement:** | 1115 |

| Name | Builder | Laid down | Launched | Comp | Fate |
|---|---|---|---|---|---|
| AGINCOURT<br>(ex-*Sultan Osman I*) | Armstrong | 14.9.11 | 22.1.13 | 8.14 | Sold for BU 12.22 |

longest battleship to serve in the RN to date and the last with 12in guns.

The ship required major alterations before she was fit to join the Grand Fleet. The massive flying deck between the funnels was removed, along with torpedo nets. The turrets were named after the days of the week instead of 'A', 'B', 'P' and 'Q' etc. As with the *Erin* the scale of protection and coal supply was not up to RN standards. In the Grand Fleet she was not highly regarded, partly because her non-standard equipment put her in dockyard hands frequently but principally because of her light protection and, as Oscar Parkes said, she

was regarded as nothing more than a 'floating magazine with a tremendous volume of fire as her best protection'. The turrets were unusual in having all loading operations controlled by a single lever. The Elswick 'W' pattern 12in gun was not interchangeable with the similar Mk X in the early dreadnoughts.

In 1916 the tripod mainmast was removed and the topmast was restepped on the derrick post amidships, a considerable improvement to her profile. In 1918 her bridgework was enlarged and searchlights were regrouped in towers around the after funnel. To quell rumours that she would turn

turtle if she fired all 14 guns together her gunnery officer ordered the 'Gin Palace' to fire full broadsides when she got her brief moment of action at the rear of the battle line at Jutland. In all 144 rounds of 12in were fired and on-lookers recorded that the massive sheet of flame looked like a battlecruiser blowing up.

Taken over 2 August 1914 and after alterations joined the 4th Battle Squadron, Grand Fleet at sea on 7 September 1914. Transferred to 1st BS 1915 and fought at Jutland (no damage or casualties). Joined 2nd BS late 1918 but put on Disposal List 1919. Recommissioned at Rosyth 1921

for experimental work and then stripped for conversion to 'Mobile Naval Base' or large depot ship. This involved the removal of all but No 1 and No 2 turrets and the provision of extra oil fuel and ammunition stowage. Work was stopped late in 1921 (a rumoured resale to Brazil did not materialise) and she was sold for BU in 1922.

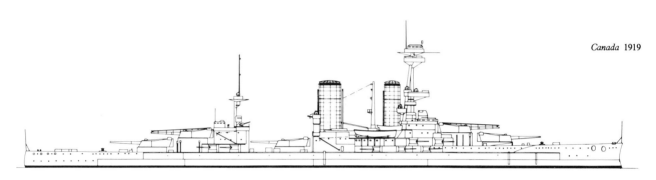

*Canada* 1919

## CANADA class *battleships*

| | |
|---|---|
| **Displacement:** | 28,600t load; 32,120t deep load |
| **Dimensions:** | 625ft pp, 661ft oa × 92ft × 29ft mean |
| | *190.5m, 201.5m × 28.0m × 8.8m* |
| **Machinery:** | 4-shaft Brown-Curtis (HP) and Parsons (LP) turbines, 21 Yarrow boilers, 37,000shp = 22¾kts. Coal 3300t, oil 520t. Range 4400nm at 10kts |
| **Armour:** | Belt 9in–4in (229mm–102mm), bulkheads 4.5in–3in (114mm–76mm), barbettes 10in–4in (254mm–102mm), turret faces 10in (254mm), CT 11in (279mm), decks 4in–1in (102mm–25mm) |
| **Armament:** | 10–14in (356mm)/45 Mk I (5 × 2), 16–6in (152mm)/50 Mk XI, 2–3in (76mm)/20cwt AA Mk I, 4–3pdr (47mm), 4–21in (533mm) TT sub (beam) |
| **Complement:** | 1167 |

| Name | Builder | Laid down | Launched | Comp | Fate |
|---|---|---|---|---|---|
| CANADA (ex-*Almirante Latorre*) | Armstrong | 12.11 | 27.11.13 | 9.15 | Returned to Chile 4.20 |
| — (ex-*Almirante Cochrane*) | Armstrong | 2.13 | — | — | Completed as carrier *Eagle* |

The Chilean Navy's response to the Argentine and Brazilian battleships of 1910–11 was typically forthright: two much larger and altogether more powerful ships were ordered in Britain, armed with 14in guns. The *Almirante Latorre* was afloat and well advanced in August 1914, but her sister *Almirante Cochrane* was still on the stocks. As Chile was a friendly neutral and supplier of nitrates vital to the munitions industry there could be no question of seizure, and the *Latorre* was formally purchased on 9 September 1914. Work was suspended on her sister, which was complete up to the forecastle deck, with boilers and engines installed and plated over but side armour not yet in place. Although suspended, her 14in guns were completed and put into reserve for her sister. She was formally taken over on 28 February 1918 for conversion to an aircraft carrier and renamed *Eagle*. The design was essentially similar to the *Iron Duke* but longer, with a shorter forecastle and a much longer quarterdeck. As they were intended to be fast the engine and boiler rooms occupied more space than in *Erin* or her British contemporaries. Although having the same freeboard as the *Iron Duke* class the *Canada*'s massive funnels and tall tripod seemed to make her lower in the water, particularly forward. During completion the funnels were increased in height and a single pole mast was stepped on the after superstructure. In 1916 the after four 6in guns were removed because they were badly affected by blast from 'Q' turret. Like the other two purchased battleships

she had a 'plough' bow. In 1918 she had aircraft platforms on 'B' and 'X' turrets.

Joined 4th Battle Squadron, Grand Fleet in October 1915. Fought at Jutland without damage or casualties, and then transferred to 1st BS. In 1919–20 refitted at Devonport and returned to Chile in April 1920 under her original name.

*Canada* as completed.
*CPL*

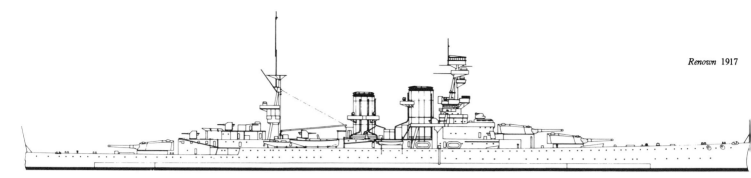

The Admiralty had decided that there would be no more battlecruisers after HMS *Tiger* but they reckoned without the return of Lord Fisher to the post of First Sea Lord in October 1914. Capitalising on the apparent vindication of the *Invincible* class at the Battle of the Falklands he was able to persuade the Cabinet to overturn its decision to stop work on capital ships. In response to questions about the war being over before the ships were finished, Fisher promised to build them as fast as the *Dreadnought* ten years earlier. That boast proved impossible but the speed with which the two novel and complex ships were built was nonetheless a great tribute to the efficiency of British shipbuilding and the DNC's staff. As was to be ex-

*Repulse* April 1939.
*CPL*

## RENOWN class *battlecruisers*

**Displacement:** 27,650t average load; 30,835t deep load
**Dimensions:** 750ft pp, 794ft oa × 90ft × 25ft 6in mean
228.6m, 242.0m × 27.4m ×7.8m
**Machinery:** 4-shaft Brown-Curtis turbines, 42 Babcock & Wilcox boilers, 112,000shp = 31.5kts. Oil 4243t. Range 3650nm at 10kts
**Armour:** Belt 6in-1.5in (152mm-38mm), bulkheads 4in-3in (102mm-76mm), barbettes 7in-4in (178mm-102mm), turret faces 11in (279mm), CT 10in (254mm), decks 3in-0.5in (76mm-13mm)
**Armament:** 6-15in (381mm)/42 Mk I (3 × 2), 17-4in (102mm)/44.3 BL Mk IX (5 × 3, 2 × 1), 2-3in (76mm)/20cwt AA Mk I, 4-3pdr (47mm) saluting, 2-21in (533mm) TT sub (beam)
**Complement:** —

| Name | Builder | Laid down | Launched | Comp | Fate |
|------|---------|-----------|----------|------|------|
| RENOWN | Fairfield | 25.1.15 | 4.3.16 | 9.16 | Sold for BU 19.3.48 |
| REPULSE | John Brown | 25.1.15 | 8.1.16 | 8.16 | Sunk 10.12.41 |

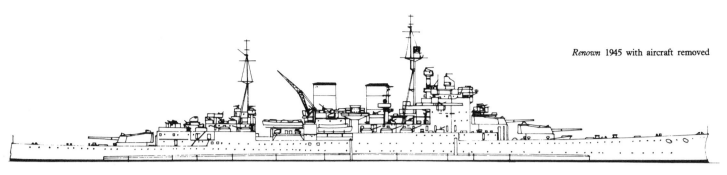

*Renown* 1945 with aircraft removed

pected Fisher's influence on the design was disastrous. He rightly sought to use as much material as possible from the two contracts already placed with Palmers and John Brown for *Revenge* class battleships, and built the design around existing gun mountings, six sets of turntables and twelve 15in guns, part of the outfit for the battleships. But the old admiral's belief that speed was the best protection led him to armour the two ships on the scale of the *Invincible*, despite the fact that they would be facing enemy capital ships armed with guns which could riddle 6in belt armour.

Speed was everything, and a speed of 32kts was to be achieved. The Engineer-in-Chief recommended the use of new lightweight machinery,

*Renown* in the 1920s.
CPL

with lighter turbines and small-tube boilers but as time was short the machinery of *Tiger* was duplicated, with three more boilers. Fisher's influence could also be detected in the choice of secondary armament. The ships were given five triple 4in mountings and two singles, arranged high up around the superstructure. The PXII mounting was very clumsy, with all three guns in separate sleeves, and they required exceptionally large crews, 32 men. In theory the arrangement of these mountings – one on either side of the forward superstructure, one on the centreline between the funnels and the mainmast, and two superfiring aft – gave a concentration of fire which was superior to a 6in battery, but this ignored realities as the triple mount-

ings could not deliver a volume of fire and the 4in shell lacked range and stopping power.

When the *Repulse* joined the Grand Fleet in August 1916 (*Renown* joined a month later) the losses at Jutland had destroyed whatever reputation the battlecruisers had ever had, and nobody could avoid the significance of the long double row of scuttles amidships, indicating a vast area of hull unprotected even by the thin strip of 6in armour. So poor an impression did they make that the C-in-C Sir John Jellicoe suggested in October 1916 that they should both receive additional protection, and a month later *Repulse* was taken in hand, followed by her sister in February 1917. This was only a palliative, taking the form of 500t of

additional plating on decks, particularly over the crowns of magazines, over the engine rooms and over the steering gear.

Both ships had funnels of equal height when completed but after trials the forward one was raised by 6ft to cure interference from smoke. *Repulse* was the first capital ship to receive a flying-off platform, in the autumn of 1917, and Sqn Ldr Rutland flew a Sopwith Pup from the ship's 'B' turret on 1 October. On 8 October Rutland flew off again, this time off the back of 'Y' turret to demonstrate the platform's reversibility. *Renown* was similarly fitted early in 1918. Both ships received the remainder of the standard modifications, but in addition extra stiffening had to be

fitted internally as they proved to have been too lightly built.

The effect of these alterations was to increase deep load displacement to 32,730t (Renown). Even after the first round of modifications their protection was a constant source of worry, and in response to complaints from the C-in-C the DNC proposed various schemes for adding grating-type armour, a proper bulge etc. DNC then suggested that one ship could be given the 9in armour belt removed from the ex-Chilean battleship *Almirante Cochrane* (which was being converted to a carrier), while the second would have to wait longer for new 9in armour to be manufactured, or have one of the less orthodox types of protection. By July 1918 it had been decided to give *Repulse* the ex-Chilean armour and to re-armour *Renown*, the work to be done at Portsmouth. In fact *Renown* had to wait until 1923, but *Repulse* went into the dockyard for reconstruction between December 1918 and January 1921. The original 6in belt armour was moved up a deck to cover the lower deck side, and was replaced by the ex-Chilean 9in. The main deck was increased to 3in flat, 4in slopes over magazines and the lower deck to 3in over the magazines. The addition of bulges increased the beam to 101ft (30.8m). 8–21in above-water TT were fitted. The alterations added 4500 tons, but because of the bulges draught went up by only 1ft, to 27ft 11in (8.5m) mean at 32,740 tons load displacement and to 31ft 6in (9.6m) mean at 37,490 tons extra deep load. The light displacement became 31,450t and the deep load 36,920t; speed fell to about 30 knots.

*Renown* received a short refit in 1919–20 to improve accommodation

for the Prince of Wales' tour of the United States and Australasia. This included removal of one triple 4in and the installation of a squash court on the port side amidships. At Portsmouth between May 1923 and August 1926 she was given a new 9in belt, but instead of moving the 6in armour up above it, as had been done in *Repulse*, it was omitted, so externally the ship could be distinguished from *Repulse* by retaining the double row of scuttles. In place of the upper belt, *Renown* was given more deck armour, data becoming main deck 4in over magazines, 2.5in–1in over boiler rooms, 3in over engine rooms, continued to side over deck slope at 4in–2.5in, main deck slope 4in by magazines, lower deck 4in–3.75in over magazines beyond 'A' and 'Y', and longitudinal bulkheads by boiler uptakes 2in. The 9in belt was vulnerable to 15in shellfire, but shells would break up in penetrating, or at worst explode a short distance inside. The thicker decks would deflect 15in shells from the magazines at all likely battle ranges, and from the machinery at 15,000 yards or below. The fitting of bulges increased the beam to 102ft 4in (31.2m) and the deep load displacement to 37,150 tons, at 31ft 9in (9.5m) mean draught. The machinery was unchanged but speed fell to 30.25 knots. The secondary and AA armament was altered to 15–4in BL Mk IX (5×3) and 4–4in QF Mk V AA (4 × 1). One 4in triple was removed in March 1932, an 8-barrelled pompom mounted in May 1932 and a second briefly from January to May 1936, whilst a catapult was fitted in May 1933.

Between September 1936 and 2.9.39 *Renown* was taken in hand at Portsmouth for a second, more drastic re-

construction to serve as fast carrier escort. New, lighter machinery, four sets of Parsons geared turbines and 8 Admiralty 3-drum boilers, saved weight for additional armour and a new dual-purpose secondary armament, deep load displacement falling to 36,080 tons at 30ft 6in (9.3m) mean draught. The new machinery developed 120,000shp for 30.75 knots, and oil capacity became 4613 tons. The elevation of the main armament was increased to 30° and the new secondary and AA armament was 20–4.5in (115mm)/45 QF Mk I or III (10 × 2), 24–2pdr pompom (3 × 8). There were 8–21in above-water TT. One cross-deck catapult was fitted, with hangars for two aircraft. The aircraft equipment was removed in 1943, although the catapult was also not carried from November 1940 to October 1941. A quadruple pompom was added in December 1943 and 64–20mm by 1944. The TT were removed in April 1945; 12–4.5in guns were also removed for installation in new fleet carriers. By 1944, because of the usual wartime additions, deep load displacement had risen to 38,395 tons.

*Repulse* had 2–4in BL Mk IX and 2–3in AA replaced by 4–4in QF Mk V AA (4×1) in November 1924, and was reconstructed at Portsmouth from April 1933 to May 1936. The protection was increased as follows: main deck over magazine 5.75in, for 20ft abaft 'Y' 4.25in, over engine rooms 3.5in continued to side, lower deck over forward magazines 4.25in, while the crushing tubes were removed from the bulges. The secondary and AA armament became 12–4in BL Mk IX (4 × 3), 4–4in QF Mk XV AA (2 × 2), 4–4in QF Mk V AA, 16–2pdr pompom (2 × 8), with 8–21in TT aw. The alter-

ations increased the displacement to 38,300 tons deep load at 32ft 2in (9.8m) mean draught, and with machinery unaltered speed fell to 28.3 knots. There was one cross-deck catapult, and hangars for two aircraft. The 4in Mk XV were replaced by 2–4in Mk V in February 1939, and a third 8-barrelled pompom replaced a 4in triple in November 1940, while 8–20mm Oerlikons were added in 1941.

Both ships joined the Grand Fleet on completion; *Repulse* was briefly in action against German light forces in Heligoland Bight on 17 November 1917 (fired 54 shells, scoring one hit on light cruiser *Königsberg*). They again saw considerable service in the Second World War, *Repulse* serving with the Home Fleet from the outbreak of war and *Renown* in home waters and with Force H at Gibraltar. *Renown* had the better of an inconclusive encounter with *Scharnhorst* and *Gneisenau* off Narvik on 8 April 1940, but contact was lost in very heavy weather. Their sub-standard protection caused concern during the hunt for the *Bismarck*; *Repulse* was ordered to keep 5000 yards outside *King George V*, and was not to engage until the flagship had opened fire, while *Renown*, escorting *Ark Royal*, was only to engage if *King George V* or *Rodney* were already heavily engaged. *Repulse* was sunk with HMS *Prince of Wales* by Japanese torpedo-bombers off Malaya in December 1941. The old ship shrugged off an initial bomb and still manoeuvred at 25 knots after the first torpedo, but capsized and sank eight minutes after four more torpedo hits. *Renown* was paid off in 1945 and sold for BU in 1948.

*Renown* September 1933.
CPL

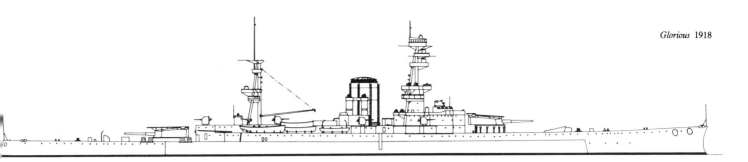

To get around the Cabinet ruling against new capital ships Fisher ordered early in 1915 three 'large light cruisers' which were in fact light battlecruisers intended to support his proposed Baltic landing. The precise role, like everything else connected with Fisher's Baltic plans, was never worked out, but it can be assumed that they were to provide gunfire support with their heavy guns and possibly to lure away German forces. To that end their high speed and shallow draught made sense, but as with the original battlecruisers, the result was a very expensive solution to the problem. The basis of the design was simply an enlargement of the current light cruisers, with 2in armour plating over 1in shell plating. Even the machinery was

## COURAGEOUS class *light battlecruisers*

| | |
|---|---|
| **Displacement:** | 19,230t load; 22,690t deep load |
| **Dimensions:** | 735ft pp, 786ft 3in oa × 81ft × 23ft 4in mean |
| | *224.0m, 239.7m × 24.7m × 7.1m* |
| **Machinery:** | 4-shaft Parsons geared turbines, 18 Yarrow small-tube boilers, 90,000shp = 32kts. Oil 3160t. |
| **Armour:** | Belt 3in–2in (76mm–51mm), bulkheads 3in–2in (76mm–51mm), barbettes 7in–3in (178mm–76mm), turret faces 13in–11in (331mm–279mm), CT 10in (254mm), decks 1.5in–0.75in (38mm–19mm) |
| **Armament:** | 4–15in (381mm)/42 Mk I (2 × 2), 18–4in (102mm)/44.3 BL Mk IX (6 × 3), 2–3in (76mm)/20cwt AA Mk I, 2–3pdr (47mm), 2–21in (533mm) TT sub (beam) |
| **Complement:** | 828–842 |

| Name | Builder | Laid down | Launched | Comp | Fate |
|---|---|---|---|---|---|
| COURAGEOUS | Armstrong, Elswick | 28.3.15 | 5.2.16 | 1.17 | Converted 1924–28 |
| GLORIOUS | Harland & Wolff | 1.5.15 | 20.4.16 | 1.17 | Converted 1924–30 |

*Courageous* as a minelayer 1917.
CPL

*Glorious* 1918.
CPL

merely that of the light cruiser *Champion*, doubled to drive four shafts, and 18 boilers instead of 8. However the design showed that the RN was at last becoming aware of the benefits of more advanced machinery, for the combination of small-tube boilers and double helical geared turbines enabled the *Courageous* class to develop 90,000shp quite easily, when compared with the 42 large-tube boilers need for 110,000shp in the *Renown* class. This feature in the design marked a victory for the DNC and E-in-C, who had been pressing the Naval Staff for some years to get away from heavy, uneconomical machinery. The main improvement was to use small-diameter, fast-running turbines in place of large-diameter turbines.

The hull form was similar to the *Renown* class, with an integral 'bulge'

taking the place of an internal anti-torpedo bulkhead. During construction an additional 1½in–1in torpedo bulkhead was worked in between the barbettes but as they ran inboard of the wing engine rooms they would have been only partially effective in limiting flooding. As Fisher had already initiated work on an 18in gun it was hoped to give the new ships an armament of two single 18in, but to get the first two ships into service quickly twin 15in were substituted.

The ships were designed to reach 32kts at a load tonnage of 17,400t, so that the trial speed of *Glorious*, 31¼kts at 21,270t with 88,550shp was highly creditable. Although not too lightly built the great length of the hull was a potential source of weakness. On 8 January 1917 while working up to full power during a trial the *Courageous*

suffered buckling of the forecastle between the breakwater and the 15in barbette, as well as leaking fuel tanks, so she was given 130t of stiffening. Although no such damage was suffered in *Glorious*, she was also stiffened early in 1918. In addition to the torpedo bulkhead mentioned earlier, after Jutland both ships were given extra 1in plating on the main deck over the magazines. The single large funnel and long forecastle made them handsome ships but they were even bigger white elephants than the *Renown* and *Repulse*, for which no proper role could be imagined. In 1917 both ships were given 12 additional fixed TT (6 × 2), 2 twin abreast the mainmast and 4 twin around the after turret, port and starboard. Although *Glorious* managed to fire a torpedo from one of her submerged TT at full speed, in practice

this was limited to 23kts as the guide-bar was bent by the water pressure. When *Courageous* received four sets of mine rails on her quarterdeck in the spring of 1917 (known as 'Clapham Junction') she could lay 222 British Elia mines or 202 of the new HII type, but there is no record of her ever laying any. *Courageous* could be distinguished from her sister by having her search-lights around the funnel on one level.

*Courageous* commissioned in January 1917 and joined the Grand Fleet, first with 3rd Light Cruiser Squadron and later 1st Cruiser Squadron. Converted to minelayer in April 1917, and order given for removal of rails 23 November 1917. On 17 November 1917 engaged (with *Glorious* and *Repulse*) German light forces in the Heligoland Bight. Expended 92 15in shells, scoring a hit on the cruiser *Pillau* (shared with *Glorious*); out of 393 4in shells fired by both ships scored no hits. After the Armistice she was attached to the Gunnery School and later became flagship of the reserve. Converted to a carrier 1924–28 and was the first RN ship loss of the Second World War, being torpedoed by *U 29* on 17 September 1939 with the loss of 23 Swordfish planes and 514 of her 1200 crew.

*Glorious* commissioned in January 1917 as flagship 3rd LCS but then joined her sister in 1st LCS. In action on 17 November 1917, firing 57 15in shells. Attached to gunnery school at Devonport in 1919 and later became flagship of reserve. Converted to carrier 1924–30 and sunk by gunfire of *Scharnhorst* and *Gneisenau* off Norway, 8 June 1940.

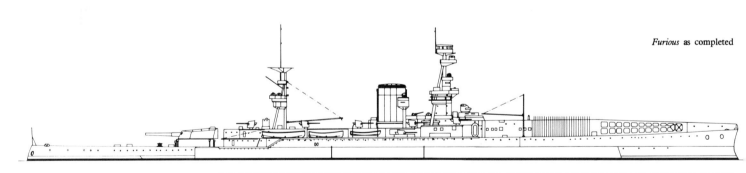

*Furious* as completed

## FURIOUS *light battlecruiser*

| | |
|---|---|
| **Displacement:** | 19,513t load; 22,890t deep load |
| **Dimensions:** | 735ft pp, 786ft 6in oa × 88ft × 21ft mean |
| | *224.0m, 239.7m × 26.8m × 6.4m* |
| **Machinery:** | 4-shaft Brown-Curtis geared turbines, 18 Yarrow boilers, 90,000shp = 31½kts. Oil 3393t. |
| **Armour:** | Belt 3in–2in (76mm–51mm), bulkheads 3in–2in (76mm–51mm), barbettes 7in–4in (178mm–102mm), turret faces 9in (229mm), CT 10in (254mm), decks 3in–0.75in (76mm–19mm) |
| **Armament:** | 2–18in (457mm)/40 Mk I, 11–5.5in (140mm)/50 BL Mk I, 2–3in (76mm)/20cwt Mk I, 4–3pdr (47mm), 2–21in (533mm) TT sub (beam) |
| **Complement:** | 880 |

| Name | Builder | Laid down | Launched | Comp | Fate |
|---|---|---|---|---|---|
| FURIOUS | Armstrong | 8.6.15 | 15.8.16 | 7.17 | Converted to carrier 1917 |

The third light battlecruiser was given two single 18in guns, but care was taken to make the turret-ring the same size as the twin 15in mounting, so that if problems were encountered with the gun it would be possible to re-arm the ship with 15in guns. In fact the 18in gun was merely a much bigger version of the 15in, and apart from its massive muzzle blast, retained the good qualities of the smaller gun. Experience with the ex-Greek cruisers *Birkenhead* and *Chester* had demonstrated the qualities of the 5.5in gun, and the single mountings proved far more satisfactory than the triple 4in guns in the *Courageous* class. They were grouped two p&s of the foremast, p&s of the funnel, one on the centreline, p&s of the mainmast, and p&s abreast of the funnel at weatherdeck level.

The ship was nearly complete at Elswick when on 19 March 1917 it was decided by the Admiralty to convert her to a carrier to remedy the Grand Fleet's crucial shortage of aircraft. The after gun had been installed but the forward turret was being assembled and the gun was still ashore. The turret was replaced by a hangar and sloping flying-off deck which extended to the forecastle, with two derricks for hoisting aircraft aboard. The ship was completed to the new design on 4 July 1917 and she joined the Fleet, but on 17 October further orders were issued to give her an after flight deck and hangar. This was a much more drastic conversion leading to reclassification as an aircraft carrier.

The hull was 7ft beamier than the *Courageous* class, but with a more pronounced 'bulge'. There was also a simpler form of main framing and structure. In appearance she would have resembled the *Courageous* class, apart from the massive 18in turrets. As with her half-sisters the torpedo armament was increased by the addition of four sets of triple 21in TT on the upper deck aft and two pairs on the upper deck forward. The triple tubes were subsequently removed, reducing the total to six TT, including the submerged tubes ahead of the forward barbette. On a full power trial she reached 31½kts with 94,000shp.

Joined Grand Fleet in July 1917 and carried out trials until November. On 2 August 1917 Sqn Cdr Dunning twice landed a Sopwith Pup on the flying-off deck but he was killed while attempting to repeat the success on 7 August. Went into dockyard hands for full conversion to carrier in December 1917.

Two views of *Furious* July 1917.
*CPL*

*Hood* 1937.
*CPL*

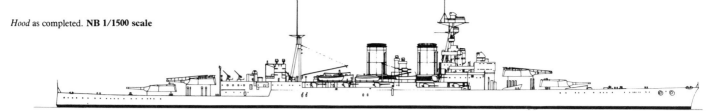

*Hood* as completed. **NB 1/1500 scale**

## HOOD class *battlecruisers*

| | |
|---|---|
| **Displacement:** | 42,670t load; 45,200t deep load |
| **Dimensions:** | 810ft pp, 860ft oa × 104ft × 28ft 6in |
| | *246.9m, 262.1m × 31.7m × 8.7m* |
| **Machinery:** | 4-shaft Brown-Curtis geared turbines, 24 Yarrow boilers, 144,000shp = 31kts. Oil 4000t. Range 4000nm at 10kts |
| **Armour:** | Belt 12in–5in (305mm–127mm), bulkheads 5in–4in (127mm–102mm), barbettes 12in–5in (305mm–127mm), turret faces 15in (381mm), CT 11in–9in (279mm–229mm), decks 3in–1.5in (76mm–38mm) |
| **Armament:** | 8–15in (381mm)/42 Mk I (4 × 2), 12–5.5in (140mm)/50 BL Mk I, 4–4in (102mm)/45 QF Mk V AA, 4–3pdr (47mm), 6–21in (533mm) TT (2 sub beam, 4 aw beam) |
| **Complement:** | 1477 |

| Name | Builder | Laid down | Launched | Comp | Fate |
|---|---|---|---|---|---|
| HOOD | John Brown | 31.5.16* | 22.8.18 | 5.20 | Sunk 24.5.41 |
| RODNEY | Fairfield | 9.10.16 | — | — | Cancelled 1918 |
| HOWE | Cammell Laird | 16.10.16 | — | — | Cancelled 1918 |
| ANSON | Armstrong | 9.11.17 | — | — | Cancelled 1918 |

*Laid down for second time 1.9.16 (see notes)

In November 1915 the Admiralty Board called for a design for an experimental battleship, with the lightest practicable draught and incorporating the latest ideas on underwater protection. The basis was to be the *Queen Elizabeth* class of fast battleships, but when the proposals were forwarded to the C-in-C, Admiral Jellicoe, he insisted that 30kt battlecruisers were more useful than battleships. The design was recast as a battlecruiser of 36,300t, with 8in belt armour and a speed of 32kts, but the loss of three battlecruisers at Jutland on the day the first ship was laid down (construction of three had been authorised in April 1916 and the fourth followed in July) caused all work to be stopped. The design was investigated and recast by early August 1916 as 37,500t, with a deeper belt. Later that month the DNC submitted his own modifications, which raised displacement to 40,600t and increased belt armour to 12in. Among other ideas looked at were triple 15in mountings, two triple and two twin, or three triples, with displacement increased to 40,900t–43,500t and speed cut to 30½kts–30¾kts. Finally, however, the 8-gun design was accepted, and so in effect the original idea of a bigger and faster *Queen Elizabeth* was finally achieved.

The most obvious lesson learned since the outbreak of war was that secondary batteries needed to be a deck higher, and so the 5.5in guns were mainly at forecastle deck level, with two singles p&s abreast of the forward funnel giving even better command in bad weather. Seakeeping was improved by giving the hull pronounced sheer and flare. This flare was also intended to ensure that an incoming shell would strike more obliquely, and so in effect increased the armour's resistance to penetration. On 8 February 1917 the War Cabinet decided to proceed only with the *Hood* as intelligence showed that the Germans had stopped work on capital ships. *Rodney, Howe* and *Anson* were therefore suspended on 9 March. They lay on the stocks until October 1918, when the contractors were authorised to clear the slips, but the task of selling off armour and machinery continued until August 1919. So many changes had been made to their design that they would have differed considerably from

the *Hood*. The belt would have been reduced to 11in, funnels would have been closer together and the mainmast would have been stepped close to the after funnel. A new type of 15in turret was also under consideration.

Before the *Hood* was completed four 5.5in guns at the after end of the battery were suppressed along with 4 of the 8 aw TT. The ship was by now considerably overweight with all the additions made in 1918–19, and it was having the effect of submerging the main belt and reducing freeboard. The 15in Mk II mounting differed from previous mountings in having 30° elevation. As in the 18in turret, sighting ports in the roof were replaced by rectangular ports cut in the face armour, and the crowns were much flatter than before. In the light of subsequent allegations about specific design faults 'known to a handful of senior officers' it is interesting to note that the DNC's advice in 1918 was that the ship reflected pre-Jutland ideas on the disposition of armour, and that the changes since August 1916 had done no more than remedy the worst defects. He went on to recommend that since it would be an unwarranted waste of money to break her up on the slip the best thing would be to get her out of the way, cancel her sisters and get on with building ships which benefited from wartime experience. The reputation of the 'Mighty *Hood*'

was largely inflated by the press, which equated size with fighting power. Notwithstanding her weak protection against long-range gunfire, she embodied several novel features, and had the armour been concentrated where it did most good she would have been a much better ship. In 1919, trials had shown that the magazines were vulnerable at ranges of 25,000 yards and over to new types of 15in AP shells then being developed for the RN, but proposals to thicken the deck from 3in to 5in (forward) and 6in (aft) were not implemented.

Post-1918 modifications were largely confined to the AA armament. The 4in Mk V AA guns were increased to 6 in December 1937 and to 8 in June 1938 when 2–5.5in were removed, but in June–August 1939 8–4in Mk XVI (4 × 2) were mounted, all the 4in Mk V removed and the 2–5.5in replaced. Finally in April 1940 the 5.5in were removed and 6–4in Mk XVI (3 × 2) added. During the 1929–31 refit 2–8 barrelled pompoms were mounted, a catapult added (removed in June 1932), and oil fuel increased to 4615 tons. A third 8-barrelled pompom was added in December 1937 and the 2 submerged TT removed, while 5 UP rocket projectors were mounted in May 1940, deep load displacement being now 48,360 tons. In March 1939 a major reconstruction was approved, involving removal of the CT and all

secondary guns; the weight saved together with new machinery would allow a new DP secondary armament, cross-deck catapult and hangar, and much strengthened anti-torpedo and deck protection, generally on the lines of a modified *Renown*, but the outbreak of war prevented plans being finalised.

HMS *Hood* commissioned on the Clyde in May 1920 as flagship of the Battle Cruiser Squadron. As the most prestigious unit of the RN she saw service all over the world but never received the modernisation which she needed. Served with Home Fleet and Force 'H' in the Second World War and blew up in action with *Bismarck* and *Prinz Eugen* on 24 May 1941. The contemporary Board of Inquiry concluded that a 15in shell from *Bismarck* penetrated *Hood*'s armour and exploded in or near her after 15in magazines, the 4in magazine very probably exploding first; at the range of loss, 18,000 yards, the main magazines should have been proof against plunging 15in fire. Expert opinion has also attributed her loss to the explosion of her above water torpedoes, accentuated by her poor material condition, or to an 8in hit from *Prinz Eugen* starting a deck fire that spread to the AA ammunition below and then to the after magazines.

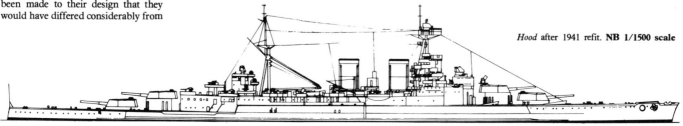

*Hood* after 1941 refit. **NB 1/1500 scale**

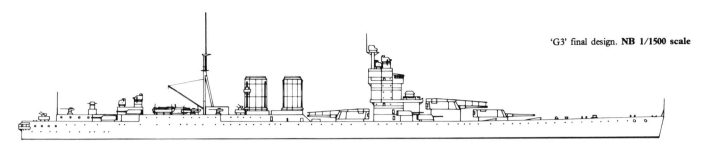

'G3' final design. NB 1/1500 scale

## 'G 3' type *battlecruisers*

| | |
|---|---|
| **Displacement:** | 48,400t legend; 53,909t deep load |
| **Dimensions:** | 820ft pp, 856ft oa × 106ft × 35ft 8in deep |
| | *249.9m, 260.9m × 32.3m × 10.9m* |
| **Machinery:** | 4-shaft single-reduction geared steam turbines, 20 small-tube boilers, 160,000shp = 31–32kts. |
| | Oil 5000t |
| **Armour:** | Belt 12in–14in (305mm–356mm), bulkheads 10in–12in (254mm–305mm), turret faces 17in (430mm), |
| | decks 4in–8in (102mm–203mm), CT 10in–14in (254mm–356mm) |
| **Armament:** | 9–16in (406mm)/45 Mk I (3 × 3), 16–6in (152mm)/50 Mk XXIII (8 × 2), 6–4.7in (120mm)/43 AA, |
| | 40–2pdr (40mm) pompom (10 × 4), 2–24.5in (622mm) TT sub (forward) |
| **Complement:** | 1716 |

The Royal Navy was well aware that it had ended the War in an inferior position *vis á vis* the American and Japanese navies. Despite the enormous preponderance of numbers, the 12in-gunned dreadnoughts were quite outclassed, and even the 13.5in- and 15in-gunned ships were outmatched by the latest 14in- and 16in- gunned 'super-dreadnoughts' laid down during the War. Drastic reconstruction would remedy the worst deficiencies of the 15in-gunned ships, but what was needed was a new class of ships capable of facing 16in and even 18in gunfire. There was also an urgent need to incorporate war lessons: the *Hood* class, despite detailed improvements, was essentially a pre-Jutland design, and by 1921 there was a large body of fresh experience based on tests against German ships. The first design required was a class of four large battlecruisers, to be laid down in 1921. The concept which evolved was much closer to a fast battleship than anything previously considered and the US Navy's 'all-or-nothing' concept of protection was embraced. The latest type of protection was to be used, namely an inclined internal armour belt and internal 'bulges' against torpedoes.

For the first time a triple turret was

adopted to concentrate armament. The secondary armament was mounted in twin turrets. Various designs were drawn up, but all had in common a concentration of heavy armour over the vitals, with turrets grouped together to permit the maximum thickness of armour. They represented as big a step forward in fighting power as the *Dreadnought* had 17 years earlier, and they showed how much the size of capital ships had increased in little more than a decade.

After lengthy consideration, design 'G 3' (out of an alphabetical series) was accepted in February 1921, the final legend being approved in August 1921. Orders followed on 26 October –

one each from Beardmore, John Brown, Fairfield and Swan Hunter (the last with machinery subcontracted to Parsons) – but the orders were suspended on 18 November by Cabinet order. The threat of these ships being built was used as a bargaining counter during the Washington Conference, but it was quite clear by the end of 1921 that Britain was in a deepening financial crisis, and the Cabinet would seemingly not have permitted the programme to go ahead, even if the Americans and Japanese had refused to negotiate reductions in their fleets. Although the ships had not started construction the details of the design were sufficiently developed to

provide a basis for the *Nelson* and *Rodney*, truncated versions carrying the same armament and scale of protection, but 8–9kts slower. Under the terms of the Treaty the four 'G 3's were cancelled on 13 February 1922. Names were never allocated, and the two sets of names often quoted are merely speculative: *St George, St Andrew, St David* and *St Patrick*; or *Invincible, Inflexible, Indomitable* and *Indefatigable*.

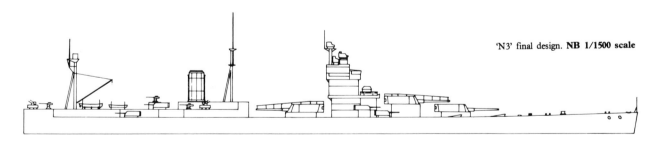

'N3' final design. NB 1/1500 scale

## 'N 3' type *battleships*

| | |
|---|---|
| **Displacement:** | 48,500t normal |
| **Dimensions:** | 790ft pp, 820ft oa × 106ft × 32–33ft |
| | *240.8m, 250m × 32.3m × 9.9m–10.1m* |
| **Machinery:** | 4-shaft single-reduction geared steam turbines, probably 80,000shp = 23½kts. |
| **Armour:** | Belt 13.25in–15in (337mm–381mm), bulkheads 14in (356mm), turret faces 18in (457mm), decks 8in |
| | (203mm), CT 15in (381mm) |
| **Armament:** | 9–18in (457mm)/45 Mk II (3 × 3), 16–6in (152mm)/50 Mk XXII (8 × 2), 6–4.7in (120mm)/43 AA, |
| | 40–2pdr (40mm) pompom (10 × 4) |
| **Complement:** | Not known |

In addition to four battlecruisers for 1921 the Admiralty hoped to lay down four battleships in 1922. The design which evolved was broadly similar to the 'G 3' battlecruiser design, but with only half the horsepower, as speed was cut to 23–23½kts (the speed of the battlefleet). The main armament was to be three triple 18in, of a new 45cal type, firing a 2837lb shell at a muzzle velocity of 2837fps. Experience with the blast effects of the triple 16in was later to suggest that the theoretical power of the 18in would have been outranked by the appalling blast-effects on decks and superstructure.

The four ships planned were still at an early design-stage when the

Washington Treaty put an end to all plans for large capital ships. Like the 'G 3' design they would apparently have been cancelled at the insistence of

the Treasury, even without the Treaty, but they remain the most powerfully armed British battleships of all time.

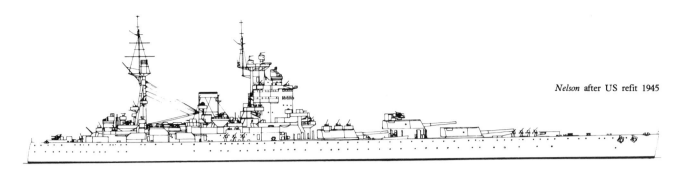

*Nelson* after US refit 1945

These ships resembled the revolutionary 'G 3' battlecruisers cancelled under the Washington Treaty, but their speed had to be reduced drastically to comply with the 35,000t standard displacement limit, and unfortunately they came out well under this. The three 16in turrets were forward, and 40° elevation was provided, whilst the 6in turrets with 60° elevation were aft on either beam, the middle ones also superfiring. Four of the 4.7in were forward of the 6in and a deck higher, the other two being on the quarterdeck. The torpedo tubes were forward, discharging at a small angle to the keel line, and equipment for oxygen enrichment of the torpedoes' air was provided.

The armour belt was internal and in-

## NELSON class *battleships*

**Displacement:** 33,313t (*Rodney* 33,730t) standard; 41,250t extra deep load with buoyancy spaces filled
**Dimensions:** 660ft pp, 710ft oa × 106ft × 28ft 1in mean, 33ft 6in mean at 41,250t
*201.2m, 216.4m × 32.3m × 8.6m, 10.2m*
**Machinery:** 2-shaft Brown-Curtis geared turbines, 8 Admiralty 3-drum boilers, 45,000shp = 23kts. Oil 3805t (*Rodney* 3770t)
**Armour:** Belt 14in–13in (356mm–330mm), bulkheads 12in–4in (305mm–102mm), funnel uptakes 9in–7in (229mm–178mm), barbettes 15in–12in (381mm–305mm), turrets 16in–7.5in (406mm–190mm), CT 14in–6.25in (356mm–159mm)
**Armament:** 9–16in (406mm)/45 Mk I (3 × 3), 12–6in (152mm)/50 Mk XXII (6 × 2), 6–4.7in (120mm)/40 QF Mk VIII HA (6 × 1), 8–2pdr pompom (8 × 1), 4–3pdr saluting, 2–24.5in (622mm) TT sub
**Complement:** 1314; 1361 as flagship

| Name | Builder | Laid down | Launched | Comp | Fate |
|------|---------|-----------|----------|------|------|
| NELSON | Armstrong | 28.12.22 | 3.9.25 | Aug 1927 | BU 1948 |
| RODNEY | Cammell Laird | 28.12.22 | 17.12.25 | Nov 1927 | BU 1948 |

*Nelson* 1933.
*CPL*

clined at 15° to the vertical. It extended from the fore 16in to the after 6in barbette and at 33ft 6in draught from the middle deck 6ft 6in above to 5ft 9in below water. The thickness was 14in abreast the main armament and 13in elsewhere with a 12in-17in forward bulkhead between the middle and platform decks and a 10in one aft between the middle and lower decks. The funnel uptakes extended to the main deck. The main turrets had 16in faces, 11in-9in sides, 9in rears and 7¼in roofs, but the secondary guns had only 1½-1in and the 4.7in had nothing until shields were added during the war. The armour deck at the belt upper edge was 6¼in over the magazines and 3¾in over the machinery, whilst the lower deck aft was 4¼in ending in a 4in stern bulkhead. These deck thicknesses are for armour only and do not include the ½in plating underneath. The internal bulges were designed to withstand a 750lb TNT charge and amidships comprised an empty outer chamber, a water filled buoyancy chamber, a 1½in torpedo bulkhead about 12ft inboard and a compartment to limit flooding from a strained torpedo bulkhead. Metacentric height was 11ft at 41,250t with a stability range of 81°. There were four boiler rooms located abaft the two engine and two gearing rooms, the total length being 138ft. Tactical diameter was 670yds.

The design was based on the heaviest armament and best magazine protection possible on the displacement, and the very limited area of side armour had to be accepted. Unfortunately, the 16in guns and mountings gave considerable trouble initially and the rate of the fire from the 6in and 4.7in mountings, both of which were power-worked, was much slower than had been expected. These defects were gradually corrected and when Rodney and Bismarck engaged in 1941 the former quickly gained the upper hand with some help from King George V. Rodney was not hit in this action, but Nelson was twice damaged by ground mines during the war, and an Italian 18in airborne torpedo which hit abreast the torpedo body room in September 1941 caused no less than 3750t of water to enter the ship. After this the torpedo installation was removed from Nelson. Various proposals were made for increasing the depth of the belt and for improving the secondary armament, but only Nelson was taken in hand in 1937-38 and alterations were limited to 3in-2¾in armour on the lower deck forward and 4in to extend the forward bulkhead to the hold.

An aircraft catapult was fitted on Rodney's 'X' turret roof in 1936 and removed in 1942-43. It had always been intended that 8-barrelled 2pdr pompoms should form the chief close

range AA armament, but these were not available until 1931 when one was mounted in each ship, replacing the eight single guns. A second 8-barrelled mounting was added in 1935-36 and a third in 1938-39. Nelson received two more in June 1940 and a sixth in January 1942, whilst Rodney had a quadruple mounting added in September 1941, and two more 8-barrelled mountings in February 1942. Nelson also received 4 quadruple US 40mm Bofors mountings in November 1944 and there is a record of a single Army Bofors being installed briefly in the spring of 1942. The number of 20mm Oerlikon guns eventually reached between 60 and 70 in each ship, and 4 UP rocket mountings were fitted in Nelson during 1940-41. As usual, displacement rose during the ships' careers: just before she was torpedoed Nelson displaced 43,4000t at a draught of 35ft 3in forward and 34ft 6in aft, and in 1945 the figure was 44,054t. Rodney displaced 43,140t in 1945.

Because Nelson had been refitted in the United States at the end of 1944 she was in sufficiently good shape to serve in the postwar fleet, unlike Rodney, in such poor repair by 1945 that she was laid up immediately. Apart from removal of the 20mm Oerlikons Nelson remained unaltered from the last days of the war.

According to Winston Churchill's

memoirs, a major modernisation was discussed to enable Nelson to serve for several years in the postwar fleet, but no other details have survived. In any case she was too slow and there was no front-line role for battleships any more. After a brief spell as flagship of the Home Fleet at the end of 1945, she joined the Training Squadron at Portland in August 1946 as Flagship, RA Training Battleships for a year. She was sold in February 1948 and used as a bombing target in the Firth of Forth before scrapping commenced in March 1949.

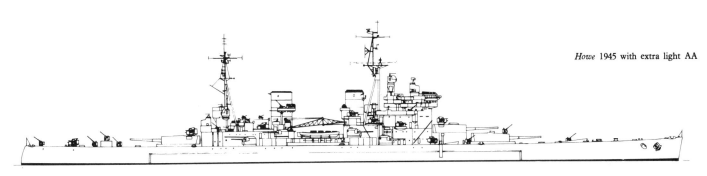

Howe 1945 with extra light AA

This class were built to the London Treaty limits of 35,000t standard and 14in guns, though additions during construction and the lapsing of the treaty resulted in them being over the old limit. The design was more conventional that that of Nelson, with a much greater area of armoured side, less protection to the main armament which was not concentrated forward, and much greater shp due to improvement in machinery weights. The 14in mountings allowed 40° elevation and were arranged with the quadruples forward and aft and the twin superfiring forward. The 5.25in, which served as anti-destroyer and heavy AA guns, had 70° elevation and were in two groups on each beam, with a fixed athwartships catapult between the groups and the inner mounting superfiring in each group.

The armour belt was external and

## KING GEORGE V class *battleships*

| | |
|---|---|
| **Displacement:** | 36,727t standard; 42,076t deep load |
| **Dimensions:** | 700ft pp, 745ft oa × 13ft × 29ft mean, 32ft 7in mean at 42,076t |
| | *213.4m, 227.1m × 31.4m × 8.8m, 9.9m* |
| **Machinery:** | 4-shaft Parsons geared turbines, 8 Admiralty 3-drum boilers, 110,000shp = 28kts. Oil 3700t, later 4030t |
| **Armour:** | Belt 15in-4.5in (381mm-115mm), bulkheads 12in-4in (305mm-102mm), barbettes 13in-11in (330mm-279mm), turrets 13in-6in (330mm-152mm), CT 4.5in-2in (115mm-51mm) |
| **Armament:** | 10-14in (356mm)/45 Mk VII (2 × 4, 1 × 2), 16-5.25in (133mm)/50 QF Mk 1 (8 × 2), 32-2pdr pompom (4 × 8), 2 aircraft |
| **Complement:** | 1422 |

| Name | Builder | Laid down | Launched | Comp | Fate |
|---|---|---|---|---|---|
| KING GEORGE V | Vickers-Armstrong, Tyne | 1.1.37 | 21.2.39 | 11.12.40 | BU 1957 |
| PRINCE OF WALES | Cammell Laird | 1.1.37 | 3.5.39 | 31.3.41 | Sunk 10.12.41 |
| DUKE OF YORK (ex-*Anson*) | John Brown | 5.5.37 | 28.2.40 | 4.11.41 | BU 1957 |
| ANSON (ex-*Jellicoe*) | Swan Hunter | 20.7.37 | 24.2.40 | 22.6.42 | BU 1957 |
| HOWE (ex-*Beatty*) | Fairfield | 1.6.37 | 9.4.40 | 29.8.42 | BU 1957 |

not inclined, except where it followed the slope of the hull. It was taken to the main deck between the 14in barbettes and was 15in tapering to $5\frac{1}{2}$in at the lower edge abreast the magazines, and 14in tapering to $4\frac{1}{2}$in abreast the machinery. There were 12in fore and 10in aft bulkheads at the ends of this belt, and the lower strake of the belt was continued for about 40ft at either end with a thickness of 13in–1in tapering to $5\frac{1}{2}$in at the lower edge. Between end barbettes the belt was exceptionally deep and at 32ft 6in mean draught extended from 10ft above to 13ft below water. The main turrets had 13in faces, 9in–7in sides, 7in rears and 6in roofs but the 5.25in had only 2in–1in protection and the previously heavy CT was replaced by a light one high up on the signal deck. The main deck had 6in armour over the magazines and 5in elsewhere, while the lower deck forward had 5in–$2\frac{1}{2}$in to the foremost watertight bulkhead and $4\frac{1}{2}$in aft to the steering gear where it was increased to 5in ending in a 4in stern bulkhead. During construction $1\frac{1}{2}$in splinter protection was added to the sides and crowns of the 14in and 5.25in magazines. The amidships protection against torpedoes was a development of that in *Nelson*, the two outer chambers of the latter being replaced by a three-compartment sandwich of which the middle compartment was filled with oil and the other two left empty. When required for fuel the oil was replaced by seawater. The protective bulkhead was increased to $1\frac{3}{4}$in and the system was designed to withstand a 1000lb TNT charge. The designed metacentric height was 6.1ft at light and 8.1ft at deep load. Each propeller shaft was driven by an independent unit of two boilers and a set of turbines, though the boilers could be cross-connected if necessary. The units driving the outer shafts were located forward of those driving the inner. Unfortunately a small tactical diameter was not among the Staff Requirements and it amounted to 930yds.

Although the 14in mountings were of more orthodox design than the 16in in *Nelson*, they gave considerable trouble to both *Prince of Wales* and *King George V* when engaging *Bismarck* and also in *Duke of York* against *Scharnhorst* two and half years later. The 5.25in turrets were cramped and too slow-firing to be ideal AA weapons, and 20–4.5in would probably have been better. The armour protection against heavy shells was never seriously tested in action, though it is interesting to note that in spite of the deep belt a 15in shell from *Bismarck* hit *Prince of Wales* far below the belt lower edge. It is, however, essential to explain how *Prince of Wales* was sunk by a probable total of 1 330lb and 3 450lb torpedo warheads charged with the type of explosive used by the Germans in World War I. The 330lb

*Howe* 1943.
*CPL*

explosion broke off the 'A' bracket of the port outer shaft which was seriously bent with the loss of the propeller, the turbines driving this shaft were not stopped immediately, and the flooding directly or indirectly caused by the rotating bent shaft effectively disabled the ship. Subsequently three torpedoes with 450lb charges hit the starboard side, one of which bent the outer shaft wedging the propeller between the inner shaft and the hull, but it should be noted that the ship capsized to port.

The aircraft catapult was removed from the four surviving ships in 1943–45, and there was a great increase in close-range AA armament during the war. The original 4 8-barrelled pompoms were increased to 6 in the last three ships as completed, and eventually the four survivors each had 8, with 6 quadruple pompoms in all but *King George V*, 2 quadruple 40mm Bofors in all and 2 single Bofors in *King George V* and 14 in *Howe*. The greatest number of 20mm Oerlikons appears to be 65. UP rocket mountings were in the first two ships for a time initially, and *Prince of Wales* when lost had 5 8-barrelled and 1 quadruple pompom with a single Bofors and probably about 10 Oerlikons.

Displacement rose and stability fell as additional weights were carried, and as completed *Howe* at extreme deep load was 44,510t with GM 7.25ft and a stability range of 65½°, whilst the corresponding displacement for *Anson* in 1945 was 45,360t.

After the war, the four survivors were immediately stripped of their smaller light AA guns, but otherwise remained unaltered until scrapped. *King George V* and *Howe* had 64-2pdr pompoms (8 × 8), but *Duke of York* and *Anson* had an extra 4-barrelled pompom on each side of the bridge and on the forecastle deck.

*King George V* served as flagship of the Home Fleet in 1946 and then as a private ship until paid off into reserve in 1950. After a spell with the Training Squadron at Portland, *Anson* paid off in 1949, while *Howe* served as a harbour TS at Portsmouth from 1950 to 1951, after a year as Flagship, RA Training Battleships (1947). *Duke of York* served with the Home Fleet as flagship until 1949 and remained in commission as flagship of the Reserve Fleet until 1951. All four were eventually laid up in the Gareloch and schemes were discussed in the mid-1950s for converting them to missile ships, but the cost would have been prohibitive and in 1957 they were sold for scrapping.

*Duke of York* 1947.
*CPL*

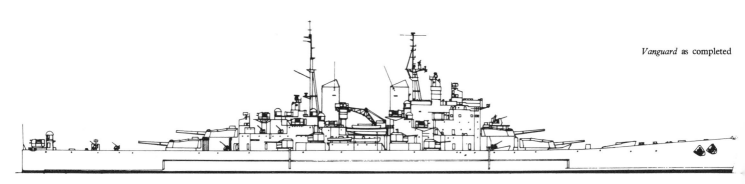

*Lion* as designed 1938

## LION class *battleships*

**Displacement:** 40,500t standard; 46,300t deep load
**Dimensions:** 740ft pp, 785ft oa × 104ft × 30ft mean, 33ft 6in mean at 46,500t
225.6m, 239.3m × 31.7m × 9.1m, 10.2m
**Machinery:** 4-shaft Parsons geared turbines, 8 Admiralty 3-drum boilers, 130,000shp = 30kts. Oil 3720t
**Armour:** Belt 15in-5.5in (381mm-140mm), bulkheads 13in-4in (330mm-102mm), barbettes (15in-12in) (381mm-305mm), turrets 15in-6in (381mm-152mm), CT 4.5in-2in (115mm-51mm)
**Armament:** 9-16in (406mm)/45 Mk II or III (3 × 3), 16-5.25in (133mm)/50 QF Mk I (8 × 2), 48-2pdr pompom (6 × 8), 2 aircraft
**Complement:** 1680 as fleet flagship

| Name | Builder | Laid down | Launched | Comp | Fate |
|------|---------|-----------|----------|------|------|
| LION | Vickers-Armstrong, Tyne | 4.7.39 | — | — | See notes |
| TEMERAIRE | Cammell Laird | 1.6.39 | — | — | See notes |
| CONQUEROR | John Brown | — | — | — | — |
| THUNDERER | Fairfield | — | — | — | — |

This class were to have been built under the escalation clause of the London Treaty which allowed 45,000t and 16in guns, and were far nearer the Navy's requirements than the *King George V*. It does not appear to have been realised that Japan, Russia and Germany had already started or were about to lay down ships approaching or exceeding 60,000t, and British political thinking of the day kept the *Lion* class to near 40,000t. In general layout and appearance they would have resembled the *King George V* but with a transom stern. The 16in guns and mountings were different from those in *Nelson*, being designed for a 2375lb instead of a 2048lb shell. The armour belt was a uniform 15in between barbettes with a 5½in lower edge, and at 33ft 6in mean draught extended from 11ft above to 12ft below water. The lower strake was continued as *King George V*. The main turrets had 15in faces, 10in-7in sides, 7in rears and 6in roofs; deck, underwater and other protection was as in *King George V* except where indicated above, with the addition of 2in between the lower deck and inner bottom below the citadel bulkheads. The turbines and boilers were arranged as in *King George V*.

Work was suspended on 3 October 1939 and, although resumed between November 1939 and May 1940 on a standby basis, little more was done before construction ceased entirely. The 218t in place for *Lion* and 121t for *Temeraire* were dismantled in 1942-43. Design work continued, however, reflecting wartime experience; by January 1942 displacement was 42,550t standard, beam 108ft, and the bow and sheer forward as in *Vanguard*. Requirements were again altered to include the lessons of the *Prince of Wales*'s loss, producing a further enlargement. In 1944 the class was finally cancelled, following the sinking of *Tirpitz*. However, even then the *Lions* were kept on the drawing-board as the Admiralty hoped to be able to restart two of them postwar; under the 1945 Programme it was proposed to lay down the *Lion* and *Temeraire* to a new design in 1946 for completion by 1952. Full details of this design have not been found, but in the light of wartime experience it was necessary to increase the beam and the depth of the anti-torpedo system. Upper limits of the proposals were 50,000t standard with dimensions of 840ft × 118ft, and figures of 56,500t deep load and 810ft × 115ft × 34ft 3in mean at this displacement have been quoted. The armament would have comprised 9-16in/45 Mk IV guns in a new type of triple mounting design to have a firing interval of 20 seconds per gun instead of the usual 30, with 24-4.5in/45 QF Mk V guns and 10 6-barrelled Bofors mountings. Oil fuel capacity would probably have been between 5000 and 6000t and speed about 29kts. The increased beam would have allowed much improved torpedo protection probably against a 2000lb TNT charge. The project seems to have been abandoned because 12in deck armour was found to be necessary against possible AP bombs, and this would have required a much larger ship. The economic condition of Britain would in any case have forced the cancellation of these ships.

*Vanguard* as completed

This ship's origins go back to an early 1939 project for utilising the 15in turrets from *Courageous* and *Glorious* in a 30kt ship for the Far Eastern fleet. The sacrifice in using these venerable turrets was less than might appear as they were a reliable and satisfactory design which could be modernised and given 30° elevation with thicker face and roof plates, and the 15in gun was only about 30fs down in muzzle velocity compared with a new British design. The one serious fault was that the turrets were designed for a ship with shell rooms below the magazines, and for the contrary arrangement, which was now standard practice, it was necessary to have the magazine handing rooms on the lower deck above the shell rooms with fixed hoists from the magazines below. Although outwardly of different appearance, *Vanguard* resembled *King George V* in many ways.

The 5.25in guns were in improved mountings and there was no provision for aircraft. The belt was reduced to 14in abreast the magazines and 13in elsewhere with a uniform 4½in lower edge, and the lower strake was continued for some distance at 13in-11in with a 4½in lower edge. The main turrets had 13in faces, 9in-7in sides, 11in rears and 6in roofs. The main deck armour was 6in over the magazines

# VANGUARD *battleship*

| | |
|---|---|
| **Displacement:** | 44,500t standard; 51,420t deep load |
| **Dimensions:** | 760ft pp, 814ft 4in oa × 108ft × 30ft 9.5in mean, 34ft 10in mean at 51,420t |
| | *231.6m, 248.2m × 32.9m × 9.4m, 10.6m* |
| **Machinery:** | 4-shaft Parsons geared turbines, 8 Admiralty 3-drum boilers, 130,000shp = 30kts. Oil 4423t |
| **Armour:** | Belt 14in-4.5in (356mm-115mm), bulkheads 12in-4in (305mm-102mm), barbettes 13in-11in (330mm-279mm), turrets 13in-6in (330mm-152mm), CT 3in-1in (76mm-25mm) |
| **Armament:** | 8-15in (381mm)/42 Mk I (4 × 2), 16-5.25in (133mm)/50 QF Mk I (8 × 2), 73-40mm Bofors (10 × 6, 1 × 2, 11 × 1), 4-3pdr saluting |
| **Complement:** | 1893 |

| Name | Builder | Laid down | Launched | Comp | Fate |
|---|---|---|---|---|---|
| VANGUARD | John Brown | 2.10.41 | 30.11.44 | 9.8.46 | BU 1960 |

and 5in over the machinery, and the lower deck was 5in-2½in forward and 4½in -2½in aft. The 5.25in guns had 2½in-1½in and there was more splinter protection than in *King George V*, including 2½in-2in on the sides between the middle and lower decks beyond the heavy belt and extending nearly to bow and stern. The torpedo protection was similar to that in *King George V* with a 1¾in-1½in protective bulkhead, and the compartment bulkheads outboard of this were taken to the middle deck instead of ending at the lower deck. At the most favourable position the system was designed to stand 1300lb TNT. At deep load metacentric height was 8.2ft with a stability range of 68°. The main machinery was arranged as in *King George V*, and

on the mile at 45,720t *Vanguard* developed 136,000shp = 31.57kts. As a result of war experience there were 4 diesel and 4 turbine-driven dynamos instead of 2 and 6 respectively.

*Vanguard* had a transom stern and a marked sheer forward, which made her a much better seaboat than previous British battleships. Tactical diameter at full speed was 1025yds. As often happened, weights increased during construction and 770t had to be added to the upper deck structure to meet the resultant higher stresses. Only two minor changes were made to the ship during her career: the removal of the 11-40mm single Bofors guns and the temporary replacement of the twin STAAG Bofors mounting on 'B' turret by an observation and saluting

platform for the Royal Tour to South Africa early in 1947. She refitted at Devonport in 1947-48 and went to the Mediterranean in January 1949 for six months. She became a training ship at Portland, acting as temporary Home Fleet flagship during exercises. After a refit at Devonport in 1954 she paid off into reserve at Portsmouth, becoming the flagship of the Reserve Fleet and NATO HQ ship. She was sold for scrapping in 1960.

*Vanguard* 1947.
CPL

# Greece

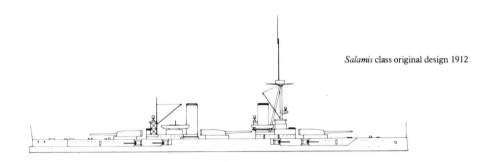

*Salamis* class original design 1912

She was ordered in July 1912, originally designed for operations in the Aegean with the following particulars: 13,500t, 458ft (pp) × 72ft × 24ft, *139.6m × 22.0m × 7.4m*, 2-shaft turbines 26,000shp = 21kts, 6–14in/45 (3 × 2), 8–6in/50 in casemates, 8–3in, 4–37mm AA and 2–450mm (17.7in) TT and protection of belt 10in, barbettes 10in and 12in CT. Design was soon enlarged by the Greeks to 16,500t and finally on 23 December 1912 the contract was changed to a battleship of the particulars mentioned above costing £1,693,000 for delivery in March 1915. Construction work suspended on 31 December 1914. After the war the Greeks refused to accept the incomplete ship and the builders sued the Greek Governmet in 1923. On 23 April 1932 the arbitrators judged that the Greeks must pay a further £30,000 (apart from £450,000 paid before the war) to Vulcan while the ship remained the builders' property. She was scrapped at Bremen in 1932. Her main and secondary armaments were ordered from Bethlehem Steel (USA) and apart from two barbettes delivered without guns her 14in guns were purchased by Britain and used in the *Abercrombie* class monitors.

## SALAMIS class *battleship*

| | |
|---|---|
| **Displacement:** | 19,500t |
| **Dimensions:** | 569ft 11in wl × 81ft × 25ft |
| | *173.7m × 24.7m × 7.6m* |
| **Machinery:** | 3-shaft AEG turbines, 18 Yarrow boilers, 40,000shp = 23kts |
| **Armour:** | Belt 250mm–100mm (9.8in–3.9in), deck 75mm–40mm (3in–1.6in), barbettes 250mm (9.8in), turrets 250mm (9.8in), CT 300mm (11.8in) |
| **Armament:** | 8–14in (356mm)/45 (4 × 2), 12–6in (152mm)/50, 12–3in (75mm) QF, 5–19.7in (500mm) TT |

| Name | Builder | Laid down | Launched | Comp | Fate |
|---|---|---|---|---|---|
| SALAMIS (ex-*Vasileus Georgios*) | AG Vulcan, Hamburg | 23.7.13 | 11.11.14 | Unfinished | BU 1932 |

---

### French PROVENCE class *battleship*

A 23,5000t battleship was ordered from C et A de St Nazaire – Penhoët in April 1914 and was to be similar to the French *Provence* class except for an additional 12–76mm guns. Work on her began on 12 June 1914 but stopped at the beginning of August and never resumed. She was to be named *Vasileus Konstantinos*. Contract dispute settled in 1925.

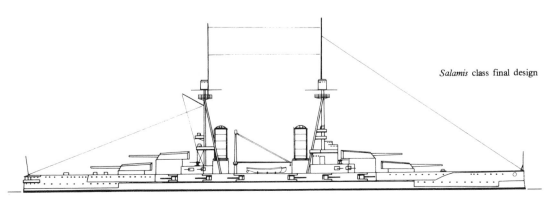

*Salamis* class final design

# Italy

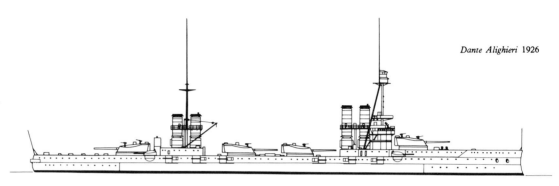

*Dante Alighieri 1926*

The first Italian dreadnought type battleship, designed by Eng Admiral Edoardo Masdea and Eng Commander Antonino Calabretta. She was the first ship in the world with triple large calibre turrets, although the Austro-Hungarian *Viribus Unitis* entered service earlier. *Dante Alighieri* was also the first dreadnought with medium calibre guns (partly) in turrets, instead of side batteries, and the first Italian capital ship with four propellers. According to contemporary reports, alterations made during construction added about 2.5ft to the draught and 1000t to displacement, so that she could only make her speed with difficulty; the design data is

## DANTE ALIGHIERI *battleship*

| | |
|---|---|
| **Displacement:** | 19,552t normal; 21,600t full load |
| **Dimensions:** | 518ft 5in wl, 551ft 6in oa × 87ft 3in × 28ft 10in |
| | *158.4m, 168.1m × 26.6m × 8.8m* |
| **Machinery:** | 4-shaft Parsons geared turbines, 23 Blechynden boilers (7 oil 16 mixed), 35,350 projected shp, max 32,190shp = 22.83kts. Range 4800nm/1000nm at 10kts/22kts |
| **Armour:** | Belt 254mm (10in), deck 38mm (1.5in), main turrets 254mm (10in), secondary turrets and casemates 98mm (3.9in), CT 305mm (12in) |
| **Armament:** | 12–12in (305mm)/46 (4 × 3), 20–4.7in (120mm)/50 (4 × 2, 12 × 1), 13–3in (76mm)/40, 3–17.7in (450mm) TT sub |
| **Complement:** | 981 |

| Name | Builder | Laid down | Launched | Comp | Fate |
|---|---|---|---|---|---|
| DANTE ALIGHIERI | Castellammare RN Yd | 6.6.09 | 20.8.10 | 15.1.13 | Stricken 1.7.28 |

*Dante Alighieri* 1923.
CPL

listed in the table.

The 12in guns had a maximum range of 24,000 metres and a rate of fire of one round per gun per minute; arcs of fire were 300° for the end and 260° for the midships turrets. The arrangement of the triple turrets was only copied in the Russian Navy. In comparison with the *Viribus Unitis* arrangement, it was unecomonic in space requirements and restricted the end-on fire; these disadvantages more than outweighed the favourable effect on stability, and the reduced possibility of more than one complete turret being destroyed by a single lucky hit. The improved KC-type armour was manufactured by Terni.

In 1913 she received a 'Curtiss' reconnaissance seaplane experimentally. In 1915 her 13–3in/40 guns were replaced by 16–3in/50 guns plus 4–3in/50 AA guns. In 1923 the foremast was replaced by a heavy tripod with a large foretop, placed just forward of the first two funnels, which were increased in height. An M18 reconnaissance seaplane was carried on No. 3 turret from 1925. In 1928 the ship became the first Italian dreadnought to be stricken from the Navy List, excluding the sunken *Leonardo da Vinci* (qv); the design was obsolete in the postwar era, and the basic layout precluded any possibility of real modernisation.

*Conte di Cavour* as reconstructed 1937.
CPL

*Conte di Cavour* after 1922
reconstruction.
*CPL*

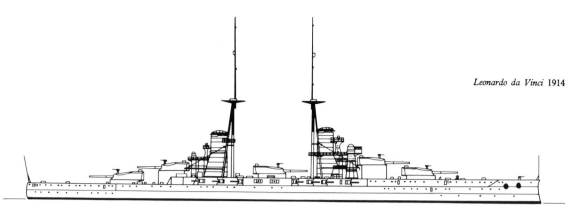

First group of Italian dreadnoughts, designed by Eng Adm Edoardo Masdea. During World War One, 4–76mm (3in)/50 AA guns were added, on the top of the main turrets. *Leonardo da Vinci* was sunk on 2 August 1916 at Taranto, by an Austrian sabotage explosion. She was refloated on 17 September 1919 upside down. It was planned to refit her, with the main armament reduced to 10–305mm (12in/)46 (suppressing the amidships turret) and mounting, as AA armament, 6–102mm (4in)/35 guns. But the project was not carried out and the ship, although righted in January 1921, was discarded from the Navy List and sold for scrapping on 26 March 1923 at Taranto. In 1921–22 *Cavour*'s and *Cesare*'s fore tripod masts were replaced by derrick stumps, and new quadrupod foremasts fitted forward of the first funnel, for protecting the gun directors from smoke and heat from the boilers. In 1925 both *Cavour* and *Cesare* were provided with an M 18 reconnaissance seaplane, on the top of the central 12in turret. In 1926 *Cavour* was fitted with a catapult, on the fore part of her deck, for launching the seaplane. Reconstruction and modernisation took place from October 1933 to June 1937 (*Cavour*) and from October 1933 to October 1937 (*Cesare*) in CRDA Trieste Yd and Cantieri del Tirreno, Genoa respectively.

The original machinery was taken out and replaced by a two-shaft geared turbine installation driven by eight boilers providing a nominal 75,000shp at 27kts; forcing provided 93,000shp for 28kts. Oil fuel stowage was 2472t, giving an endurance of 6400nm at 13kts. Internally, the ships were rebuilt to include the Pugliese underwater protection system, more ex-

## CAVOUR class *battleships*

| | |
|---|---|
| **Displacement:** | 22,992t normal; 24,500t full load (*Cesare* 23,193t–24,801t; *Leonardo* 23,087t – 24,677t) |
| **Dimensions:** | 554ft 1in wl, 557ft 5in oa × 91ft 10in × 30ft 6in (*Cesare* 30ft 10in) |
| | 168.9m, 176.0m × 28.0m × 9.3m (9.4m) |
| **Machinery:** | 4-shaft Parsons geared turbines, 8 oil and 12 mixed Blechynden boilers (*Cesare* 12 and 12 Babcock & Wilcox), 31,278shp = 22.2kts (*Cesare* 30,700shp = 21.56kts; *Leonardo* 32,300shp = 21.6kts). Range 4800nm/1000nm at 10kts/22kts |
| **Armour:** | Belt 254mm (10in), deck 111mm (4.4in), turrets 254mm (10in), battery 127mm (5in), CT 279mm (11in) |
| **Armament:** | 13–12in (305mm)/46 (3 × 3, 2 × 2), 18–4.7in (120mm)/50, 13–3in (76mm)/50 (*Leonardo* 14–3in (76mm)/50), 3–17.7in (450mm) TT sub |
| **Complement:** | 1232 –1235 |

| Name | Builder | Laid down | Launched | Comp | Fate |
|---|---|---|---|---|---|
| CONTE DI CAVOUR | La Spezia RN Yd | 10.8.10 | 10.8.11 | 1.4.15 | Sunk 12.11.40, BU 1947–52 |
| GIULIO CESARE | Ansaldo, Genoa | 24.6.10 | 15.10.11 | 14.5.14 | To USSR 1948 |
| LEONARDO DA VINCI | Odero, Sestri Ponente | 18.7.10 | 14.10.11 | 17.5.14 | Sunk 2.8.16 |

tensive sub-division and a unit machinery arrangement in which the port engine room was aft and the starboard engine room forward of the boiler rooms. Externally, a new superstructure was fitted and a new section added to the bow, increasing the overall length to 611ft 6in (186.4m), the latter assisting in the speed improvement by increasing the length-to-beam ratio.

The deck over machinery was increased to 80mm and over the magazines to 100mm thickness and the barbette armour to 280mm, while various other minor improvements were made to the protection, including a new, 260mm CT and 25mm torpedo bulkheads. The secondary gun battery and its casemate armour were removed and the embrasures plated in to give the ships flush sides to forecastle level. A new secondary battery of 12–120mm/50 (6 × 2) was mounted amidships, on the forecastle deck, and

the original light and AA weapons replaced by 8–100mm/47 (4 × 3), 12–37mm/54 (6 × 2) and 12–13.2mm MG (6 × 2). The midships triple 305mm/46 gun mounting was removed and the remaining 10 guns of the main armament were bored out and relined to 320mm/43.8 calibre while the mountings were modified to give 27° elevation for a range of 31,000yds. The modernisation increased the deep displacement to 29,032 and the draught, at normal load, to 34ft 1in (10.4m). On trials *Cavour* made 28.08kts with 93,433shp and *Cesare* 28.25kts with 93,490shp.

On completion of this refit the *Cesare* carried 2 aircraft catapults but these were removed after trials. Both vessels had their 13.2mm MG replaced by 12–20mm/65 AA (6 × 2) during the early years of the war and *Cesare* had a further 4 (2 × 2) added in 1942. *Cavour* was sunk by an 18in aerial torpedo at Taranto in November

1940, and when salvaged had her armament removed except for the 37mm/54 AA guns – a further 4–37mm/54 (2 × 2) were added on the quarterdeck for her transfer to Trieste for repair and reconstruction. When refitted she was to have mounted 12–135mm/45 (6 × 2), in place of the 120mm, 12–65mm/64 AA (12 × 1) in place of the 100mm and 13–20mm/65 AA (5 × 2, 3 × 1) guns, a second director on the bridge and radar but was scuttled on the Italian surrender in 1943. The wreck was captured and raised by the Germans but was sunk again during an air raid on Trieste. The ship was refloated in 1947 and scrapped 1950–52. *Cesare* was renamed *Z11* after the war and on 15.12.48 was transferred to Russia as part of war reparations. The Russians renamed her *Novorossiysk*; she was lost or irreparably damaged in the Black Sea in 1955 (see Russia/Soviet Union section).

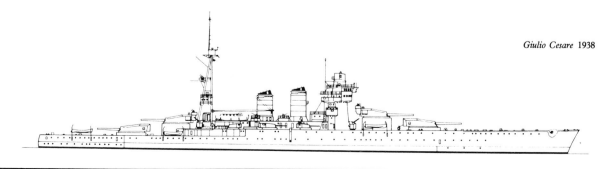

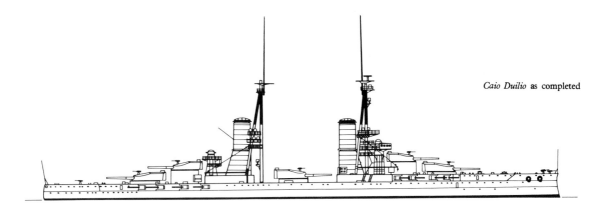

*Caio Duilio* as completed

This class was an improvement of the *Cavour* class. Its construction, the work of Eng Vice-Admiral Giuseppe Valsecchi, involved a larger medium calibre, and the medium guns were disposed in a better arrangement against destroyer and torpedo-boat attacks. The central 12in turret was lowered (in comparison with the *Cavours*) by one deck level and the foremast was placed ahead of the fore funnel, after *Cavour* class experience. While completing, *Doria*'s funnels were slightly lengthened for improving the draught of the boilers. After World War One the 6–3in/50 AA guns were replaced by 6–3in/40 AA guns plus 2–40mm/39 Vickers MGs. In 1925 both were fitted with an M 18 reconnaissance seaplane, and one year later both were provided with a catapult on the forecastle for the seaplane.

Modernisation and reconstruction took place from 8 April 1937 to 26 October 1940 (*Doria*) and from 1 April 1937 to 15 July 1940 in CRDA Trieste Yd and Cantieri del Tirreno, Genoa respectively. Modifications closely followed those in the *Cavour* class, the midship structure and machinery compartments being gutted and the midships turret and secondary battery removed to allow the fitting of the same type and arrangement of machinery, underwater protection sub-division and superstructure. The forecastle deck was extended aft to the

## DORIA class *battleships*

| | |
|---|---|
| **Displacement:** | 22,956t normal; 24,729t full load (*Duilio* 22,994t–24,715t) |
| **Dimensions:** | 554ft 1in wl, 557ft 5in oa × 91ft 10in × 30ft 10in (*Duilio* 557ft 1in × 91ft 10in × 30ft 10in) |
| | *168.9m, 176.0m × 28.0m × 9.4m (176.0m × 28.0m × 9.4m)* |
| **Machinery:** | 4-shaft Parsons geared turbines, 8 oil and 12 mixed Yarrow boilers, 30,000shp = 21kts (*Duilio* 31,009shp = 21.3kts). Range 4800nm at 10kts and about 1000nm at full speed |
| **Armour:** | Belt 254mm (10in), deck 98mm (3.9in), turrets 280mm (11in), battery 130mm (5.1in), CT 280mm (11in) |
| **Armament:** | 13–12in (305mm)/46 (3 × 3, 2 × 2), 16–6in (152mm)/45, 13–3in (76mm)/50, 6–3in (76mm)/50 AA, 3–17.7in (450mm) TT sub |
| **Complement:** | 1233 |

| Name | Builder | Laid down | Launched | Comp | Fate |
|---|---|---|---|---|---|
| ANDREA DORIA | La Spezia RN Yd | 24.3.12 | 30.3.13 | 13.3.16 | Stricken 1.11.56 |
| CAIO DUILIO | Castellamare RN Yd | 24.2.12 | 24.4.13 | 10.5.15 | Stricken 15.9.56 |

mainmast and made flush with the side and the overall length increased to 613ft 2in (186.9m) by an addition to the bow, but the speed was slightly less at 75,000shp = 26kts (normal) and 87,000shp = 27kts (forced). The protection was modified as in *Cavour* except that the barbettes were not altered, they already being slightly thicker than in the earlier class. The main guns were also modified as in *Cavour* but the remaining armament was altered to 12–135mm/45 (4 × 3)

mounted forward abreast the bridge, 10–90mm/50 AA (10 × 1) amidships, 15–37mm/54 AA (6 × 2 + 3 × 1) and 16–20mm/65 AA (8 × 2), all recently-introduced weapons. On completion of reconstruction the deep displacements were 28,882t (*Doria*) and 29,391t (*Dulio*) with normal draught at 28ft 3in (8.6m). War modifications were few and consisted mainly of the addition of 4–37mm/54 AA (2 × 2) guns and radar; 4 of the 20mm (2 × 2) were removed in 1944.

*Duilio* was damaged by a single 18in torpedo at Taranto in November 1940 but was repaired, at Genoa, by May 1941. She was under refit from March 1942 until the Italian surrender, when both ships transferred to Allied control. They were returned in 1944 and employed as training ships in the postwar fleet; *Duilio* was flagship of the CinC Italian Navy 1947–49, *Doria* in 1949–50 and again in 1951–53. *Doria* was laid up in reserve from June 1953, followed by *Duilio*.

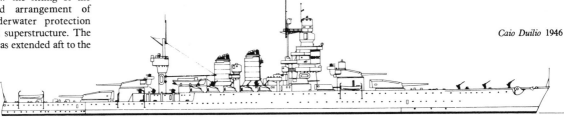

*Caio Duilio* 1946

*Andrea Doria* early 1920s.
CPL

*Caio Duilio* 1944.
CPL

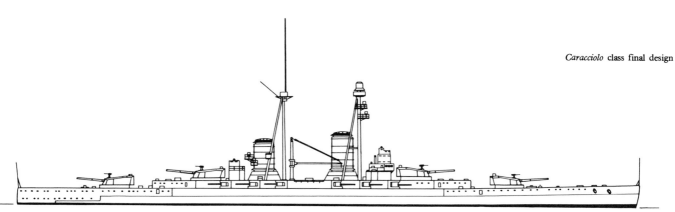

*Caracciolo* class final design

Designed by Eng Rear-Admiral Edgardo Ferrati. The original plan for these four super-dreadnoughts (the first in the Italian Navy) was for ships armed with 12–15in guns and with 20–6in guns for the medium calibre. The final project provided for battleships similar to the British *Queen Elizabeth* class, with the armament listed in the table. The wide separation of the turrets fore and aft is noteworthy; the possibility of a single hit disabling half the main armament was greatly reduced. But for lack of steel and other materials, and, on the other hand, for the need of destroyers, submarines and light craft, the Italian Navy was compelled to abandon the completion of these powerful battleships. *Caracciolo*: construction was suspended in March 1916 when about 9000 tonnes of the hull had been built. Work resumed in October 1919 and the ship was launched, but the hull was sold, on 25 October 1920, to the 'Navigazione General Italiana' shipping company, which intended to convert her to a merchant ship. But the hull was dismantled and scrapped.

## CARACCIOLO class *battleships*

| | |
|---|---|
| **Displacement:** | 31,400t normal; 34,000t full load |
| **Dimensions:** | 661ft 5in wl, 695ft oa × 97ft 1in × 31ft 2in |
| | *201.6m, 212.0m × 29.6m × 9.5m* |
| **Machinery:** | 4-shaft Parsons geared turbines, 20 oil Yarrow boilers, 105,000shp = 28kts. Range 8000nm at 10kts |
| **Armour:** | Belt 303mm (11.9in), decks 50mm (2in), turrets 400mm (15.8in), battery 220mm (8.7in), CT 400mm (15.8in) |
| **Armament:** | 8–15in (381mm)/40 (4 × 2), 12–6in (152mm)/45, 8–4in (102mm)/45, 12–40mm/39 AA, 8–17.7in (450mm) or 21in (533mm) TT |

| Name | Builder | Laid down | Launched | Comp | Fate |
|---|---|---|---|---|---|
| FRANCESCO CARACCIOLO | Castellammare RN Yd | 16.10.14 | 12.5.20 | — | Stricken 2.1.21 |
| CRISTOFORO COLOMBO | Ansaldo, Genoa | 14.3.15 | — | — | Stricken 2.1.21 |
| MARCANTONIO COLONNA | Odero, Sestri Ponente | 3.3.15 | — | — | Stricken 2.1.21 |
| FRANCESCO MOROSINI | Orlando, Leghorn | 27.6.15 | — | — | Stricken 2.1.21 |

*Colombo*: work was suspended in March 1916, when about 12.5 per cent of the hull had been built, and 5 per cent of the machinery finished: total construction about 5.5 per cent.

*Colonna* and *Morosini*: work suspended soon after beginning. The ships were planned to be commissioned: the first three in 1917, the fourth in 1918. Ten of the 15in guns intended for these ships were installed in Italian monitors.

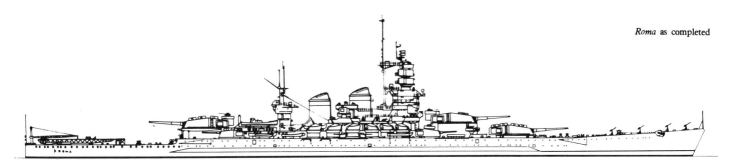

Design work on these ships began in 1930 under the direction of Umberto Pugliese. They were the first capital ships to be built by Italy since the First World War and the first battleships to be laid down by a major naval power since 1922. They contained many novel features, initiated the prewar development of the fast battleship, and were primarily intended as an answer to the French *Strasbourg* class. Although the initial intention may have been to keep to the existing international limit of 35,000t it can safely be assumed that by 1934, when *Littorio* and *Vittorio Veneto* were authorised, the designed displacement was at least 40,000t as even at this figure the completed ships can be seen to be substantially overweight. In contrast, the main armament was restricted to 381mm calibre, instead of the 406mm allowed by treaty, due to the limit-

## LITTORIO class *battleships*

| | |
|---|---|
| **Displacement:** | 40,724t (*Veneto* 40,517t, *Roma* 40,992t) standard; 45,236t (*Veneto* 45,029t, *Roma* 45,485t) full load |
| **Dimensions:** | 735ft pp, 780ft (*Roma, Impero* 789ft 6in) oa × 107ft 5in × 31ft 5in mean at standard load<br>*224.0m, 237.8m (240.7m) × 32.8m × 9.6m* |
| **Machinery:** | 4-shaft Belluzo geared turbines, 8 Yarrow boilers, 128,200hp = 30kts. Oil 4140t |
| **Armour:** | Belt 350mm (13.8in), bulkheads 210mm–70mm (8.3in–2.8in), main deck 162mm–90mm (6.4in–3.5in), funnel uptakes 105mm (4.1in), barbettes 350mm–280mm (13.8in–11in), turrets 350mm–200mm (13.8in–7.9in), secondary turrets 150mm (5.9in), CT 260mm–60mm (10.2in–2.4in) |
| **Armament:** | 9–15in (381mm)/50 Mod 34 (3 × 3), 12–6in (152mm)/55 Mod 34/35 (4 × 3), 4–4.7in (120mm)/40 Mod 91/92, 12–3.5in (90mm)/50 Mod 38/39 AA, 20–37mm/54 AA (8 × 2, 4 × 1), 16–20mm/65 AA (8 × 2), 3 aircraft |
| **Complement:** | 1830–1950 |

| Name | Builder | Laid down | launched | Comp | Fate |
|---|---|---|---|---|---|
| IMPERO | Ansaldo, Genoa | 14.5.38 | 15.11.39 | — | BU incomplete 1948–50 |
| LITTORIO | Ansaldo, Genoa | 28.10.34 | 22.8.37 | 6.5.40 | BU 1948–55 |
| ROMA | CRDA, Trieste | 18.9.38 | 9.6.40 | 14.6.42 | Sunk 9.9.43 |
| VITTORIO VENETO | CRDA, Trieste | 28.10.34 | 22.7.37 | 28.4.40 | BU 1948–51 |

*Vittoria Veneto* on trials 1940.
*CPL*

ations of existing Italian ordnance manufacturing plant. To compensate for this a long, 50cal, high velocity design was adopted, firing a 885kg AP shell at 2800fs, giving a maximum range of 46,800yds at 35° elevation. The 391mm triple turrets weighed 1560t and magazine stowage was provided for 74rpg (55 AP, 19 HE). The 152mm/55 secondary guns were carried in triple mountings weighing 133t and providing 45° maximum elevation. The 120mm guns were old Armstrong weapons carried for firing starshell but the AA guns, like the main and secondary, were all of new design.

The side armour, designed to defeat 15in AP at 17,500yds and beyond, was sloped at 11° and layered from outboard as follows: 70mm hard faced steel to decap AP shells/250mm gap/280mm KC armoured belt/ 50mm wood backing/25mm skin plating/140cm gap/36mm splinter screen; a second, 1in, splinter screen was positioned further inboard but sloped in the opposite direction where it also served to deflect projectiles from above. The belt was 12ft 4in high, of which 5ft was below the load waterline, and closed by 70mm bulkheads fore and aft, beyond which was a waterline belt of 60mm forward and 125mm aft. The magazines were protected by a 162mm armoured main deck and 210mm-100mm bulkheads while, between these, the main deck over the machinery reduced to 110mm and, at the sides over the wing compartments, to 90mm. A 45mm forecastle, and 70mm side above the belt, served to provide fuze initiation and decapping of bombs and shells. Aft, the steering and one of the auxiliary machinery rooms were protected by a 105mm lower deck, 210mm after bulkhead and 100mm forward bulkhead, the latter forming the lower section of the 70mm after bulkhead of the citadel. The 381mm barbettes were 350mm thick above the forecastle and 280mm below while the turrets had 350mm faces and 200mm sides and roofs. The secondary

turrets were protected with 150mm faces, 130mm-75mm sides, 150mm roofs and 150mm-100mm barbettes. The central bridge tower was protected from main deck to director with 50mm to 130mm plates and had a central communication tube of 200mm-160mm thickness. The underwater protection system, developed by Pugliese, was particularly original; from the base of the belt a 40mm torpedo bulkhead extended inboard before curving downward to meet the outer bottom. Within the space formed by this bulkhead and the void double bottom was a liquid-filled compartment containing a void longitudinal drum of 380cm diameter with 6mm walls. In the event of a torpedo hit the drum was designed to collapse, absorbing the majority of the force of detonation, while the curved torpedo bulkhead arrested the remaining blast and splinters. This system, designed to resist 772lb TNT, is said not to have performed as well as expected due to insufficient care in the construction of the compartments. As defence against explosions under the hull the area between the wing compartments was protected by a Ferrati triple bottom with outer liquid and inner void spaces.

The turbines were divided between two engine rooms separated by four boiler rooms, the after turbines driving the centre and the forward turbines the wing shafts. Endurance was 4700nm at 14kts. Six turbo and 3 diesel generators provided a total power output of 4050kW. On trials *Littorio* made 137,649hp = 31.3kts at 41,122t and *Veneto* 132,771hp = 31.4kts at 41,472t; their maximum continuous sea speed was 28kts. To improve the speed they were designed with bulbous bows, but these were found to cause vibration and wetness and the bow was modified and lengthened 6ft to reduce these problems.

In the second pair, *Impero* and *Roma* (provided under the 1938 Programme), the sheer forward was increased adding 6ft to the freeboard at

the stem and further increasing the length. A 68ft catapult was mounted on the quarterdeck and 3 reconnaissance aircraft could be carried; in 1942 some of these were replaced by fighters. War modifications included the addition of 12-20mm/65 (6 × 2) in *Littorio* and *Roma* (in the latter case before completion) and 16-20mm/ 65 (8 × 2) in *Veneto*. *Littorio* was the first Italian battleship fitted with radar, receiving a Gufo EC3 in September 1941; it was later replaced by an improved version and eventually became fully operational at the end of 1942. *Veneto* and *Roma* were fitted with Gufo, and *Littorio* received a second set, in 1943.

*Littorio* was hit by 3 torpedoes at Taranto on 11 November 1940, two on the starboard side forward and one on the port side aft; she was under repair until April 1941. She subsequently received minor damage in the Battle of Sirte in March 1942 and in air attacks on June 1942 and April 1943. On 30 July 1943, 5 days after the overthrow of Mussolini, she was renamed *Italia*. *Veneto* was hit by an aerial torpedo, on the port side abaft 'Y' turret, during the Battle of Matapan in March 1941, and was under repair until August 1941. Two months later she was torpedoed by the submarine *Urge*, on the port side abreast 'Y' turret, and was again out of action until March 1942. *Veneto* and *Roma* received minor bomb damage during air raids on La Spezia in June 1943. While on route to Malta to surrender on 9 September 1943, *Italia* and *Roma* were hit by 1400kg German AP glider bombs. *Roma* was hit twice, the first bomb striking amidships, passing through the ship and exploding under the bottom, and the second hitting abreast the bridge and detonating the forward magazines with the result that the ship broke in two and sank. In *Italia* a single bomb passed through the deck and side and exploded in the sea, causing heavy damage to the hull forward of 'A' turret. The incomplete *Impero* was captured by the Germans and used as a

target but was sunk in an air attack on 20 February 1945. She was raised in 1947 and towed to *Venice* for scrapping. The surviving pair returned to Italy in 1946 but in 1947 were assigned, as war reparations, to the USA (*Italia*) and UK (*Veneto*) who ordered their scrapping. *Vittorio Veneto* was discarded on 1 February 1948, *Littorio* on 1 June 1948. A considerable amount of disarming and equipment stripping took place before the ships began breaking up proper in the early 1950s.

# Japan

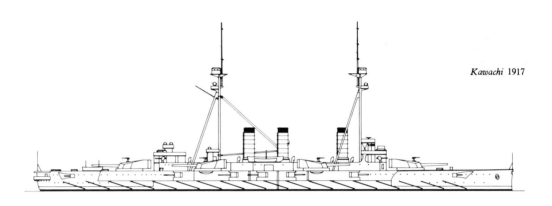

*Kawachi* 1917

This was a modified *Aki* type, designated Design A-30 by the Japanese Navy. Construction was delayed by a severe world depression. The 12in guns were ordered in England, but the 25,000shp Brown-Curtis turbines were built under licence by Kawasaki. Note that only about 20 per cent of the material was imported, compared to about 60 for the *Satsuma*. *Kawachi* had a straight stem and *Settsu* a clipper bow. Although nominally dreadnoughts, these ships did not have a really uniform main battery, since the guns differed in length, and therefore in performance, particularly at very long range. *Kawachi* sank by magazine explosion (700 dead) in Tokuyama

## SETTSU class *battleships*

**Displacement:** 21,443t normal (*Kawachi* 20,823t)
**Dimensions:** 500ft pp, 526ft oa × 84ft 2in × 27ft 10in (*Kawachi* 27ft)
*152.4m, 160.3m × 25.7m × 8.5m (8.2m)*
**Machinery:** 2-shaft Curtis turbines, 16 Miyabara boilers, 25,000shp = 20kts. Coal 2300t, oil 400t. Range 2700nm at 18kts
**Armour:** Belt 12in–4in (305mm–102mm), barbettes and turrets (280mm), deck 1.2in (30mm), CT 10in (254mm)
**Armament:** 4–12in (305mm)/50 (2 × 2), 8–12in (305mm)/45 (4 × 2), 10–6in (152mm)145, 8–4.7in (120mm)/40, 12–3in (76mm)140, 4–3in (76mm)/28, 5–18in (457mm) TT
**Complement:** 986 (*Kawachi* 999)

| Name | Builder | Laid down | Launched | Comp | Fate |
|------|---------|-----------|----------|------|------|
| SETTSU | Kure N Yd | 18.1.09 | 30.3.11 | 1.7.12 | Sunk 24.7.45 |
| KAWACHI | Yokosuka N Yd | 1.4.09 | 15.10.10 | 31.3.12 | Sunk 12.7.18 |

Below: *Settsu* as a target ship, 1940.
*CPL*

Bay. She was stricken on 2 September 1918 and later BU.

*Settsu* had 4–3in AA guns (and no single-purpose 3in) in 1921, mounted in pairs atop her end turrets. By this time, too, 2–18in TT had been removed.

*Settsu* was disarmed at Kure in 1922 (stricken 1 October 1923) under the terms of the Washington Treaty, but in 1924 she was armoured as a light bombing target. Her middle funnel was removed, as was her belt armour, and her speed reduced to 16kts (16,130t). She was converted to radio control (with the destroyer *Yukaze* as control ship) and armoured against 8in shell fire (and 10kg bombs dropped from 12,000ft) in 1937–8; one boiler was removed. However, in 1940 a new boiler and engines were installed and the former second funnel replaced while her forefunnel was considerably reduced. She was used to train carrier pilots and sunk in shallow water by US TF 38 aircraft. Salvaged and BU at Harima.

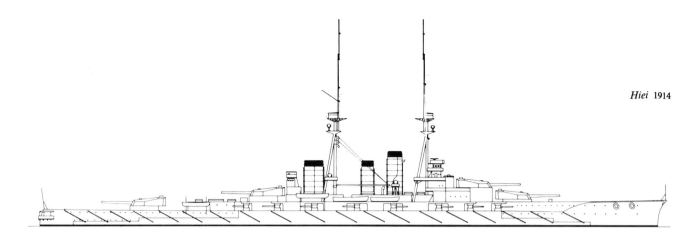

*Hiei* 1914

All four ships named after mountains. *Kongo* was the last Japanese capital ship constructed outside the country; the design, which the Japanese Navy designated B-46, was Vickers Design 472C, by Sir George Thurston. It appears that earlier versions of the design, sketched in the summer of 1910, showed a main battery of 8-12in guns (plus 16-6in and 8-21in TT), but otherwise corresponded roughly to the design as completed; an alternative battery was 10-12in. The contract, signed in November 1910, stipulated protection against 14in fire between 20,000 and 25,000 metres. The design is usually described as a battlecruiser version of the contemporary Turkish *Reshadieh*, which became HMS *Erin* during World War One. They were the first ships in the world to be armed

## KONGO class *battlecruisers*

| | |
|---|---|
| **Displacement:** | 27,500 normal; 32,300t full load |
| **Dimensions:** | 659ft 4in pp, 704ft oa × 92ft × 27ft 7in |
| | *201.0m, 214.6m × 28.0m × 8.4m* |
| **Machinery:** | 4-shaft Parsons (*Haruna* Brown-Curtis) turbines, 64,000shp = 27.5kts. Coal 4000t (1100t normal load), oil 1000t. Range 8000nm at 14kts |
| **Armour:** | Belt 8in-3in (203mm-76mm), barbettes 10in (254mm), turrets 9in (229mm), decks 2.25in-1.625in (57mm-41mm), CT 10in (254mm) |
| **Armament:** | 8-14in (356mm)/45 (4 × 2), 16-6in (152mm)/50, 8-3in (76mm)/40, 8-21in (533mm) TT sub (16 torpedoes) |
| **Complement:** | 1221 (*Kongo* 1201) |

| Name | Builder | Laid down | Launched | Comp | Fate |
|---|---|---|---|---|---|
| KONGO | Vickers | 17.1.11 | 18.5.12 | 16.8.13 | Sunk 21.11.44 |
| HIEI | Yokosuka N Yd | 4.11.11 | 21.11.12 | 4.8.14 | Sunk 13.11.42 |
| HARUNA | Kawasaki, Kobe | 16.3.12 | 14.12.13 | 19.4.15 | Sunk 28.7.45 |
| KIRISHIMA | Mitsubishi, Nagasaki | 17.3.12 | 1.12.13 | 19.4.15 | Sunk 15.11.42 |

*Kongo* as finally rebuilt.
*CPL*

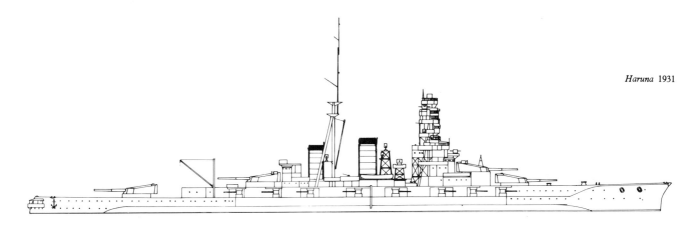

*Haruna* 1931

with the new 14in/45 gun, and their 32,200t full load displacement made them quite large for their time. Protection consumed 23.3 per cent of their displacement. Due to lack of slips, the last two ships were ordered from private yards, the first Japanese capital ships to be so constructed. Much of the material was supplied by Vickers, amounting to 31 per cent of *Haruna*, for instance.

*Kongo* was the only ship to mount paired 12pdr guns atop her turrets, and she and *Hiei* were the only two ships with 'knuckled' 14in turrets. In addition, *Kongo* differed from her sister ships in having her forefunnel closer to the foremast. In the other ships the forefunnel was much closer to the second funnel, and in *Haruna* and *Kirishima* it was also taller.

The machinery of *Hiei* was delivered by Vickers; she was the first ship fitted with the Japanese Kampon watertube boilers. *Haruna* was unique in having Curtis turbines. On trial, in May 1913, *Kongo* made 27.54kts on 78,275shp at 27,580t. *Kongo* tested the prototype Japanese flying-off platform in September 1917. That year *Haruna* was damaged by a mine laid in the S Pacific by the German auxiliary cruiser *Wolf*.

In common with other Japanese capital ships of this period, these ships received massive new tops (incorporating director fire control) after World War One, as well as forefunnel smoke hoods to reduce smoke interference. At this time a mainmast fighting top was removed from *Hiei*.

The ships then underwent two separate series of major recon-

structions. The first was carried out at Yokosuka (*Haruna*, March 1924–31 July 1928 and *Kongo*, September 1929–31 March 1931) and Kure (*Kirishima*, March 1927–31 March 1930). The number of boilers was reduced from 36 to 16 (6 all-oil and 10 mixed-firing), although some reports list 10 boilers for *Kongo, Kirishima*, coal bunkerage being reduced to 3292t and oil fuel stowage increased to 2661t for an endurance of 9500nm at 14kts; 787t was saved on boiler weights. The forefunnel was removed and bridge structure built up; the former second funnel was enlarged and heightened, while bulges were fitted and the horizontal armour greatly strengthened, the total weight of armour being increased from 6502t to 10,313t. Four torpedo tubes were removed, and the

elevation of the 14in guns increased from 33 to 43 degrees (range from 20,000 to 25,000 metres). Three aircraft were carried between Nos 3 and 4 turrets, but no catapult was fitted. Other revised data were: displacement 29,330t standard, 31,785t normal; beam 95ft 3in (29.0m), draught 28ft 4in (8.6m); armour: lower deck 4.7in over magazines, 3.1in over machinery, turret roofs increased by 3in, barbettes by ?1in; armament 8-14in/45 (4 × 2), 16-6in/50 (16 × 1), 7-3in/40 AA, 4-21in TT sub, 3 aircraft; complement 1118. The ships were reclassified as battleships after their reconstruction.

Between 1930 and 1931 December 1932 *Hiei* was demilitarised under the 1930 London Treaty, as were the USS *Wyoming* and the British *Iron Duke*. *Hiei*'s main characteristics became:

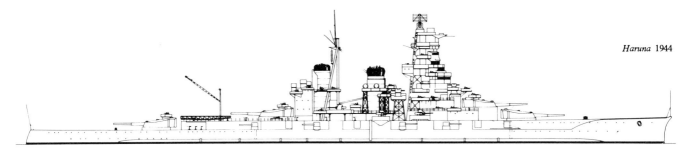

*Haruna* 1944

displacement 19,500t standard; draught 20ft 9in (6.3m); performance 13,800shp = 18kts with only 11 of the 36 boilers; armour belt removed; armament 6-14in (356mm)/45 (No 4 turret removed), 16-6in (152mm)/50, 4-3in/40 AA. The 6in guns were subsequently also removed. The forefunnel was removed and the former second funnel heightened. *Hiei* was the only training battleship to be returned to front-line duty, work beginning in November 1936.

All four ships were further rebuilt during the 1930s as fast battleships for escorting carrier task groups; the work was carried out at Kure (*Haruna*, August 1933–30 September 1934 and *Hiei*, November 1936–31 January 1940), Sasebo (*Kirishima*, June 1934–8 June 1936) and at Yokosuka (*Kongo*, June 1935–8 January 1937). The hull

was rebuilt aft, increasing the length, and the machinery completely renewed, the original power being more than doubled. The after funnel was raised to the same height as the forward funnel (slightly higher, in *Haruna*). 419 extra tons of armour were worked into and around the barbettes; a new fire control system was fitted, the elevation of the remaining 6in guns increased from 15 to 30 degrees, the AA armament increased, and a catapult fitted between Nos 3 and 4 turrets. Other revised data became: displacement 31,720t (*Kongo*), 32,350t (*Hiei*), 32,156t (*Haruna*), 31,980t (*Kirishima*) standard, 35,740t (*Kongo*), 36,400t (*Hiei*), 36,023t (*Haruna*) trial; length 720ft 6in (219.6m) wl, 738ft 7in (222.0m) oa, draught 31ft 11in (9.7m); 11 oil-fired boilers, 136,000shp = 30.5kts, 6330t oil

fuel, range 10,000nm at 18kts; armament 8-14in/45 (4 × 2), 14-6in/50 (14 × 1), 8-5in (127mm)/40 DP (4 × 2), 4-40mm AA, 8-13.2mm AA (40mm and 13.2mm replaced by 20-25mm AA in 1936), 3 aircraft; complement 1437. On post-reconstruction trials *Hiei* made 29.9kts on 137,970shp at 36,332t. *Kongo* made 30.27kts on 137,188shp at 37,003t. The fire control arrangements and bridge structure layout in *Hiei*, the last to be rebuilt, were used to test the bridge structure designed for *Yamato*. Armament changes to *Kongo* and *Haruna* during the war were as follows: in 1943, the light AA armament was increased to 34-25mm; in 1944 radar was added, and the secondary and light armament became 8-6in, 12-5in/40 DP (6 × 2), 34-25mm AA. In October 1944 the light AA armament was 100-25mm,

and in *Haruna* in 1945 118-25mm, with some depth charges.

*Kongo* blew up and sank two hours after being hit by one torpedo from the US submarine *Sealion*. *Hiei*, crippled by over 50 shell hits of 8in calibre downwards in the first Battle of Guadalcanal, was finished off by four airborne torpedoes. *Kirishima* was totally disabled by gunfire from USS *Washington* in the second Battle of Guadalcanal (she was hit by 9 16in and over 40 5in shells, at only 8400yds range), and had to be scuttled. *Haruna*, sunk in shallow water near Kure by US aircraft, was broken up in 1946.

*Hiei* August 1925.
*CPL*

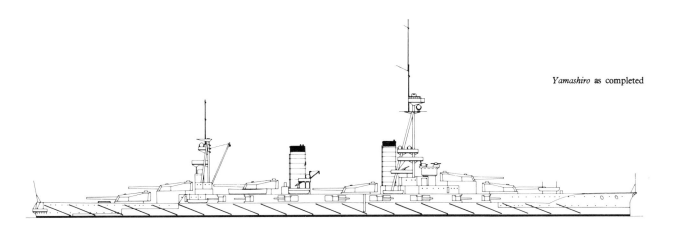

*Yamashiro* as completed

This was a battleship version of the *Kongo* design; it was designated A-64 by the Japanese Navy. Relatively great length was needed to accommodate 6 twin 14in turrets; the Vickers files show that designs for triple turrets (at least in 12in calibre) were available to the Japanese, so that the choice of twins must have been deliberate. A postwar Japanese account suggested that it was superior in attack, whereas the US triple system was superior in defence. That may mean that a ship with six individual turrets would be better able to deal with multiple targets.

By 1923 both had increased numbers of foremast platforms, and fore-

## FUSO class *battleships*

| | |
|---|---|
| **Displacement:** | 30,600t normal; 35,900t full load |
| **Dimensions:** | 630ft pp, 665ft oa × 94ft × 28ft 6in |
| | *192.1m, 202.7m × 28.7m × 8.7m* |
| **Machinery:** | 4-shaft Brown-Curtis turbines, 24 Miyabara boilers, 40,000shp = 22.5kts. Coal 5022t, oil 1026t. Range 8000nm at 14kts |
| **Armour:** | Belt 12in–4in (305mm–102mm), barbettes and turrets 12in–8in (305mm–203mm), casemates 6in (152mm), decks 3in–1.25in (75mm–32mm), CT 12in (305mm), director tower 6in (152mm) |
| **Armament:** | 12-14in (356mm)/45 (6 × 2), 16-6in (152mm)/50, 4-3in (76mm)/40 AA, 6-21in (533mm) TT sub |
| **Complement:** | 1193 |

| Name | Builder | Laid down | Launched | Comp | Fate |
|---|---|---|---|---|---|
| FUSO | Kure N Yd | 11.3.12 | 28.3.14 | 18.11.15 | Sunk 25.10.44 |
| YAMASHIRO | Yokosuka N Yd | 20.11.13 | 3.11.15 | 31.3.17 | Sunk 25.10.44 |

*Yamashiro* 1928.
CPL

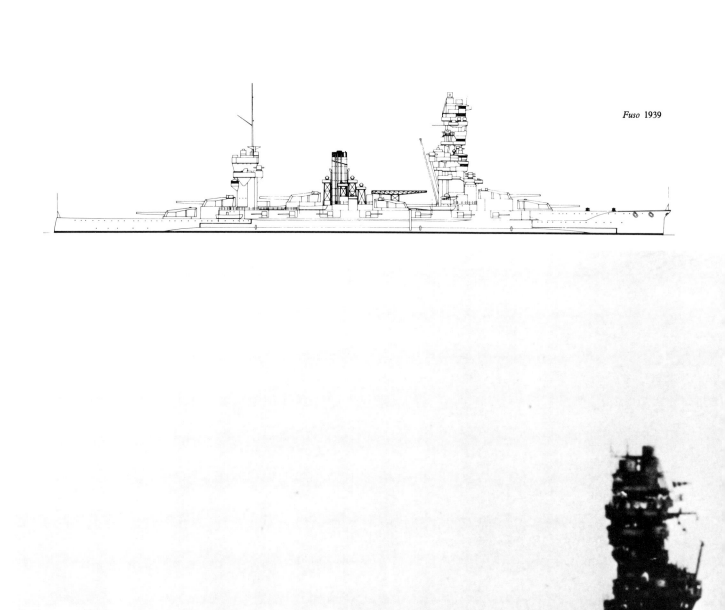

*Fuso* 1939

funnel caps to reduce smoke interference. *Yamashiro* alone was fitted with a large searchlight platform forward of her second funnel; 6–3in AA were later fitted. *Yamashiro* had the prototype Japanese flying-off platform atop her No 2 turret; later she carried her airplane atop her No 4 turret (each carried 3 aircraft from 1927 onwards).

They were the first Japanese ships reconstructed during the 1930s with new machinery and tower (pagoda) foremasts, from 1930 to 12 May 1933 (*Fuso*) and to 30 March 1935 (*Yamashiro*); however, *Fuso* needed a second reconstruction, which was completed on 19 February 1935. The hull was lengthened aft, bulges fitted, horizontal protection increased to a cumulative total of almost 7in over vitals, 14in gun elevation increased from 30 to 43 deg (range 25,000 metres or 13.5nm rather than 20,000 metres or 10.8nm) and 6in gun elevation from 15 to 30 deg. The total weight of armour went up from 8588t to 12,199t. The fitting of new geared turbines and 6 oil-fired boilers increased power to 75,000shp and designed speed to 24.7kts; on post-reconstruction trials *Fuso* made 24.682kts on 76,889shp at 38,368.6t displacement. This compared to *Yamashiro*'s August 1915 performance of 23.3kts on 47,730shp at 30,577t. The fore funnel was removed, and towering pagoda bridges replaced the previous built-up tripods. *Fuso* was initially fitted with a catapult atop No 3 turret, but it was relocated to the quarterdeck during the second reconstruction, presumably to reduce topweight. Her sister's catapult was always on the quarterdeck. After reconstruction, *Fuso*'s No 3 14in turret trained forward on the centreline; *Yamashiro*'s trained aft, the original arrangement, allowing a larger base to the bridge. Other revised data were: displacement 34,700t standard, 38,536t trial; dimensions 689ft wl, 698ft oa × 100ft 6in × 31ft 9in (210.0m, 212.8m × 30.6m × 9.7m); 5100t oil fuel; armour: main deck 2in, lower deck 1.3in–4.7in; armament 12–14in/45, 14–6in/50, 8–5in (127mm)/40 DP (4 × 2), 16–25mm AA, 3 aircraft; complement 1396.

The light AA armament was increased to 20–25mm in 1941, and to 37–25mm in June 1944. A post-Midway proposal to convert these ships to hybrid battleship-carriers on the same lines as *Hyuga* and *Ise* (see next entry) was dropped after the aircraft and pilot losses in the Battle of the Philippine Sea. Like the *Ise*s, both saw little action during World War II prior to their loss at Surigao Strait, part of the Leyte Gulf operations. *Fuso* broke in two and sank after taking two torpedo hits from US destroyers, and *Yamashiro* went down from four destroyer torpedoes and numerous 16in and 14in shells.

*Fuso* after 1933 refit.
*CPL*

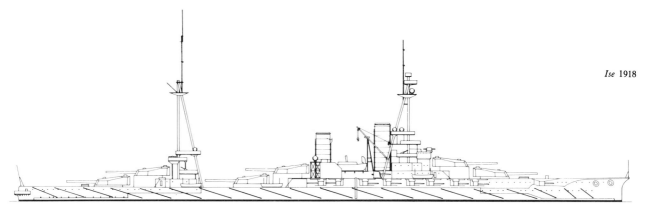

*Ise 1918*

Design A-92, a modified *Fuso*, slightly lengthened, with rearranged main turrets, concentrated in pairs for better fire control and protection. The secondary battery was to have been the 6in/50 of the *Fuso*, but a new Japanese 5.5in/50 was substituted. Contemporary accounts suggest that its somewhat lighter shell was better adapted to the smaller stature of the average Japanese seaman: the secondary gun was generally defined as the largest weapon the shell for which could be carried by a single man, for maximum rate of fire. Moreover, casemate protection was reduced, and 4 of the guns were entirely unarmoured.

Protection was generally similar to that of the *Fuso*, but the middle (protective) deck sloped down to meet the lower edge of the belt armour over both boiler rooms and magazines; in the earlier ships it was flat over the boiler rooms. Splinter protection was considerably increased, at a cost of about a thousand tons. Small-tube Kampon boilers were adopted for greater steaming efficiency. On trials in September 1917 *Ise* made 23.64kts on 56,498shp at 31,153t.

Both were fitted with numerous foremast platforms and then with fore-funnel smoke hoods in 1926-7, and 3 aircraft were added, with a flying-off platform atop No 5 turret (superfiring aft); 4-3in AA guns were fitted about 1921.

Both ships were reconstructed prior to World War II (*Ise* between 1935 and

## ISE class *battleships*

| | |
|---|---|
| **Displacement:** | 31,260t normal; 36,500t full load |
| **Dimensions:** | 640ft pp, 675ft oa × 94ft × 29ft 1in |
| | *195.1m, 205.8m × 28.7m × 8.8m* |
| **Machinery:** | 4-shaft Curtis (*Hyuga* Parsons) turbines, 24 Kampon boilers, 45,000shp = 23kts. Coal 4706t, oil 1411t. Range 9680nm at 14kts |
| **Armour:** | Belt 12in–4in (305mm–102mm), barbettes and turrets 12in–8in (305mm–203mm), decks 3in–1.25in (76mm–32mm), CT 12in (305mm) forward, 6in (152mm) aft |
| **Armament:** | 12-14in (356mm)/45 (6 × 2), 20-5.5in (140mm)/50, 4-3in (76mm)/40 AA, 6-21in (533mm) TT sub |
| **Complement:** | 1360 |

| Name | Builder | Laid down | Launched | Comp | Fate |
|---|---|---|---|---|---|
| ISE | Kawasaki, Kobe | 10.5.15 | 12.11.16 | 15.12.17 | Sunk 28.7.45 |
| HYUGA | Mitsubishi, Nagasaki | 6.5.15 | 27.1.17 | 30.4.18 | Sunk 24.7.45 |

23 March 1937, and *Hyuga* between 1934 and 7 September 1936), being altered similarly to the *Fuso* class. Main battery elevation was increased to 43 deg, except for the two turrets aft where the hull depth was insufficient for the alterations, and both were fitted with quarterdeck catapults. Horizontal protection over the vitals was increased to a cumulative total of almost 7in, and the total weight of armour from 9525t to 12,644t. Other revised data were: displacement 35,800t (*Hyuga* 36,000t) standard; 39,535t (*Hyuga* 39,031t) trial, dimensions 700ft wl, 708ft oa × 104ft × 30ft 2in (213.4m, 215.8m × 31.7m × 9.2m); 8 boilers, 80,000shp = 25.3 knots, 5313t oil fuel; armour: main deck 2in, lower deck 1.3in–4.7in; armament 12-14in/45, 16-5.5in/50,

8-5in (127mm)/40 DP (4 × 2), 20-25mm AA, 3 aircraft; complement 1376. On post-reconstruction trials, *Hyuga* made 25.264kts on 81,050shp at 40,706t.

As a result of the carrier losses at Midway, both were converted in 1943 (conversions completed, respectively, 5 September and 30 November) into hybrid battleship-carriers; 'X' and 'Y' turrets were removed, and a hangar and aircraft handling deck built onto the quarterdeck. The 22 planes were to be launched from 2 powerful catapults and recovered from the sea by crane, as the deck was much too short for flying operations. The 5.5in guns were removed and the AA armament increased. Data were revised as follows: displacement 35,350t standard,

38,065t trial; length 720ft 5in (219.6m) overall, draught 29ft 7in (9.0m); 4249t oil fuel; armament 8-14in/45, 16-5in (127mm)/40 DP (8 × 2), 57-25mm AA; complement 1463. The light AA armament was increased to 104-25mm in June 1944, and 6-4.7in (120mm) 28-barrelled rocket launchers were added in September 1944. The air group was initially to have consisted of 22 dive bombers ('Judy'), later changed to floatplane dive bombers ('Paul'). In fact no aircraft appear to have been carried. The two catapults were removed in October, and definitely no aircraft were aboard in the Leyte Gulf operations, during which both served as decoys. Both were sunk in shallow water at Kure by US aircraft, and were broken up after the war.

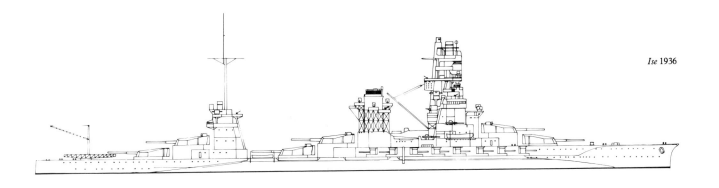

*Ise* 1936

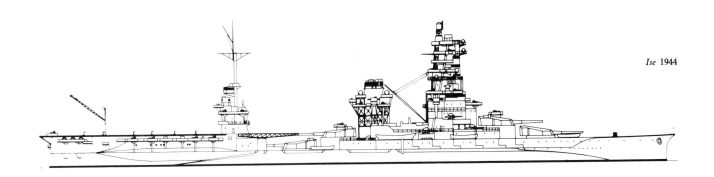

*Ise* 1944

*Ise* 1937.
CPL

*Hyuga* 1926.
CPL

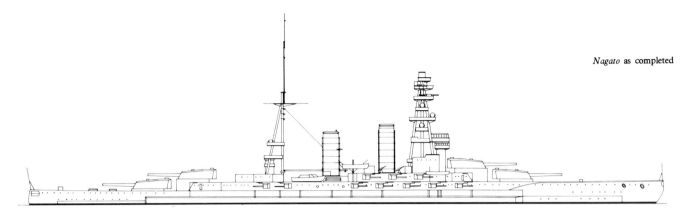

Design A-102, the first purely Japan-ese battleships, designed by Capt Y Hiraga. Hiraga's originality showed, for example, in the unusual bow pro-file, similar to that adopted in con-temporary light cruisers. The design was completed in the spring of 1916, the Japanese claiming later that it ante-dated the US *Maryland* by four months. Thus, these can be considered the first battleships in the world to mount 16in guns; the decision in favour of this weapon over the existing 14in/50 was made by the Navy Minister, Admiral Tomosaburo Kato.

They were also extremely fast, and were, in effect, Japanese equivalents of the British *Queen Elizabeth*s. It is not clear whether this was merely a con-

## NAGATO class *battleships*

| | |
|---|---|
| **Displacement:** | 33,800t normal; 38,500t full load |
| **Dimensions:** | 660ft 4in pp, 700ft oa × 95ft × 30ft |
| | *201.4m, 213.4m × 29.0m × 9.1m* |
| **Machinery:** | 4-shaft geared Gihon turbines, 15 oil-burning and 6 mixed-firing Kampon boilers, 80,000shp = 26.5kts. Oil 3400t. Coal 1600t. Range 5500nm at 16kts |
| **Armour:** | Belt 12in–4in (305mm–102mm), main deck 1.7in (44mm), lower deck 3in–2in (76mm–51mm), barbettes 12in–3in (305mm–76mm), turret faces 14in (356mm), CT 14.6in–3.8in (371mm–97mm) |
| **Armament:** | 8–16.1in (410mm)/45 (4 × 2), 20–5.5in (140mm)/50, 4–3in (76mm)/40 AA, 8–21in (533mm) TT (4 sub, 4aw) |
| **Complement:** | 1333 |

| Name | Builder | Laid down | Launched | Comp | Fate |
|---|---|---|---|---|---|
| NAGATO | Kure N Yd | 28.8.17 | 9.11.19 | 25.11.20 | Sunk 29.7.46 |
| MUTSU | Yokosuka N Yd | 1.6.18 | 31.5.20 | 22.11.21 | Sunk 8.6.43 |

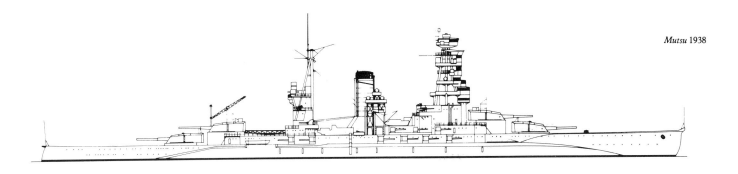

*Mutsu* 1938

1928

1937

tinuation of the long-standing Japanese policy of high battleship speed though wartime British battleship designs to which the Japanese probably had access, called for relatively high speed. What was remarkable was how well the speed of these ships were concealed; for years they were generally described as capable of 23kts. The US Navy apparently learned of their higher speed (as reconstructed) only in 1937, one immediate result being the redesign of the new *South Dakota*. On trials in October 1920 *Nagato* made 26.7kts on 95,500shp at 34,000t.

Visually they were dominated by the uniquely Japanese heptapodal mast, with two legs sloping forward, two aft, one to either beam, and a thick central leg containing an elevator connecting the main director position in the foretop to the upper deck. This structure was adopted for maximum steadiness and survivability under shellfire, after a series of experiments; it was described by the Japanese as virtually shellproof. The heptapod, then, may be considered, along with the US cage, an alternative to the more conventional tripod. Note that, although their legs were sometimes shot through, no British tripod fell in wartime. It is, then, somewhat surprising that the Japanese, who probably had access to this data, chose so heavy an alternative. When completed, these ships already showed numerous foremast platforms

(for heavy and light directors, lookouts, and searchlights), the lineal ancestors of the 'pagodas' soon installed on other battleships.

As might have been expected, the intermediate platforms experienced smoke interference. A smokehood was installed on the forefunnel in 1921 (*Mutsu* 1923), and in 1924 the forefunnel was bent aft.

The armour arrangement resembled that of contemporary US 'all or nothing' battleships, and so represented a break with previous Japanese (and British) practice: the ends were 'soft' and there was no side armour above the main belt. However, unlike US ships, they continued to devote considerable armour to the lower deck, which in American practice was a relatively thin splinter deck. Moreover, they had both a flat protective deck over the belt *and* an upper armoured deck over the otherwise unprotected lower secondary guns. The arrangement of the torpedo bulkhead was also unusual: its upper end sloped up and out to meet the lower edge of the downward-sloping armour deck. This complete armoured enclosure of the vitals was typical of all later Japanese capital ship designs of this period. The armoured citadel was 440ft long.

Both were taken in hand in 1934 for major reconstructions (completed 31 January and 30 September 1936), being altered similarly to the *Fuso*

class; however, unlike the three earlier classes, the machinery was not substantially increased in power, although the ships were reboilered and the turbines slightly uprated. Deck protection over machinery and magazines was increased and additional armour added to the barbettes above and below the main deck; the turret roofs were probably made thicker. The total weight of armour went up from 10,396t to 13,032t. The elevation of the main battery was increased to 43 degrees (range increased from 20,000 to 28,000 metres, but one source claims 37,000 metres maximum range; the correct calibre of the main armament, almost always listed as 16in (406mm), was established by post-war US investigations). Other revised data were: displacement 39,120t standard, 42,753t trial; length 725ft 4in wl, 738ft oa × 108ft 2in × 31ft 2in (221.2m, 224.9m × 33.0m × 9.5m); 10 boilers, 82,000shp = 25kts, 5600t oil fuel; armour: main deck 1.7in–2.7in, lower deck 5in over magazines, barbettes 12in + 4.9in (above main deck), 3in + 8.4in (below main deck); armament 8–16.1in/45 (4 × 2), 18–5.5in/50 (18 × 1), 8–5in (127mm)/40 DP (4 × 2), 20–25mm AA, 3 aircraft, 1 catapult; complement 1368. The 1in deck over the casemates was increased to 2.5in. Unlike the four earlier ships, they had their catapults on their weather decks just forward of No 3 turret, which in *Mutsu* carried an aircraft crane. *Mutsu*

was accidentally destroyed in the Inland Sea by a magazine explosion probably originating in some incendiary shrapnel shells. The light AA armament in *Nagato* was increased to 68–25mm in June 1944, two more 5.5in being removed and to 98–25mm in 1945, when trial displacement reached 42,893t. *Nagato* survived the war, although considerably damaged, and was expended as a target in the atomic bomb tests at Bikini; her major wartime engagement was the unsuccessful battle against the US escort carriers off Samar in the Philippines. She had been torpedoed near Truk by the US submarine *Skate* on 25 December 1943.

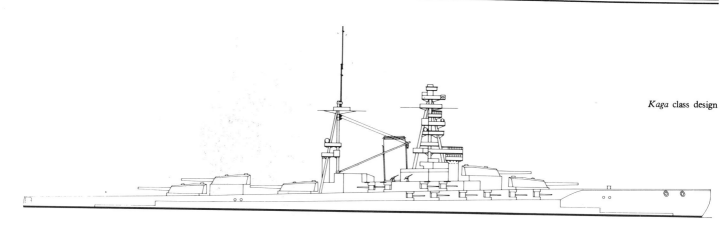

*Kaga* class design

Design A-127, designed by Y Hiraga, essentially an enlarged *Nagato* with a flush deck for maximum girder strength. Note the adoption of 24in torpedo tubes, all above water; the design initially called for 4 submerged and 4 above water tubes, but the former were dropped due to problems of firing at high speed. The Japanese also considered turbo-electric drive after American announcements of success with the plant in *New Mexico*, estimating 70,000shp = 25.25kts, 2500nm endurance at full speed, 7800nm at 14kts. It was rejected, but the turbo-electric oiler *Kamoi* was ordered in 1921 from the US to test it.

Hiraga adopted sloping belt armour to resist 16in shells between 12,000 and

## KAGA class *battleships*

| | |
|---|---|
| **Displacement:** | 39,900t normal; 44,200t full load |
| **Dimensions:** | 715ft pp, 760ft oa × 100ft × 30ft 10in |
| | *218.0m, 231.7m × 30.5m × 9.4m* |
| **Machinery:** | 4-shaft geared Curtis turbines, 12 Kampon (8 oil-firing, 4 mixed firing) boilers, 91,000shp = 26.5kts. Oil 3600t, coal 1700t. Range 6500nm/14kts, 5500nm/16kts, 2250nm/26.5kts. |
| **Armour:** | Belt 11in (280mm) sloped at 15 degrees, bulkhead 11in–9in (280mm–229mm), barbettes and turrets 12in–9in (305mm–229mm), deck 4in (102mm), CT 14in (356mm) |
| **Armament:** | 10–16.1in (410mm)/45 (5 × 2), 20–5.5in (140mm)/50, 4–3in (76mm)/40 AA, 8–24in (610mm) TT aw |
| **Complement:** | 1333 |

| Name | Builder | Laid down | Launched | Comp | Fate |
|---|---|---|---|---|---|
| KAGA | Kawasaki, Kobe | 19.7.20 | 17.11.21 | (25.12.22) | Completed as carrier |
| TOSA | Mitsubishi, Nagasaki | 16.2.20 | 18.12.21 | (3.23) | Sunk 9.2.25 |

20,000 metres. The lower armour deck, which had been the main protective deck in earlier ships, was virtually eliminated in this class, in favour of a heavy flat deck covering the belt, as in contemporary US battleships. Below these was a 1½in splinter deck. The former heavy lower armour deck was reduced to an almost vertical inward-sloping continuation of the 3in torpedo bulkhead, connected to the lower edge of the belt proper by a short upward-sloping deck. The upper end of this torpedo-bulkhead/splinter bulkhead was a short vertical 1½in splinter bulkhead above the splinter deck, which was itself above the waterline. This system was repeated in slightly modified form in the *Amagi* and *Kii* classes.

Both ships were cancelled as a result of the Washington Treaty (building stopped on both 5 February 1922), *Tosa* (stricken 1 April 1924) being expended as a target in the Bungo Straights. Accounts of tests against her show shells striking below the waterline; the Japanese interest in internal armour may correspond to this threat. She was also tested against mines and torpedoes. *Kaga* was to have been scrapped, but was completed as a carrier after the *Amagi* was damaged in the Tokyo earthquake of 1923. The completion dates in parentheses are those originally planned. It was planned to replace the 3in AA with a new 4.7in/45.

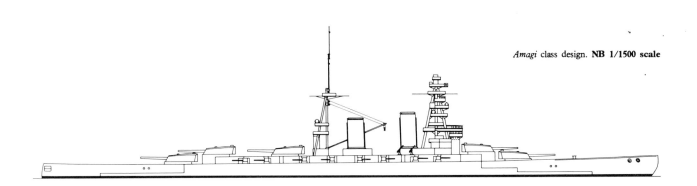

*Amagi* class design. **NB 1/1500 scale**

## AMAGI class *battlecruisers*

| | |
|---|---|
| **Displacement:** | 41,217t normal; 47,000t full load |
| **Dimensions:** | 820ft 3in wl, 826ft 1in oa × 101ft × 31ft |
| | *250.0m, 251.8, × 30.8m × 9.5m* |
| **Machinery:** | 4-shaft geared Gihon turbines, 19 Kampon boilers (11 oil firing, 8 mixed firing), 131,200shp = 30kts. Oil 3900t, coal 2500t. Range 8000nm at 14kts. |
| **Armour:** | Belt 10in (254mm) sloped 12 degrees, bulkhead 2.9in (73mm), barbettes 11in–9in (280mm–229mm), decks 3.9in (98mm), CT 14in–3in (356mm–76mm) |
| **Armament:** | 10–16.1in (410mm)/45 (5 × 2), 16–5.5in (140mm)/50, 4 (later 6)–4.7in (120mm)/45 AA, 8–24in (610mm) TT aw |
| **Complement:** | ? |

| Name | Builder | Laid down | Launched | Comp | Fate |
|---|---|---|---|---|---|
| AMAGI | Yokosuka N Yd | 16.12.20 | — | (11.23) | Wrecked 1.9.23 |
| AKAGI | Kure N Yd | 6.12.20 | — | (12.23) | Completed as carrier |
| ATAGO | Kawasaki, Kobe | 22.11.21 | — | (before 12.24) | BU 1924 |
| TAKAO (ex *Ashitaka*) | Mitsubishi, Nagasaki | 19.12.21 | — | (before 12.24) | BU 1924 |

This design B-64 of 1919, by Y Hiraga, was an enlarged *Kago* with thinner belt and deck. Although 16.1in/45 was planned, they might have been armed with a 16.1in/50 tested in 1920. The secondary battery was reduced to 16 guns; note the use of a new AA gun. Hiraga considered turbo-electric drive (105,000shp = 28kts, 9600nm at 14kts). All construction as battlecruisers ceased on 5 February 1922 under the Washington Treaty when *Amagi* was 40 per cent complete. Planned completion dates in parentheses.

Both *Akagi* and *Amagi* were to have been completed as aircraft carriers, corresponding to USS *Lexington* and *Saratoga*, but the latter was destroyed in the Tokyo earthquake and the fast battleship *Kaga* substituted. Conversion work had already begun, but the hull structure was too badly strained to be usable. She was stricken 31 July 1922 and BU began on 14 April 1924. *Atago* and *Takao* were cancelled 31 July 1922, stricken 14 April 1924 and BU on the slip. All named after mountains except *Takao*, a town.

## KII class *battleships*

**Displacement:** 42,600t normal; 48,500t full load
**Dimensions:** 770ft pp, 820ft oa × 101ft × 31ft 9in
*234.8m, 250.0m × 30.8m × 9.7m*
**Machinery:** 4-shaft geared Gihon turbines, 19 Kampon boilers, 131,200shp = 29.75kts. Oil 3900t, coal 2500t. Range 8000nm at 14kts.
**Armour:** Belt 11.5in (292mm) sloped 12 degrees, barbettes 11in–9in (280mm–229mm), bulkheads 2.9in (73mm), deck 4.6in (117mm), CT 14in (356mm)
**Armament:** 10–16.1in (410mm)/45 (5 × 2), 16–5.5in (140mm)/50, 4(later 6)–4.7in/45 AA, 8–24in (610mm) TT aw
**Complement:** ?

| Name | Builder | Laid down | Launched | Comp | Fate |
|------|---------|-----------|----------|------|------|
| KII | Kure N Yd | — | — | — | — |
| OWARI | Yokosuka N Yd | — | — | — | — |
| No 11 | Kawasaki, Kobe | — | — | — | — |
| No 12 | Mitsubishi, Nagasaki | — | — | — | — |

These ships mark the decision of the Naval Staff to merge the battleship and battlecruiser categories; they were designated simply 'High Speed Battleships'. Designed by Y Hiraga, they were based on *Amagi* class with slightly thicker belt and deck armour, the latter 4.6in rather than 3.9in. All were cancelled (under the Washington Treaty). The first two were ordered on 12 October 1921; stopped 5 February 1922, and cancelled 14 April 1924. Second pair cancelled 19 November 1923. None was laid down.

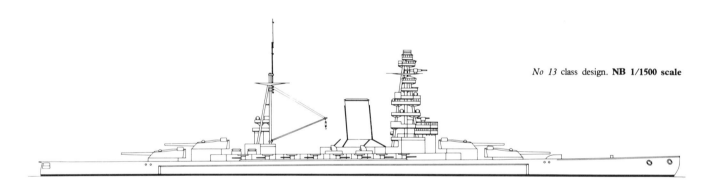

*No 13* class design. **NB 1/1500 scale**

## No 13 class *battlecruisers*

**Displacement:** 47,500t normal
**Dimensions:** 850ft pp, 900ft oa × 101ft × 32ft
*259.1m, 274.4m × 30.8m × 9.8m*
**Machinery:** 4-shaft geared Gihon turbines, 22 Kampon boilers, 150,000shp = 30kts
**Armour:** Belt 13in (330mm) sloped at 15 degrees, deck 5in (127mm)
**Armament:** 8–18in (457mm)/45 (4 × 2), 16–5.5in (140mm)/50, 8–4.7in (120mm)/45 AA, 8–24in (610mm) TT aw
**Complement:** ?

| Name | Builder | Laid down | Launched | Comp | Fate |
|------|---------|-----------|----------|------|------|
| No 13 | Yokosuka N Yd | — | — | — | Cancelled 19.11.23 |
| No 14 | Kure N Yd | — | — | — | Cancelled 19.11.23 |
| No 15 | Mitsubishi, Nagasaki | — | — | — | Cancelled 19.11.23 |
| No 16 | Kawasaki, Kobe | - | - | - | Cancelled 19.11.23 |

This Y Hiraga 1921 design was based on *Amagi/Kii*, but scaled up to take the new 18in gun. They were to have been rated 'fast battleships'. The first ship would have been laid down mid-1922. The class was scheduled for completion by 1927. Protection was scaled up to match the new gun, hence the thicker side and deck. Note that the 18in gun was not available in 1921, although a 19in gun had been tested at Kure in 1916-17.

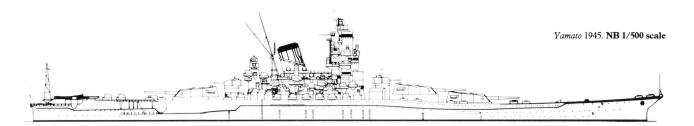

*Yamato* 1945. **NB 1/500 scale**

The ultimate battleships, with the greatest displacement, biggest guns and heaviest armour of all times. Aware that the United States would always be able to outbuild her, Japan's intention was to go for quality at the expense of quantity, by constructing a few very large, powerful units; they should hopefully act as a constraint on US ambitions, as eventual US replies would be too large to pass through the Panama Canal locks. *Yamato* and *Musashi* were ordered in the 1937 3rd Supplementary Programme, the second pair in the 1939 4th Supplementary Programme. Their history, even in the design stage, consisted of a series of superlatives; no fewer than 23 different projects, with numerous further proposals and variations, were considered before plans were finalised.

## YAMATO class *battleships*

**Displacement:** 62,315t standard; 67,123t trial; 69,990t full load
**Dimensions:** 800ft 6in pp, 839ft 11in wl, 862ft 9in oa × 121ft 1in × 34ft 1in
244.0m, 256.0m, 263.0m × 36.9m × 10.4m
**Machinery:** 4-shaft Kampon geared turbines, 12 boilers, 150,000shp = 27kts. Oil 6300t
**Armour:** Belt 16.1in (410mm), barbettes 21.5in–2in (550mm–50mm), turrets 25.6in–7.5in (650mm–190mm), deck 9.1in–7.9in (230mm–200mm), conning tower 19.7in–11.8in (500mm–300mm)
**Armament:** 9–18.1in (460mm)/45 (3 × 3), 12–6.1in (155mm)/60 (4 × 3), 12–5in (127mm)/40 DP (6 × 2), 24–25mm AA, 4–13.2mm AA, 7 aircraft
**Complement:** 2500

| Name | Builder | Laid down | Launched | Comp | Fate |
|------|---------|-----------|----------|------|------|
| YAMATO | Kure N Yd | 4.11.37 | 8.8.40 | 16.12.41 | Sunk 7.4.45 |
| MUSASHI | Mitsubishi, Nagasaki | 29.3.38 | 1.11.40 | 5.8.42 | Sunk 24.10.44 |
| SHINANO | Yokosuka N Yd | 4.5.40 | (8.10.44) | (19.11.44) | Converted 1942–44 |
| No 111 | Kure N Yd | 7.11.40 | — | — | BU incomplete 1942 |

*Yamato* on trials 1941.
CPL

*Yamato* fitting out.
*CPL*

Very serious consideration was given to fitting new 10,000bhp 2-cycle double-acting diesels for long endurance, with steam turbines on the inner shafts for high speeds. *Yamato* and *Shinano* were built in new or enlarged docks, while *Musashi* was launched from a conventional slipway at a record 35,737t. Elaborate precautions, including a 408t camouflage net for *Musashi*, were needed to keep their building secret, and official figures (1942) grossly understated their particulars: 42,000t standard displacement, dimensions 235 × 31.5m × 9.2m, 9-16in guns, 90,000shp = 25kts. To help maintain secrecy, the 46.0cm (18.1in) guns were always referred to as the 40.6cm (16in) Type 94. A special heavy-lift ship, *Kashino*, was constructed to transport 18.1in guns and mountings to the shipyards.

In general, the design philosophy led to reliance on massive armour thicknesses, i.e. direct protection. Less attention was paid to indirect protection, such as splinter decks or extensive subdivision; thus there were only 1147 watertight compartments, compared with 1089 in the 40% smaller *Nagato*. Protection was designed to give immunity against 18in shells between 22,000 yards and 33,000 yards, and against a 1t bomb dropped from 15,000ft. Below the belt (inclined at 20 deg to the vertical) was a 7.9in–3in (200mm–75mm) anti-torpedo bulkhead (14 deg inclination) which extended down to the outer bottom along machinery spaces, but was carried under the magazines fore and aft as extra protection against mines. The bulkhead was designed to withstand an attack with a 400kg (880lb) charge, the weight of a destroyer torpedo warhead, but the connection of the belt armour to the anti-torpedo bulkhead was weak and the inboard bulkheads inelastic, so that the anti-torpedo protection fell below expectations. No attempt was made to provide a sandwich (liquid layer) anti-torpedo system, in line with contemporary RN or US practice, but the Japanese system was also intended to protect against diving shells, regarded as a serious threat after the 1924 tests on *Tosa*. A single torpedo hit from USS *Skate* in December 1943 produced a 5m × 25m hole in *Yamato*'s bulge and breached the anti-torpedo bulkhead, allowing flooding of the No 3 turret upper magazine. Although remedial measures were taken, post-war U.S. investigators concluded 600lb torpex warheads would still rupture the torpedo defence system. Small armoured boxes with 11.8in-7.9in (300mm-200mm) plating protected the steering gear. A 15in solid plate perforated with 7in diameter holes formed a grating to allow the passage of smoke from the boilers. The VH armour used in plates over 11in (280mm) thick was surface tempered by suitable heat treatment but not carbonised ('cemented'); it was probably about 10% less resistant than equivalent British or US armour, and, because of problems in the heat treatment, distinctly brittle, particularly in

the very thick turret face plates.

Each triple turret had a total revolving weight of 2530t, and the range at 45 deg elevation with a 3220lb projectile was 45,960 yards, rate of fire being 1.5–2 rounds per gun per minute. 100 rounds per gun were stored, 60 in the rotating turret structure and 40 in the shell rooms. Muzzle velocity (AP projectile) was 780 m/sec (2556ft/sec), and the projectile was designed to penetrate a 22.3in vertical plate at ranges up to 20,000 metres, and a horizontal plate of 9.1in at ranges over 30,000 metres. Blast effects were very severe, and all secondary and AA guns had to be in enclosed mountings; boats and aircraft were stored below decks at the stern with a large lift. There were two catapults; hangar capacity was

seven aircraft, but the usual number carried was four. *Yamato* is reported to have fired 108 18.1in salvoes in the action off Samar against US escort carriers, destroyers and destroyer escorts during the Leyte Gulf operations.

The design displacement figures listed above were exceeded, actual figures being 63,000t (approx) standard, 68,010t trial, 71,659t full load. The 6–6.1in guns amidships were removed in 1943, to make room for an additional 12-5in/40 DP (6 × 2), although these were only fitted in *Yamato*. The light AA armament in this ship was increased to 36–25mm in 1943, 98–25mm in April 1944, 113–25mm in July 1944 and 150–25mm in 1945. The data for *Musashi* were 36–25mm in 1943,

54–25mm early in 1944, 115–25mm in April 1944 and 130–25mm in July 1944.

The construction of *Shinano* and *No 111*, which would have had marginally thinner armour than the first pair and a modified AA armament, was suspended in December 1941 and cancelled in 1942. *Shinano*, about 50 per cent complete, was completed as an aircraft carrier, but *No 111*, 30 per cent complete, was dismantled in the building dock. *No 797*, of similar type, proposed in the 1942 5th Supplementary Programme, was cancelled before being named or ordered. Two further ships, *No 798* and *799*, with 6–20in guns and probably 18in side armour, were also proposed and cancelled in 1942.

Neither completed ship had an

opportunity of justifying its existence, both perishing under the fury of American air attacks after brief careers. *Musashi* was sunk by between 10 and 19 torpedoes and 17 bombs in the Battle of the Sibuyan Sea, part of the Leyte Gulf operations, and *Yamato* by between 9 and 13 torpedoes and 6 bombs while approaching Okinawa.

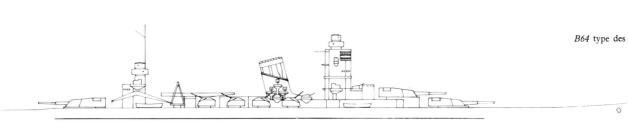

*B64* type des

## B64 type

| | |
|---|---|
| **Displacement:** | 32,000t standard; 34,800t trial |
| **Dimensions:** | 787ft 5in wl, 802ft 6in oa × 89ft 3in × 28ft 10in |
| | *240.0m, 244.6m × 27.2m × 8.8m* |
| **Machinery:** | 4-shaft geared turbines, 8 boilers, 160,000shp = 33.0kts. Oil 4545t |
| **Armour:** | Belt 7.5in (190mm), deck 5in (127mm) |
| **Armament:** | 9–12.2in (310mm)/50 (3 × 3), 16–3.9in (100mm)/65 AA (8 × 2), 12–25mm AA, 8–13.2mm AA, 8–24in TT, 3 aircraft |
| **Complement:** | ? |

The design of this type was begun in 1939, and tests on the 12.2in (31cm) gun and the proposed underwater protection system were carried out in 1940–41. Plans were finalised in 1941, but in 1942, when more details of the US *Alaska* class became known, the proposed main armament was altered to 9–14.2in (36cm) in three triple turrets (B65 type). The construction of

two ships, *Nos 795* and *796*, to this design was approved in the 1942 Programme, but they were never named, ordered or laid down, because of more important wartime priorities.

The ships would have been rated as 'super A-type (ie heavy) cruisers', not battlecruisers (cf *Alaska* class), and in appearance would have been less massive *Yamato*s.

# Netherlands

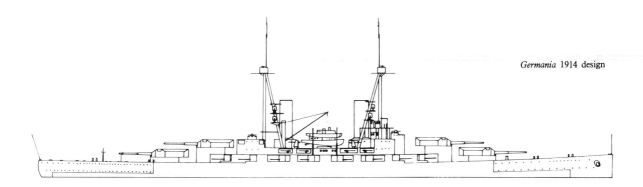

*Germania* 1914 design

## Projected *battleships*

| | |
|---|---|
| **Displacement:** | 24,605t normal; 26,851t full load |
| **Dimensions:** | 603ft 8in wl × 91ft 10in × 29ft 8in max |
| | *184.0m × 28.0m × 9.0m* |
| **Machinery:** | 3-shaft turbines, 6 double-ended boilers, 38,000shp = 22kts. Fuel 2400t max |
| **Armour:** | Belt 250mm–150mm (9.8in–5.9in), bulkheads 200mm (7.9in), barbettes 300mm–110mm (11.8in–4.3in), torpedo bulkheads 40mm (1.6in), deck 50mm–25mm (2in–1in), CT 11.8in–7.9in (300mm–200mm) |
| **Armament:** | 8–14in (356mm) (4 × 2), 16–5.9in (150mm), 12–75mm, 5 TT sub |
| **Complement:** | — |

The rise of Japan in the 1900s spurred Dutch plans to reinforce the defences of the Netherlands (East) Indies. 1912 proposals to construct four new coast defence ships (7600t, 4–11in guns, 18kts) were clearly insufficient; their rejection by Parliament caused a political crisis, and led to the formation of a Royal Commission to study the whole question of East Indies defence. The Commission recommended the construction of nine dreadnought battleships (20,668t, 21kts, 8–13.5in, 16–5.9in, 12–75mm guns), and the Dutch Government, after slightly enlarging the recommended proposals, invited detailed designs from Germania, Blohm & Voss and Vickers. The data for the Germania design, which seemed best to meet Dutch requirements, are listed in the table; the others were generally similar. The battery in the Blohm & Voss design was too low, while the Vickers design, although having the advantage of a raised forecastle, was probably too narrow. Noteworthy features were the above-average speed and below-average belt armour, for possible gunnery duels in the generally good visibility of the Java Sea, and the strong protection against torpedoes and mines. Curiously, although recent German tests had shown shells should be stowed longitudinally to prevent detonation by a torpedo, the Germania design retained the older system of transverse stowage. Had the programme been approved, the first ship would have been laid down in December 1914 and completed in 1918. However, no decisions to place orders or even on financing the programme were taken before the events of August 1914 killed it.

## Projected *battlecruisers*

| | |
|---|---|
| **Displacement:** | 27,950t standard |
| **Dimensions:** | 777ft 8in wl × 98ft 5in × 25ft 7in |
| | *237.1m × 30.0m × 7.8m* |
| **Machinery:** | 4-shaft geared turbines, 8 Werkspoor boilers, 180,000shp = 34kts. Oil 2900t |
| **Armour:** | Belt 225mm (8.9in), bulkheads 225mm (8.9in), barbettes 250mm (9.8in), turrets 250mm–100mm (9.8in–3.9in), torpedo bulkheads 40mm (1.6in), decks 100mm, 30mm (3.9in, 1.2in) |
| **Armament:** | 9–11in (280mm)/45 (3 × 3), 12–4.7in (120mm)/45 (6 × 2), 14–40mm AA (7 × 2), 8–20mm AA |
| **Complement:** | 1050 |

Three battlecruisers were proposed for the reinforcement of the East Indies Squadron in 1939 and authorised in February 1940. They were intended to strengthen the cruiser and destroyer force and support them against the more powerful and numerous Japanese cruisers which, in particular, outclassed the existing Dutch cruisers. The first was to have been completed in 1944 but the German invasion halted all further development of the class. German assistance was initially sought for design work and the first proposal was for ships very similar to the *Scharnhorst* class and armed with the same 280mm guns in three triple turrets. Displacement was 27,500t standard, speed 33kts with 155,000shp and secondary armament 8–120mm (4 × 2). Subsequently the design was enlarged (with the particulars given above) to include more powerful machinery arranged on the unit system, necessitating two funnels instead of one, and two more twin 120mm mountings; the German main armament was retained. The side armour was sloped to increase its angle of impact with projectiles. A 100mm main deck joined the tops of the side armour while a 30mm splinter deck, sloped at the sides to join the bottom of the belt, was provided below it. Underwater protection was provided by wing compartments divided longitudinally and bounded on the inboard side by a 40mm bulkhead. The outboard side extended beyond the base of the belt to form a slight bulge giving a hull section reminiscent of the British *Repulse* and *Renown*. In general the ships, if built, would have been contemporaries of the US *Alaska* class which they resembled in size, speed, armament and concept.

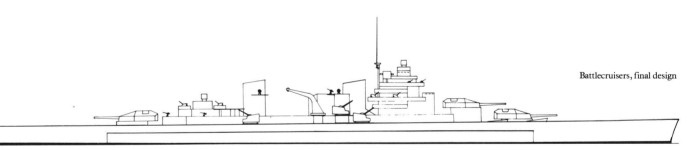

Battlecruisers, final design

# Russia

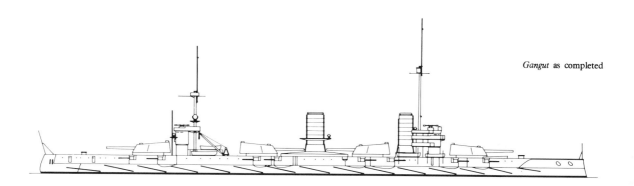

*Gangut* as completed

Despite strong opposition from the Duma, the first Russian dreadnoughts were authorised at the end of 1908 by the Czar Nicholas II. Their principal characteristics had been worked out during 1906–7 by the Naval Staff and provided for 21.5kt battleships armed with 12-12in in triple turrets and 16-120mm in casemates. Because of lack of experience, tenders for the design were invited in early 1908. In response 6 Russian and 21 foreign yards and designers presented a total of 51 designs. The German Blohm and Voss Yd design was considered the best one by the Naval Technical Committee while the Naval General Staff preferred that presented by Cuniberti. The latter was rejected however on the grounds that the 120mm guns were placed in turrets and not in casemates as had been required.

The prospects of an order for battleships from Germany attracted political opposition in both Russia and France. The Russian Prime Minister decided to purchase the German drawings while the battleships themselves were to be built in Russia according to a design of the Baltic Yd. The design had to be re-worked completely and the assistance of the British John Brown Yd was utilised together with design material received from abroad as far as possible. Finally the compromise between battleship and battlecruiser (called Baltic-dreadnought at that time) was achieved, strongly reflecting Cuniberti's ideas in the general layout.

The four triple turrets with the excellent Obukhov 12in pieces placed on the centreline, gave an effective

## GANGUT class *battleships*

| | |
|---|---|
| **Displacement:** | 23,360t normal; 25,850t full load |
| **Dimensions:** | 590ft 6in wl, 594ft 6in oa × 87ft 3in × 27ft 6in mean, 30ft 2in max |
| | *180.0m, 181.2m × 26.6m × 8.4m, 9.2m* |
| **Machinery:** | 4-shaft Parsons turbines, 25 Yarrow boilers, 42,000shp = 23kts. Oil fuel 1170t max, coal 3000t max |
| **Armour:** | Belt 225mm–100mm (8.9in–3.9in), decks 76mm–38mm (3in–1.5in), barbettes 200mm (7.9in), turrets 305mm–203mm (12in–8in), CT 250mm (9.8in) |
| **Armament:** | 12-12in (305mm)/52 (4 × 3), 16-4.7in (120mm)/50, 4-47mm, 4-18in (457mm) TT (sub) |
| **Complement:** | 1126 |

| Name | Builder | Laid down | Launched | Comp | Fate |
|---|---|---|---|---|---|
| GANGUT | Admiralty Yd, St Petersburg | 16.6.09 | 7.10.11 | 12.14 | BU 1958–59 |
| PETROPAVLOVSK | Baltic Yd, St Petersburg | 16.6.09 | 9.9.11 | 12.14 | Constructive total loss 23.9.41 |
| POLTAVA | Admiralty Yd, St Petersburg | 16.6.09 | 10.7.11 | 17.12.14 | Stricken 1925 |
| SEVASTOPOL | Baltic Yd, St Petersburg | 16.6.09 | 27.6.11 | 17.11.14 | BU 1957 |

broadside a third heavier than in contemporary British and German capital ships. Positioning of the 120mm battery was not so successful as the casemates had been arranged immediately below the 12in muzzles.

The powerplant consisted of two groups of boiler rooms separated by B turret, while the machinery room was placed abaft the Y mounting. Introduction of the light Yarrow boilers instead of the Belleville ones, in common use in the Russian battlefleet, allowed an increase of speed of 1.5kts, giving a 2kts–3kts margin over other dreadnoughts. The high speed achieved (*Poltava* developed 52,000shp = 24.3kts on 24,000t displacement

during trials) involved substantial weight penalties for the power and sacrifices had to be made in the armour.

As a result of Russo-Japanese War experience it was decided to extend the armour over the whole hull area, as had been done in the revised *Andrei Pervozvanni* design. Because of this the belt was 1in–3in thinner than in other 12in gun capital ships building at that time. The belt covered the hull from the level of the main deck to 5½ft below the normal load waterline where it tapered to 6in. Beyond the end turrets the belt was reduced to 4in–5in. The sides above the main deck were given 5in armour (reduced to 3in forward of

the bow casemates), while additional protection against fragments of shell from AP projectiles penetrating the belt was provided by a longitudinal 1.5in–1in bulkhead placed 11ft inboard from the outer plating (reports that this bulkhead was 3in–4in cannot be confirmed). The horizontal armour consisted of a 1in–1.5in armoured deck, inclined to the lower edge of the main belt. The main deck was covered with 1in plates while the upper deck reached 1½in. The funnel uptakes received 3in armour while the turret roofs and both CTs 3in and 4¾in respectively. The bow 4in armoured bulkhead was placed immediately forward the bow turret while the after

*Poltava* about 1917.
CPL

4in–5in bulkhead was positioned abaft the rudders. The underwater protection was provided by the 4ft double bottom which reached as far as the armoured deck. The 1½in torpedo bulkheads were constructed as extensions of the longitudinal ones.

The longitudinal construction of the main members of the hull and use of high tensile steel throughout caused much inconvenience for the designers. In the summer of 1910 doubts had arisen about the hull's general strength and building had to be stopped for a time to introduce necessary corrections. Other unusual features included provision of an ice-breaking

bow and cage masts. The latter were abandoned during construction in favour of pole ones after excessive vibrations had been experienced during trials of the *Andrei Pervozvanni* class.

The design faults and shipyard shortcomings as well as inertia in the state bureaucracy delayed completion of the ships by 2 years which made the class obsolescent and outclassed by the advent of 13.5in gun battleships. Building costs soared by 29 million roubles for each ship, sufficient to obtain 2 similar ships from abroad in 1912. After completion the four ships formed the First Battleship Division

operating from Helsingfors (Helsinki). They were not to be risked unnecessarily and the strategic plans proposed their employment in defence of the Nargen-Porkalla-Udd position at the entrance to the Gulf of Finland. Subsequently their service was restricted to confined waters, only *Gangut* and *Petropavlovsk* ventured as far as Gotland when screening minelaying forces.

The *Gangut* class did not incorporate numerous changes during the First World War. The most noticeable was omission of 4–47mm, one planned atop each turret, and only during 1917 did all ships receive 4 light AA guns

placed in pairs on the outermost turrets (*Poltava* and *Sevastopol* 75mm ones, the others 63mm pieces). The torpedo nets were removed by the end of 1916 and at that time the director control of the Geisler system was introduced for the main guns and placed on both CTs instead of the large rangefinders.

After the February Revolution the crews succumbed to Bolshevik agitation, and during July/August 1917 the First Battleship Division came under Bolshevik control. With other ships stationed at Helsingfors the dreadnoughts were demobilised in January 1918 and three months later they were evacuated to Kronstadt. Owing to lack of maintenance and trained crews, only *Petropavlovsk* could be commissioned in the Red Navy (November 1918), participating in the Civil War with the Active Squadron of the Baltic Fleet. Her 12in gunfire covered the retreat of Soviet minesweepers into Kronstadt, forcing British destroyers to break off their pursuit on 31 May 1919. On 17 August she was claimed sunk in shallow water by three torpedoes from the British *CMB 31* and *CMB 88*, but Soviet sources state she was undamaged by the attack, the torpedoes passing under the keel and exploding against the quayside.

The remaining three were laid up at the end of 1918. Because of total negligence, a fire which broke out in *Poltava*'s forward boiler room on 24 November 1919 damaged the ship so severely that she was found not worth repairing. It was decided in 1925 to disarm her and expend her for experimental purposes, but three years later plans were changed again and repairs started. However, work proceeded slowly and after the construction of new battleships was decided in the mid-1930s, *Poltava* was once again hulked, and used as a stationary bar-

*Oktyabrskaya Revoluciya* (ex-*Gangut*) with *Marat* (ex-*Petropavlovsk*) behind, about 1935. *CPL*

racks at Leningrad while being cannibalised piecemeal for spare parts. The hulk was towed to Kronstadt in 1941 and expended as a blockship, raised in 1944 and BU by the mid-1950s. Persistent reports that she was renamed *Frunze* in 1926 cannot be confirmed.

After the Civil War, the remaining ships were in desperate need of repairs; *Marat* (ex-*Petropavlovsk* from 31 May 1921), being in the best condition, was recommissioned in 1922 with 6–75mm AA mounted in threes on the foremost turrets and a light rangefinder platform added on the foremast, followed by *Parizhskaya Kommuna* (ex-*Sevastopol* from 31 March 1921) in 1923. The latter was quickly taken in hand for a refit; she was recommissioned again on 17 September 1925 with a clipper bow, forefunnel raised and curved aft, an additional rangefinder and augmented AA armament. *Gangut* was renamed *Oktyabrskaya Revoluciya* on 27 May 1925 and was recommissioned on 23 March 1926. *Parizhskaya Kommuna* was transferred to the Black Sea 1929–30.

After their 1930s modernisation, all three battleships appeared with a clipper bow, an additional forecastle deck added, forefunnels heightened and curved aft, an enlarged bridge, improved fire control, heavy masts, and cranes for handling seaplanes or light MTBs. The mixed-firing boilers originally fitted were replaced by oil-fired units, *Oktyabraskaya Revoluciya* being re-engined with the turbines probably intended for the battlecruiser *Izmail*. *Parizhskaya Kommuna* was fitted with bulges. Both battleships of the Baltic Fleet undertook shore bombardment during the Winter War with Finland in 1939–40. Shortly before the German invasion some 120mm guns were removed (2 from *Oktyabraskaya Revoluciya*, 4 from *Parizhskaya Kommuna*, ? from *Marat*) together with the large cranes and seaplanes so that the AA armament could be augmented to 6–3in/55 and 36–13.2mm (*Parizhskaya Kommuna* 16–13.2mm) MG. After the outbreak of war all three ships were used as floating batteries, their crews being reduced by one-third and some 120mm guns removed for ground defence.

*Marat* was damaged 23.9.41 by bombers from *Stukageschwader* 2 in Kronstadt; the forward part of the hull as far back as the forefunnel was submerged, but as the rest of the hull remained above water the ship was used as a gun battery, reverting to her original name of *Petropavlovsk* in 1943. After the war she was towed to Leningrad and reclassified as the artillery ship *Volkhov*; BU from 1952. *Oktyabrskaya Revoluciya* was heavily damaged by German bombers in Kronstadt 21.9.41; towed to Leningrad for repairs, she was again bombed 4.4.42. However, she was serviceable once more by November 1942 and took part in the Soviet offensive off Leningrad in 1944. Her armament by now consisted of 12–12in, 10–120mm, 6–3in AA, 10–0.5in MG, 89–0.3in MG and 4–450mm TT, and she carried a crew of 1411. By the end of the war she received 8–3in AA in twin mounts, 16–37mm AA with protective shields and type 279 air warning radar supplied by the British. She was used as a training ship after the war, being reported operational in 1950 and at Kronstadt from at least November 1954; superstructure and turrets were being removed in July 1956, and the hulk was last reported in May 1958. *Parizshkaya Kommuna* was employed 1941–42 in coastal bombardment duty but following bomb damage was withdrawn to Poti and remained there until the end of hostilities in the Black Sea, reverting to her original name of *Sevastopol* in 1943. In 1944 she had 12–12in, 12–120mm, 6–3in AA, 12–37mm AA and 14–0.5in MG, with a crew of 1546. British Type 290/291 air warning radar was installed. She became a training ship after the war and was BU at her name port (also reported in existence but inactive 1958).

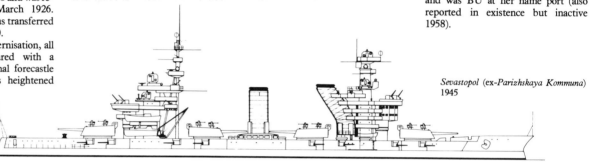

*Sevastopol (ex-Parizhskaya Kommuna)*
1945

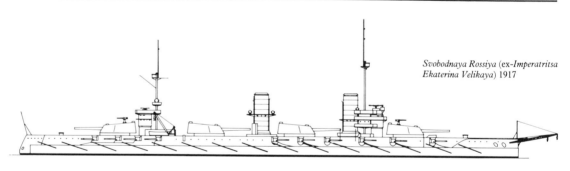

*Svobodnaya Rossiya (ex-Imperatritsa Ekaterina Velikaya) 1917*

Authorised under the 1911 Programme. The preliminary characteristics issued by the Technical Committee provided for 20,000t, 20.5kt battleships armed with 12in guns. The Naval Staff rejected this idea and demanded 14in, 22kt ships to follow development trends of the day and to counter the *Reshadieh* class battleships ordered by Turkey. Unfortunately for the Russians, the 14in guns were then only in the earliest stage of development in the Obukhov Works and it was therefore decided to mount 12in to avoid delays. The general layout was modelled on the *Gangut* class, but the new capital ships were to be pure battleships unlike the previous class and with protection substantially improved. The 11in belt was backed by a 2in longitudinal bulkhead extended down to form the armoured torpedo bulkhead. The horizontal armour remained the same as in the previous class while special attention was paid to

## IMPERATRITSA MARIYA class *battleships*

| | |
|---|---|
| **Displacement:** | 22,600t normal (*Ekaterina II* 23,783t); 24,000t full load (24,960t) |
| **Dimensions:** | 550ft 6in oa (*Ekaterina II* 557ft) × 89ft 6in (91ft 6in) × 27ft 6in |
| | *167.8m (169.8m) × 27.3m (27.9m) × 8.4m* |
| **Machinery:** | 4-shaft Parsons (*Volya* Brown-Curtis) turbines, 20 Yarrow boilers, 26,500shp (*Ekaterina II* 27,000shp) = 21kts. Oil fuel 720t, coal 3000t max |
| **Armour:** | Belt 280mm–127mm (11in–5in), decks 76mm (3in), barbettes 254mm (10in), turrets 305mm (12in), CT 305mm (12in) |
| **Armament:** | 12–12in (305mm)/52 (4×3), 20 (*Volya* 18)–5.1in (130mm)/55, 8–75mm, 4–47mm, 4 MG, 4–18in (457mm) TT (sub) |
| **Complement:** | 1220 |

| Name | Builder | Laid down | Launched | Comp | Fate |
|---|---|---|---|---|---|
| IMPERATRITSA MARIYA | Russud Yd, Nikolayev | 30.10.11 | 1.11.13 | 6.7.15 | Lost 20.10.16 |
| VOLYA (ex-*Imperator Aleksandr III*) | Russud Yd, Nikolayev | 30.10.11 | 15.4.14 | 28.6.17 | Sold 1924 |
| IMPERATRITSA EKATERINA VELIKAYA (ex-*Ekaterina II*) | Naval Yd, Nikolayev | 30.10.11 | 6.6.14 | 18.10.15 | Sunk 18.6.18 |

turret protection. The medium battery of the newly introduced 130mm/55 guns was placed in casemates covered with 5in armour. Disposition of casemates showed signs of improvement as compared with the *Gangut* class but interference with the main calibre guns was not avoided in all cases.

Financial problems hampered Naval Staff requirements, and the speed was reduced to 21kts and the displacement limited to 21,500t normal. The same reason caused abandonment of the 1911 proposals for 24kts and increased protection. The authorised displacement was increased by 1100t to fulfil requirements already settled on, while *Imperatritsa Ekaterina* exceeded twice this figure. Such a divergence between her and the remaining pair was due to the various supervisory firms of the Russud Yd and Naval Yd, backed by John Brown and Vickers respectively. Initially cage masts were planned but pole ones were fitted instead.

The first pair was completed in 1915 (*Ekaterina II* was renamed on 27 June 1915) with their light guns outfit varying from the designed one in the light of war experience. *Imperatritsa Mariya* received only 4–75mm AA mounted one atop each turret while *Imperatritsa Ekaterina Velikaya* had one 75mm AA mounted atop the forward turret with 2 other pieces placed atop the after turret, one on each side of the roof. Commissioning of 2 dreadnoughts shifted the balance of power in the Black Sea to the Russian side and enabled the Black Sea Fleet to bombard the Turkish and Bulgarian shore installations. *Imperatritsa Mariya* capsized at Sevastopol as a result of internal explosions caused by unstable propellant. The wreck was raised in 1918 and broken up in 1922.

Despite being given top priority in July 1915, *Imperator Aleksandr III* entered service only after the February Revolution, being renamed *Volya* on 29 April 1917, while *Imperatritsa*

*Ekaterina Velikaya* became *Svobodnaya Rossiya* on the same day. *Volya* varied from the prototype in details, having an AA armament consisting of 4–75mm placed one by one atop the foremost turrets on the centreline, while the forward casemate on either side was plated over. This was introduced when it became evident that *Imperatritsa Mariya* had a tendency when in a seaway to ship a large amount of water through her forward casemates. The hull of *Svobodnaya Rossiya* being 7ft longer presented no such problems so the forward 130mm guns were retained. After the October Revolution *Svobodnaya Rossiya* went over to the Bolshevik side and in April 1918 followed the order to leave Sevastopol for Novorossisk to escape the advancing Germans. When Novorossisk fell the destroyer *Kerch* sank her with torpedoes. *Volya* on the contrary flew the Independent Ukraine colours from 29 April 1918, but being forced

by the Bolshevik ships to leave Sevastopol returned there two weeks later to be seized by the Germans, who commissioned her on 15 October 1918 as *Volya* (not *Wolga* as was erroneously stated by most sources). She was able to perform only one trial cruise off the Bosphorus and in November 1918 passed under British control. In April 1919 she was sent to Izmid in Turkey to prevent capture by the Reds. She was transferred to Wrangel's fleet on 17 October and commissioned as *General Alekseev*, performing well until the capitulation in the Crimea. To Bizerta after the White collapse in October 1920, decommissioned 1924, BU by 1936 by the French.

*Imperator Aleksandr III* as completed.
CPL

## IMPERATOR NIKOLAI I *battleship*

**Displacement:** 27,300t normal
**Dimensions:** 616ft 9in oa, 597ft wl × 94ft 9in × 29ft 6in
*188.0m, 182.0m × 28.9m × 8.0m*
**Machinery:** 4-shaft Brown Curtiss turbines, 20 Yarrow boilers, 27,300shp = 21kts. Oil fuel 720t, coal 2300t
**Armour:** Belt 305mm–100mm (12in–3.9in), decks 102mm (4in), barbettes 254mm (10in), turrets 305mm (12in), CT 305mm (12in)
**Armament:** 12-12in (305mm)/52 (4 × 3), 20-5.1in (130mm)/55, 8-75mm, 4-47mm, 4-18in (457mm) TT
**Complement:** 1252

| Name | Builder | Laid down | Launched | Comp | Fate |
|------|---------|-----------|----------|------|------|
| IMPERATOR NIKOLAI I | Russud Yd, Nikolayev | 28.1.15 | 18.10.16 | — | BU incomplete 1923/4 |

Authorised in June 1914 to counter the additional Turkish battleship purchased from Brazil. She was practically a repeat of the *Imperatritsa Mariya* class with the protection increased by 50 per cent in weight proportions. The main belt was backed by a 3in longitudinal bulkhead that was extended down to form the torpedo bulkhead. The 1½in armoured deck was overhung by the 2½in battery deck while the casemates had 3in protection only. At an early stage a changeover to 14in guns was considered but rejected for the same reasons as for the previous class. Later during the war even 8–16in in four turrets were proposed but it was not certain where such guns would be obtained. As a result of war experience the light guns outfit was changed to 4–4in AA. Being known under the false name *Ivan Grozni* to confuse the enemy she received secondary priority in July 1915 when the failure of Turkish plans to strengthen their battlefleet became evident. She was renamed *Demokratiya* on 29 April 1917 and her incomplete hull fell into German hands in February 1918 and was destroyed by the Allies in 1919 to prevent completion by the Reds.

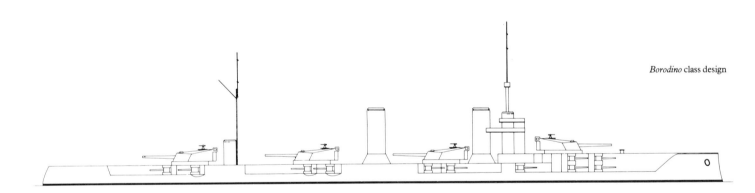

*Borodino* class design

## BORODINO class *battlecruisers*

**Displacement:** 32,500t normal; 38,000t full load
**Dimensions:** 728ft pp, 750ft oa × 100ft × 33ft 6in
*221.9m, 228.6m × 30.5m × 10.2m*
**Machinery:** 4-shaft Parsons turbines, 25 Yarrow boilers, 68,000shp = 26.5kts. Oil fuel 1575 max, coal 1950t max
**Armour:** Belt 238mm–100mm (9.4in–3.9in), deck 60mm (2.4in), barbettes 248mm (9.8in), turrets 305mm (12in), CT 400mm (15.7in)
**Armament:** 12-14in (356mm)/52 (4 × 3), 24-5.1in (130mm)/55, 8-75mm, 4-63mm AA, 4 MG, 6-21in (533mm) TT (sub)
**Complement:** *c*1250

| Name | Builder | Laid down | Launched | Comp | Fate |
|------|---------|-----------|----------|------|------|
| BORODINO | Admiralty Yd, St Petersburg | 19.12.13 | 1.7.15 | — | BU incomplete 1923 |
| IZMAIL | Baltic Yd, St Petersburg | 19.12.13 | 27.6.15 | — | BU incomplete 1931 |
| KINBURN | Baltic Yd, St Petersburg | 19.12.13 | 30.10.15 | — | BU incomplete 1923 |
| NAVARIN | Admiralty Yd, St Petersburg | 19.12.13 | 9.11.16 | — | BU incomplete 1923 |

Authorised under the 1912 Programme for deployment with the Baltic Fleet. The preliminary characteristics provided for 28kt battlecruisers armed with 9-14in guns in 3 triple turrets. The increased main armament calibre stemmed from rumours about the same move in the German Navy. In 1912 the fourth triple turret was added and speed reduced by 1.5kts to the same as the German battlecruisers. At that time emphasis was laid on standardisation of silhouette with the *Gangut* class dreadnoughts. The latter's flush deck hull had to be abandoned in favour of a raised forecastle for higher speed. Although designated battlecruisers, the new ships were better armoured than the *Gangut* class, but were still inferior to contemporary German battlecruisers. The designers did not avoid repeating

the *Gangut* class error of placing 130mm casemates directly below the heavy turrets.

Unfortunately for themselves, the Russians tried to expedite construction of the *Borodino* class by ordering turbines abroad, those of *Navarin* from Vulkan, Germany and those of *Kinburn* (?) from Parsons, England. After August 1914 they had to be re-ordered from the Franco-Russian Works as had been done originally for the remaining pair. The Germans used the confiscated turbines from *Navarin* in the minelaying cruisers *Bremse* and *Brummer*. The shortage of materials and labour problems forced the Russians to concentrate on construction of *Izmail* only after June 1915, while the others were given lower priority. Development and production of 14in/52 Model 1912 guns in

the Obukhov Works encountered numerous problems despite Vicker's assistance. Later during the First World War proposals were made to replace them with the well-proven 12in/52 apparently because of delays in completing the 14in pieces.

At the beginning of 1917 construction of the less advanced trio was suspended while *Izmail* was scheduled for completion at the beginning of 1918. Because of the Bolshevik Revolution, work on *Izmail* practically stopped and she was laid up. Her three sisters were sold to Germany in 1922 while concrete plans about completion and modernisation of *Izmail* were considerd (completion as an aircraft carrier was proposed also) in the late 1920s but were not carried out.

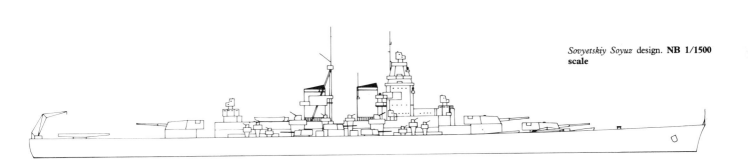

## SOVYETSKIY SOYUZ class *battleships*

**Displacement:** 58,220t standard; 64,120t deep load
**Dimensions:** 856ft 4in wl, 889ft 1in oa × 119ft 5in wl, 127ft 7in ext × 33ft 6in
*261.0m, 271.0m × 36.4m, 38.9m × 10.2m*
**Machinery:** 3-shaft geared turbines, 12 boilers, 231,000shp = 28kts
**Armour:** Belt 425mm–375mm (16.7in-14.8in), decks 25mm (1in) upper, 150mm (5.9in) main, 50mm (2in) lower, turrets 495mm (19.5in) face, CT 425mm (16.7in)
**Armament:** 9–16in (406mm)/50 (3 × 3), 12–6in (152mm)/57 (6 × 2), 8–3.9in (100mm)/56 AA (4 × 2), 32–37mm AA (16 × 2), 8–0.5mm MG, 4 aircraft
**Complement:** ?

| Name | Builder | Laid down | Launched | Comp | Fate |
|---|---|---|---|---|---|
| SOVYETSKAYA BYELORUSSIYA | 402 Yd | 28.11.39 | — | — | BU 1945–46 |
| SOVYETSKIY SOYUZ | Ordzhonikidze Yd | 28.8.38 | (11.41) | — | BU 1948–49 |
| SOVYETSKAYA UKRAINA | Marti Yd, Nikolayev | 28.11.38 | (11.42) | — | BU 1946 |

Four ships of this class were authorised on 21.1.38 by the Council for Work and Defence, despite the fact that their displacement exceeded the limit allowed by the 1936 London Naval Treaty; data as supplied on 5 September 1938 under the terms of the Anglo-Soviet Naval Agreement were displacement 44,190t standard, dimen-

sions 242.0m × 36.3m × 8.9m, 150,000shp = 29kts, 9-16in, 12-6in, 12-3.9in, 20-3in guns, 2 aircraft. Commissioning was initially planned for 1941, but progress fell behind schedule. The general characteristics were sketched by Admiral I S Isakov; the design, which was influenced by the Ansaldo project 'UP 41' supplied

in 1936, was known as 'Project 23' and was modified several times after the keels had been laid down. The Pugliese system was chosen for underwater protection as well as a triple bottom. The heavy AA armament was a remarkable feature for its time but it seems to reflect the lack of air cover that could be expected for these ships.

Design assistance was also obtained from the US firm Gibbs & Cox from 1936, but subsequent attempts by the Soviet Government to obtain 16in guns and mountings, ammunition and armour plate from the USA (and in 1937 even a complete battleship) were unsuccessful, negotiations ending in September 1939. The American influence on the design was less marked that the Italian.

On 3 units were laid down – *Sovyetskiy Soyuz* for the Baltic Fleet, *Sovyetskaya Ukraina* for the Black Sea Fleet, and *Sovyetskaya Byelorussiya* for the Northern Fleet. The fourth ship, *Sovyetskaya Rossiya*, was planned for the Molotovsk 402 Yd but construction advanced no further than the collection of material at the Marti Yd in Nikolayev; construction was cancelled in 1940.

Material for *Sovyetskaya Byelorussiya* had been supplied by the Baltic Works in Leningrad. Construction work on the three hulls was practically halted late in 1940, despite the fact that the hulls for the first pair were well advanced. In June 1941, *Sovyetskiy Soyuz* was nearly ready for launching (proposed launch dates are given in the table), with armour and turbines, but not turrets, in place. The hull was slightly damaged in the fighting, and materials were removed for use ashore. There were hopes of completing the ship after the war, but the rusty hull was BU in 1948–49. The hull of *Sovyetskaya Ukraina*, two-thirds complete and 75% ready for launching, was captured by the Germans at Nikolayev, only having been slightly damaged by the withdrawing Soviet forces. The Germans considered the launching of the hull but this plan was abandoned, and some of the material and that from two destroyer hulls was used to build the troopships *Totila* and *Teia*. The slip, with the remains of the hull, was damaged by the Germans before their evacuation of Nikolayev, and all three hulls were dismantled on the slipways during the late 1940s.

Four turbine sets were ordered from Brown, Boveri, of Switzerland, and three were delivered; further sets were built in the Soviet Union.

The armour plating for at least one ship and two or possibly three gun turrets were constructed at Leningrad, but the latter were never fitted. The prototype 16in gun was completed in 1940 and underwent extensive trials. Although not initially an unqualified success, it was used against the Germans from August 1941 at ranges up to 46km. Three more guns, under construction in June 1941, were not completed.

## KRONSHTADT class *large cruisers*

| | |
|---|---|
| **Displacement:** | 34,680t standard; 37,750t deep load |
| **Dimensions:** | 780ft 0in wl, 813ft 8in oa × 103ft × 29ft 10in |
| | *238.0m, 248.0m × 31.4m × 9.1m* |
| **Machinery:** | 4-shaft geared turbines, 231,000shp = 33kts |
| **Armour:** | Belt 230mm (9in), deck 90mm (3.5in), turrets 305mm (12in) |
| **Armament:** | 9–12in (305mm) (3 × 3), 8–6in (152mm)/57 (4 × 2), 8–3.9in (100mm)/56 (4 × 2), 24–37mm AA (6 × 4), 8–0.5in MG, 4 aircraft |
| **Complement:** | ? |

| Name | Builder | Laid down | Launched | Comp | Fate |
|---|---|---|---|---|---|
| KRONSHTADT | Marti Yd, Leningrad | 15.7.39 | — | — | BU 1950s |
| SEVASTOPOL | Marti Yd, Nikolayev | 1939 | — | — | BU 1940s |

These ships were authorised by the Council for Work Defence on 21 January 1938. The preliminary design, disregarding the Washington Treaty, called for a displacement of 22,000t, a speed of 33kts, a main armament of 9–10in guns, and a belt 5½in thick. However, the Defence Committee put forward a new requirement on 29 July 1938, presumably affected by the German *Scharnhorst* class battlecruisers. The new design was approved 12.4.40, eight months after the keel of the first unit had been laid down. Two ships were laid down; the incomplete hull of *Sevastopol* was captured by the Germans at Nikolayev and scrapped.

## ex-British ROYAL SOVEREIGN class *battleship*

The British battleship *Royal Sovereign* was temporarily transferred to the Soviet Union in order to fulfil the Soviet claim to a share of the Italian Navy. Handed over on 30 June 1944 in UK, renamed *Arkhangelsk*, and officially commissioned with the Northern Fleet on 29 August 1944, she found herself a prime target for German U-boats and midget submarines and did not venture out of the Kola Inlet until the end of hostilities in Europe. She was returned to the Royal Navy on 4 February 1949 as the Italian battleship *Giulio Cesare* had been delivered instead.

## ex-Italian CAVOUR class *battleship*

The Italian battleship *Giulio Cesare* was handed over as a war prize on 15.12.48, replacing *Royal Sovereign*. The Russians renamed her *Novorossiysk*. She is believed to have been sunk at Sevastopol on 29.10.55 by an old German ground mine or alternatively by an internal explosion. It has also been claimed, however, that she was broken up in 1955 (it is perhaps a case of confusion in that she may have been damaged by a mine or explosion and subsequently scrapped). It is further reported that the episode was the occasion for the removal of Adm Kuznetzov as Soviet Navy C-in-C; he was replaced by Adm Gorshkov.

## STALINGRAD class *battlecruisers*

| | |
|---|---|
| **Displacement:** | *c*40,000t full load |
| **Dimensions:** | 787ft 5in wl, 836ft 7in oa × 103ft × 29ft 2in |
| | *240.0m, 255.0m × 31.4m × 8.9m* |
| **Machinery:** | 210,000shp = 33kts |
| **Armament:** | 1–2 SSM launchers, 6–12in (305mm)/50 (2 × 3), 8–6in (152mm)/57 (4 × 2), 12–3.9in (100mm)/70 (6 × 2), 32–45mm/85 (8 × 4) |

| Name | Builder | Laid down | Launched | Comp | Fate |
|---|---|---|---|---|---|
| MOSKVA | Baltic | Oct 1952 | | | BU 1950s |
| STALINGRAD | Nikolayev | 1951 | 1954 | | BU 1950s |

There is no firm data on this class, but large hulls about 700ft long were reported at both Leningrad and at Nikolayev, and the Soviets themselves had referred to these ships as successors of the prewar *Kronshtadt* class. Many sources refer to a 4-ship programme as part of a 10-year building programme begun in 1950, which would have included 40 cruisers: 24 *Sverdlov*s, these 4, and 12 of a new heavy cruiser type, presumably armed either with the existing 7.1in gun or with a new 8in. The data listed is unofficial and should be treated with caution. They are probably based on the assumption that the *Stalingrad* design would be a modified version of the prewar *Kronshtadt* with better protection and AA armament. In addition it is possible that they would have been armed partly with a naval version of the land- and air-based Kennel anti-ship weapon; contemporary intelligence reports did mention a missile armament. Estimates based on the prewar design gain credence in view of the fact that both the *Sverdlov* and *Skory* designs were direct modifications of prewar types.

# Spain

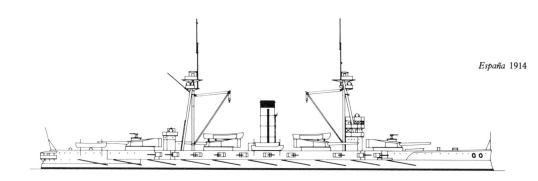

*España* 1914

These ships were authorised by the Navy Law of 7 January 1908 and built by the SECN syndicate; they were the smallest battleships of the dreadnought type ever constructed, the speed, protection and freeboard (about 15ft amidships) being well below average. To avoid rebuilding existing docks, they were built shorter than if a fully rational design were possible. The main belt was 6ft 7in deep (2ft above water) and extended between the end barbettes. The Bullivant net defence was fitted. For the end 12in turrets, the arcs of fire were about 270°, and for the echelon turrets 180° and 80°; the guns were 24ft 6in above water, manoeuvred by hydraulic power, with all-round loading at any elevation. The Vickers-type directors were in the lower top on each mast. *Jaime I* first went to sea in 1917, but her completion was much delayed by non-delivery of material, particularly armament, from Britain 1914–19. *España* hit an uncharted reef off Cape

## ESPAÑA class *battleships*

| | |
|---|---|
| **Displacement:** | 15,452t normal; 15,700t max |
| **Dimensions:** | 435ft wl, 459ft 2in oa × 78ft 9in × 25ft 6in max |
| | *132.6m, 140.0m × 24.0m × 7.8m* |
| **Machinery:** | 4-shaft Parsons turbines, 12 Yarrow boilers, 15,500shp = 19.5kts. Coal 900t normal, 1900t max + 20t oil. Range 5000nm/3100nm at 10kts /16.75kts |
| **Armour:** | Belt 8in–4in (203mm–102mm), upper belt 6in (152mm), barbettes 10in (254mm), gunhouses 8in (203mm), deck 1.5in (38mm), CT 10in (254mm), anti-torpedo bulkheads 1.5in (38mm) |
| **Armament:** | 8-12in (305mm)/50 (4 × 2), 20-4in (102mm)/50, 4-3pdr, 2 MG, 2 landing |
| **Complement:** | 854 |

| Name | Builder | Laid down | Launched | Comp | Fate |
|---|---|---|---|---|---|
| ESPAÑA | Ferrol DYd | 6.12.09 | 5.2.12 | 23.10.13 | Wrecked 26.8.23 |
| ALFONSO XIII | Ferrol DYd | 23.2.10 | 7.5.13 | 16.8.15 | Mined 30.4.37 |
| JAIME I | Ferrol DYd | 5.2.12 | 21.9.14 | 20.12.21 | Lost 17.6.37 |

Tres Forcas (Morocco), near Melilla, in dense fog. *Alfonso XIII* (renamed *España* in April 1931) was laid up at Ferrol in 1934 awaiting disposal; she was refitted by the Nationalists in 1936 after an attempt by the crew to join the

Republic had been thwarted, but drifted onto a mine laid by her own side off Cape Penas, near Santander, and sank. The Republican *Jaime I* (or *Jaime Primero*) suffered an accidental magazine explosion and caught fire

while under repair (following bomb damage) at Cartagena, and was scuttled; although refloated in 1938, she was officially discarded on 3 July 1939 as beyond economic repair, and was BU 1939–40.

## Projected *battleships*

| | |
|---|---|
| **Displacement:** | *c*21,000t normal |
| **Machinery:** | 4-shaft Parsons turbines = *c*21kts |
| **Armament:** | 8-13.5in (343mm)/45 (4 × 2), 20-6in (152mm) |

The construction of three battleships, A (possibly to have been named *Reina Victoria Eugenia*), B and C was proposed in 1913; they were to be laid down in 1914–15 and completed in 1920. The World War caused the

whole project to be abandoned; full particulars are not available, but the ships would probably have resembled contemporary British practice, with two closely-spaced funnels and superimposed turrets fore and aft.

*Jaime I.* Date unknown.
CPL

# Turkey

## RESHADIEH class *battleships*

**Displacement:** 23,000t (normal); 24,700t (*Fatih*, normal)
**Dimensions:** 525ft pp, 559ft 6in oa × 91ft 7in × 28ft 10in (design)
*160.0m, 170.5m × 27.9m × 8.8m*
565ft oa × 90ft × ? (*Fatih*)
*172.2m × 27.4m × ?m*
**Machinery:** 4-shaft Parsons turbines, 15 Babcock & Wilcox boilers, 26,500shp = 21kts (designed), 27,500shp = 21kts (*Fatih*, designed)
**Armour:** See *Erin* for particulars
**Armament:** 10–13.5in (343mm)/45 (5 × 2), 16–6in (152mm)/50, 4–3in (76mm), 4–21in (533mm) TT (as designed)

| Name | Builder | Laid down | Launched | Comp | Fate |
|------|---------|-----------|----------|------|------|
| RESHADIEH (ex-*Reshad V*) | Vickers | 1.8.11 | 3.9.13 | — | Confiscated 1.8.14 |
| RESHAD-I-HAMISS | Armstrong | 6.12.11 | — | — | Cancelled 1912 |
| FATIH | Vickers | 11.6.14 | — | — | Dismantled 1914 |

The first two ships were ordered in June 1911 by the Turkish Navy. Following the outbreak of the First Balkan War, Armstrong demanded better guarantees of payment and work was suspended, not being resumed afterwards (according to some sources the ship was never laid down, because of pressure of work at the builders). The order was cancelled, whereas work on the Vickers ship was continued, at increased pace from May 1913 onwards. *Reshadieh* was requisitioned for the Royal Navy as HMS *Erin* in August 1914, when almost complete. *Fatih* was ordered from Vickers on 29 April 1914 in reply to the Greek order for a second dreadnought. The name is from Vickers' records; Admiralty papers list her as *Sultan Mehmed Fatieh*. She was to have been delivered by 29 April 1917 and would have been a slightly enlarged *Reshadieh*, generally similar in respect of layout, armour and protection. She was dismantled on the slipway after the outbreak of war in August 1914. For further remarks, see *Erin*.

## SULTAN OSMAN I *battleship*

A 27,500t battleship laid down for Brazil as *Rio de Janeiro* on 14 September 1911 by Armstrong, bought by Turkey half finished on 9 January 1914 for £2,725,000 and construction proceeded for Turkey's account as *Sultan Osman I*. The 500-strong Turkish crew arrived on the Tyne on 27 July 1914. Handing over and start of voyage home planned for 3 August 1914 but occupied and confiscated by the Royal Navy on 2 August, then commissioned as HMS *Agincourt*.

## German MOLTKE class *battlecruiser*

The German battlecruiser *Goeben* served with the Turkish Navy, under the Turkish flag as *Yavuz Sultan Selim* from 16 August 1914, but with German command and crew; Turkish control did not become effective until 2 November 1918. *Yavuz Sultan Selim* made a 25-minute surprise bombardment of Sevastopol on 29 October 1914, firing 47-11in and 12-5.9in shells, shots that precipitated Turkey's war with Russia. Two 12in shells from a fort holed her aft funnel killing 14 men. A 12in Russian battleship shell knocked out her 3rd port 5.9in casement and ammunition in a foggy 18 November action but *Goeben* hit the battleship *Ivstafi* four times in 19 rounds of 11in. She fired 15 more at Batumi on 10 December. She was heavily damaged on 26 December 1914 by 2 Russian mines in the Bosphorus, about 2000 tons of water entering the ship, but was repaired using cofferdams. In 1915 two 150mm guns were landed and sent to the Dardanelles (she was hit by 2 12in shells in a 10 May 1915 action with the Black Sea Fleet), in 1916 the 4 aft 88mm/45 guns were replaced by 88mm AA. Again damaged by 3 British mines and bombs on 20 January 1918 during the sortie from the Dardanelles in which she sank the monitors *Raglan* and *M28*; one mine hole was repaired using a cofferdam. Altogether she fought 17 surface actions and 60 air raids, being hit by 6 12in shells, 5 mines and 3 bombs. None of the mines ruptured the anti-torpedo bulkhead. Interned at Ismit after the Allies reached Constantinople, and lay there until 1926, becoming completely unserviceable. In 1927–30 (thanks to a new 26,000t floating dock from Germany) she was overhauled, rebuilt (two British mine holes had not been fully repaired) and refitted at Ismit by A C de St-Nazaire-Penhoet. Reconstruction was delayed when the dock proved unequal to her weight, and several compartments collapsed. Revised data were: displacement 22,734t standard, draught 27ft (8.2m) mean; speed 27.1 knots on four hour trial with new boilers; armament, with new French fire control system, 10-11in, 10-5.9in, 2-88mm, 4-88mm AA, 4 MG, 2-500mm TT; complement 1300. In 1936 she was renamed *Yavuz*, received a short refit in 1938 (she took the body of Kemal Ataturk from Istanbul to Ismit in November) and was again refitted in 1941, when 4-88mm AA, 10-40mm AA and 4-20mm AA were added and the mainmast landed to make space for an AA fire control position. The final light AA armament was reported as 22-40mm, 24-20mm. From 1948 stationary at Ismit (received the hull number B70 after Turkey joined NATO in 1952), decommissioned 20 December 1960, deleted on 14 November 1964. Several attempts were made to preserve her, including an unsuccessful offer of sale to W Germany in 1963. Sold 1971, BU June 1973–February 1976.

*Yavuz Sultan Selim* (ex-*Goeben*) about 1919

# United States of America

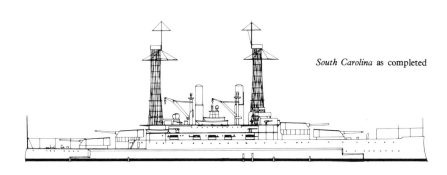

*South Carolina* as completed

## SOUTH CAROLINA class *battleships*

| | |
|---|---|
| **Displacement:** | 16,000t normal; 17,617t full load |
| **Dimensions:** | 450ft wl, 452ft 9in oa × 80ft 5in × 24ft 7in |
| | *137.2m, 138.0m × 24.5m × 7.5m* |
| **Machinery:** | 2-shaft VTE, 12 Babcock & Wilcox boilers, 16,500ihp = 18.5kts. Range 5000nm at 10kts |
| **Armour:** | Belt 10in–8in (254mm–203mm); 12in–10in/305mm–254mm over magazines, 11in–9in/279mm–229mm over machinery), casemate 10in–8in (254mm–203mm), barbettes 10in–8in (254mm–203mm), turret faces 12in (305mm), CT 12in (305mm), decks 2.5in (64mm), 2in–1.5in (51mm–38mm) |
| **Armament:** | 8-12in (305mm)/45 (4 × 2), 22-3in (76mm)/50, 2-21in (533mm) TT sub (beam) |
| **Complement:** | 869 |

| No | Name | Builder | Laid down | Launched | Comp | Fate |
|---|---|---|---|---|---|---|
| BB26 | SOUTH CAROLINA | Cramp | 18.12.06 | 11.7.08 | 1.3.10 | Stricken 1924 |
| BB27 | MICHIGAN | New York SB | 17.12.06 | 26.5.08 | 4.1.10 | Stricken 1923 |

The first US single-calibre battleships, they actually preceded HMS *Dreadnought* in design, but not in construction. They were the last American battleships, restricted to 16,000t by Congressional mandate, and they conformed to the speed standard of earlier American battleships, 18kts. As a result, they could not operate tactically with the later dreadnoughts, and were often listed with the pre-dreadnoughts. They did not, for example, serve with the later ships in European waters during World War One.

Their concept resulted from gunnery advances, largely due to then-Captain William S Sims. The Bureau of Construction and Repair (C & R) was asked to design a new type of battleship in 1904, and Sims and his colleagues found the bureau much too slow to act; that was probably the origin of the reform movement which, four years later, made the General Board responsible for ship characteristics. Very little of the design background of the class has survived, possibly in part because C&R itself found the episode so embarrassing.

It appears that the bureau's initial approach was a relatively conventional design with twin 12in turrets on the centreline fore and aft, and four single turrets replacing the twin 8in mounts of earlier pre-dreadnoughts. These designs apparently encountered severe structural problems, presumably particularly because Congress limited new battleships to a maximum of 16,000t. Chief Constructor Washington L Capps then chose the radical superfiring arrangement for which the ships were subsequently known. In March 1907 it was tested aboard the monitor *Florida*: one of the two 12in guns in the ship's turret was removed and mounted to superfire above and behind, and a dummy wooden gun mounted in its place; animals and then men were place in the turret to test the blast effects of superfiring. By this time *South Carolina* could not really have been altered; presumably the issue was whether the ship could fire four guns ahead or astern.

This class also introduced the cage masts characteristics of US dread-

mast was tested aboard the monitor *Florida* in May 1908, and adopted for the entire fleet that summer. The two ships served in the 1914 Vera Cruz incident.

Both ships were considered heavy rollers. This tendency probably con-tributed to the collapse of *Michigan*'s foremast in a gale in January 1918. Like the pre-dreadnoughts, *South Carolina* was employed as a convoy escort during 1917–18.

Both were sold off under the Washington Treaty of 1921.

*South Carolina* April 1921. *CPL*

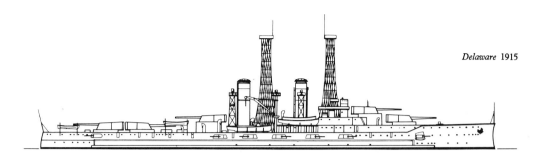

The first US battleships to match the standard of the British dreadnoughts, these ships combined the new single-calibre main battery with steam turbines, to achieve the new standard speed of about 21kts. Under the authorising Act, the Navy had to ask for private designs, comparing them with the C&R design. This procedure delayed the ships until late 1907. Although none of the private designs was even remotely satisfactory, it appears that Fore River later developed its version into what became the Argentine battleship *Rivadavia*.

The *Delaware* design was actually completed in 1905–06, the Chief Constructor producing both a 10-gun 20,500t version and a 12-gun 24,000t design. The larger ship was rejected as

## DELAWARE class *battleships*

**Displacement:** 20,380t normal; 22,060t full load (excluding 380t oil fuel)
**Dimensions:** 510ft wl, 519ft oa × 85ft 4in × 27ft 3in
*155.5m, 158.2m × 26.0m × 8.3m*
**Machinery:** 2-shaft Curtis turbines (*North Dakota* VTE), 14 Babcock & Wilcox boilers, 25,000shp = 21kts. Range *c*6000nm at 10kts
**Armour:** Belt 11in–9in (279mm–229mm), lower casemate 10in–8in (254mm–203mm), upper casemate 5in (127mm), barbettes 10in–4in (254mm–102mm), turret faces 12in (305mm), CT 11.5in (292mm), decks 2in (51mm)
**Armament:** 10–12in (305mm)/45 (5 × 2), 14–5in (127mm)/50, 2–21in (533mm) TT sub (beam)
**Complement:** 933

| No | Name | Builder | Laid down | Launched | Comp | Fate |
|------|------------------|--------------|-----------|----------|---------|---------------|
| BB28 | DELAWARE | Newport News | 11.11.07 | 6.2.09 | 4.4.10 | Stricken 1924 |
| BB29 | NORTH DAKOTA | Fore River | 16.12.07 | 10.11.09 | 11.4.10 | Stricken 1931 |

*Delaware* 1918.
CPL

150 · ALL THE WORLD'S BATTLESHIPS

too expensive for the firepower it provided, even though it was ultimately shaved to 22,000t.

The 20,500t design was severely criticised. Its secondary battery was carried at gun deck (ie below main deck) level, and the two guns sponsoned out in the bows were not only wet, they also broke up the bow wave and thus wasted power. Pre-dreadnought guns similarly situated were so wet that they could not be used effectively in a seaway as the fleet learned during its World Cruise in 1907-9. Moreover, the secondary guns were entirely unprotected. In addition, steam lines passed around the magazine of No 3 turret. Although

magazine refrigeration was fitted, the magazine could not be kept cool enough, and there was a real fear that its powder might become unstable, particularly in the tropics.

In this case the first attempt was made to do away with permanent bridgework; it was hoped that, even in peacetime, the ships could be operated from within their spacious conning towers. As in the *South Carolina*s, plans originally showed a pair of military (pole) masts, with a fire control bridge slung between them, itself between the two funnels. When cage masts were adopted, the poles were relegated to the status of kingposts for boat cranes.

The two ships were competitive sisters, *Delaware* having conventional reciprocating engines, and *North Dakota* Curtis turbines. At this stage of development, the principal effect of the turbine was a sharp reduction in fuel economy at cruising speed (estimated at 45 per cent at 14kts). *Delaware*, on the other hand, was the first American battleship that could steam for 24 hours at full speed without needing repairs, even though she had to rely on earlier reciprocating engines. The American reversion to reciprocating engines several classes later is understandable in view of the concentration on very long endurance for Pacific operations. *North Dakota*

was re-engined with geared turbines in 1917.

*Delaware* served with the 6th Battle Squadron of the Grand Fleet in 1917-18. Both were retained in service until the completion of *Colorado* and *West Virginia*, then discarded in 1924. *North Dakota* became a target, and was scrapped in 1931.

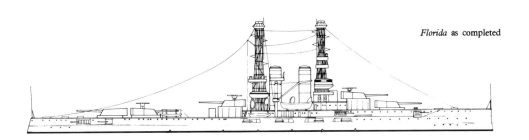

*Florida* as completed

These were essentially repeat *Delaware*s, the major change being enlargement of the machinery spaces to fit either Parsons or Curtis turbines. As a result of criticism of the *Delaware* class at the Newport Conference in 1908, this design was modified to incorporate light armour protection (in the form of an upper casemate) for its secondary battery. By way of weight compensation, the proposed 6in battery was cut back to 5in/51s, very high-powered weapons which replaced the 5in/50s of the previous class.

The two ships were the first battleships off Vera Cruz in the 1914 crisis, both landing marines and soldiers (1000) under *Florida*'s captain on 21 April for the 3 days fighting that cost 94 US casualties and hundreds of Mexican lives. *Florida* served with 6th Battle Squadron in the Grand Fleet during 1917-18, and from September 1918 *Utah* was based at Bantry Bay, Ireland.

These were the earliest US battleships retained under the Washington Naval Treaty, and both, like the four later ships of the *Wyoming* and *Texas* classes, were reconstructed in the mid-1920s, the objectives being primarily better protection (deck and underwater); in addition all were to be converted to burn oil fuel. All six ships were built to a single basic design,

## FLORIDA class *battleships*

| | |
|---|---|
| **Displacement:** | 21,825t normal; 23,033t full load |
| **Dimensions:** | 510ft wl, 521ft 8in oa × 88ft 3in × 28ft 3in |
| | *155.5m, 159.0m × 26.9m × 8.6m* |
| **Machinery:** | 4-shaft Parsons turbines, 12 Babcock & Wilcox boilers, 28,000shp = 20.75kts. Range 6720nm at 10kts |
| **Armour:** | As *Delaware* class except 1.5in (38mm) deck. STS replaced Nickel Steel (NS) for deck and turret protection |
| **Armament:** | As *Delaware* class except 16-5in (127mm)/51 |
| **Complement:** | 1001 |

| No | Name | Builder | Laid down | Launched | Comp | Fate |
|------|---------|--------------|-----------|----------|---------|--------------|
| BB30 | FLORIDA | New York N Yd | 9.3.09 | 12.5.10 | 15.9.11 | Stricken 1931 |
| BB31 | UTAH | New York SB | 15.3.09 | 23.12.09 | 31.8.11 | Sunk 7.12.41 |

which had a thin watertight 'splinter deck' at about the waterline, separating the main belt from the upper belt; upon reconstruction 3.5in was added to the second deck between the end barbettes, with local strengthening, to cover the upper belt, as in the later oil-burning battleships, and 1.75in was added to the third deck fore and aft of the main belt (the *Florida*s already had 1.5in forward on this deck). Turret and conning tower roofs, already doubled up during or just after World War I, were reinforced with an additional layer of 1.75in STS. The 3.5in deck armour consisted of two layers, only one of which was STS; however, *Utah*

had two layers of STS, the upper layer reduced to 1.25in; this deck was increased by another layer of 1.25in STS over the boilers. Both were reboilered with four oil-fired boilers originally ordered for the scrapped battleships and battlecruisers of the 1916 Programme; performance figures became 28,000shp = 21kts. An important factor in this reboilering was that it reduced the volume of the boiler rooms so that the effective depth of torpedo protection added by the bulges was considerably increased. Other revised data became: displacement (*Florida*) 21,986t standard, 27,726t full load, beam 106ft (32.3m), draught 31ft 8in

(9.6m) full load, secondary armament (12-5in/51 SP, 8-3in (76mm)/50 AA, complement 1171.

An essential objective of modernisation was the provision of aircraft, using a catapult on the midships turret; this required the elimination of the mainmast. Although the Forces Afloat demanded two fire control positions, this was not possible for the *Utah*s, which had to make do with the foremast position. Plans to increase the elevation of the main armament from 15 degrees were cancelled after Britain protested.

Advantage was taken of modernisation to re-site the hull secondary bat-

*Utah* July 1930.
*CPL*

*Utah* as an AA training ship, August 1941.
*CPL*

teries, which had been quite wet. However, the new bulges did not improve sea-keeping performance, and the ships remained wet; they also tended to be quite stiff. *Florida* was discarded under the 1930 London Treaty and

*Utah* was converted into a target ship. Late in the 1930s *Utah* was used to test the new US anti-aircraft guns and fire control systems; she was sunk by two torpedoes while serving in this capacity at Pearl Harbour.

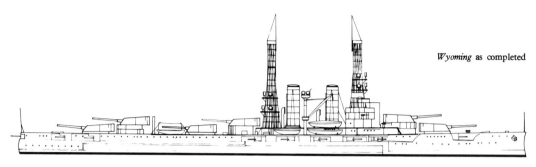

*Wyoming* as completed

*Arkansas* as completed.
*CPL*

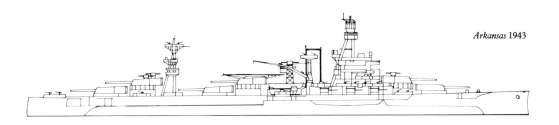

*Arkansas 1943*

## WYOMING class *battleships*

| | |
|---|---|
| **Displacement:** | 26,000t normal; 27,243t full load |
| **Dimensions:** | 554ft wl, 562ft oa × 93ft 2in × 28ft 7in |
| | *168.9m, 171.3m × 28.4m × 8.7m* |
| **Machinery:** | 4-shaft Parsons turbines, 12 Babcock & Wilcox boilers, 28,000shp = 20.5kts. Range 8000nm at 10kts |
| **Armour:** | Belt 11in–9in (279mm–229mm), lower casemate 11in–9in (279mm–229mm), upper casemate 6.5in (165mm), barbettes 11in (279mm), turret faces 12in (305mm), CT 11.5in (292mm) |
| **Armament:** | 12–12in (305mm)/50 (6 × 2), 21–5in (127mm)/51, 2–21in (533mm) TT sub (beam) |
| **Complement:** | 1063 |

| No | Name | Builder | Laid down | Launched | Comp | Fate |
|---|---|---|---|---|---|---|
| BB32 | WYOMING | Cramp | 9.2.10 | 25.5.11 | 25.9.12 | Stricken 1947 |
| BB33 | ARKANSAS | New York SB | 25.1.10 | 14.1.11 | 17.9.12 | Target 26.7.46 |

This design was developed as one of three alternatives, after President Theodore Roosevelt asked in 1908 whether the United States should not go from 12in to 14in guns: a 12–12in design, an 8–14in design, and a 10–14in design. At this time there was a widespread feeling that the standard battleship calibre would soon rise above 12in. For example, there were already reports that Britain had a 13.5in gun under construction. The 12in alternative was chosen in 1909 largely because it entailed the least

delay, and because it was the largest ship that could be docked in existing facilities on both coasts, whereas the 10–14in ship could be docked only at Pearl Harbour and Puget Sound, and at New York only if the dock there could be lengthened by 5ft. Therefore the decision was to build and test the 14in gun, and to enlarge docking facilities, so that the more satisfactory ship could be built later. That became the *New York* class, built under the 1910 (FY 11) program. The *Wyoming* design was accepted as an interim sol-

ution, particularly after the Bureau of Ordnance had developed a new 50-calibre 12in gun to arm it.

All of these designs were flush-deckers. The World Cruise had already shown the problems of mounting secondary guns too low, and the solution adopted was to slope the main deck from a high bow aft, gaining about 4ft in secondary battery height amidships. *Arkansas* was flagship of the Atlantic Fleet in 1914 and off Vera Cruz landing marines. She served in the 6th Battle Squadron, Grand Fleet,

*Wyoming* June 1942.
*CPL*

*Arkansas* 1942.
CPL

*Wyoming* after final refit 1944.
CPL

during World War One.

Both ships were rebuilt in the 1920s, with oil fuel and bulges ('blisters') for improved torpedo protection, changes being generally as in the *Florida*s. The original upper deck had already been thickened by 1in STS over magazines, so there the total thickness was 3.5in. In addition to the 1.25in extra over the boilers, 0.76in was added over the engines. The requirement for two fire control positions, after elimination of the lattice mainmast to make room for a catapult, meant mounting one on a dwarf tripod aft; the lattice foremast was retained.

With four oil-fired boilers, performance figures became 28,000shp = 21kts, and other revised data became: displacement (*Arkansas*) 26,066t standard, 30,610t full load, beam 106ft (32.3m), draught 29ft 11.75in (9.1m) full load, secondary armament 16–5in/51 SP, 8–3in (76mm)/50 AA, complement 1242.

*Wyoming* was converted into a training ship under the 1930 London Treaty, her side armour and some of her guns being removed. World War II proposals to convert her first into a

expeditionary force support ship and then back into a battleship failed, and she spent the war as a combination training ship and AA experimental unit. *Arkansas* was little modernised in 1941–45, apart from a new tripod foremast and bridgework in 1942 and numerous light AA guns. In 1945 she retained 6–5in/51 SP and 8–3in/50 AA, and had also 9 quadruple 40mm and 28 single 20mm AA. *Arkansas* was expended in the 1946 atom bomb tests, becoming a total loss as a result of test 'Baker', 25 July 1946.

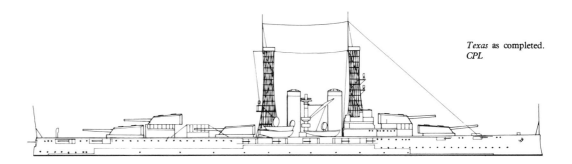

This was the 10–14in design which had originally been developed in 1908-9 as an alternative to *Wyoming*. The prototype 14in/45 gun was test-fired in January 1910, and this design approved in March. Plans for two-shaft (Curtis) and four-shaft (Parsons) turbine installations were developed, but trials of *North Dakota* appeared to show that turbines were generally un-satisfactory: it was estimated that the new ship would be able to make only about 5605nm at 12kts on turbines, compared to 7060 with reciprocating engines. The former figure would be insufficient to take the ship from the US West Coast to the Philippines. The General Board therefore chose recipro-

## NEW YORK class *battleships*

| | |
|---|---|
| **Displacement:** | 27,000t normal; 28,367t full load |
| **Dimensions:** | 565ft wl, 573ft oa × 95ft 6in × 28ft 6in |
| | *172.3m, 174.7m × 29.1m × 8.7m* |
| **Machinery:** | 2-shaft VTE, 14 Babcock & Wilcox boilers, 28,100ihp = 21kts. Range 7060nm at 10kts |
| **Armour:** | Belt 12in–10in (305mm–254mm), lower casemate 11in–9in (279mm–229mm), upper casemate 6.5in (165mm), armour deck 2in (50mm), turret faces 14in (356mm), top 4in (102mm), side 2in (51mm), rear 8in (204mm), barbettes 10in and 12in, CT 12in, top 4in |
| **Armament:** | 10–14in (356mm)/45 (5 × 2), 21–5in (127mm)/51, 4–21in (533mm) TT sub (beam) |
| **Complement:** | 1042 |

| No | Name | Builder | Laid down | Launched | Comp | Fate |
|------|----------|--------------|-----------|----------|---------|-------------|
| BB34 | NEW YORK | New York N Yd | 11.9.11 | 30.10.12 | 15.4.14 | Sunk 8.7.48 |
| BB35 | TEXAS | Newport News | 17.4.11 | 18.5.12 | 12.3.14 | Memorial 1948 |

*Texas* 1942.
*CPL*

*Texas* 1918.
CPL

cating engines, even though it was aware that they had no great potential for further development.

The first US battleship AA guns were turret-top 3in guns mounted aboard *Texas* in 1916. *Texas* was also the first US battleship with flying-off platforms for aircraft, fitted in British waters, possibly as early as March 1918. She flew off her first airplane at Guantanamo Bay (Cuba) in March 1919. Both ships served with 6th Battle Squadron, Grand Fleet, during World War One. *New York* went straight to

Vera Cruz on commissioning, arriving on 4 May 1914.

In the mid-1920s, *New York* and *Texas* underwent similar changes to the four previous coal-burners. Protection and fire control changes were as in *Florida*, with an additional 0.75in over the engines but without the extra 1.25in on the boilers. The oil-fired boilers, taken once again from the scrapped capital ships of the 1916 Programme, were six in number, for a performance of 28,000ihp = 21kts. However, these were the only former coal-

burners to be fitted with new fire controls, together with new tripod foremasts: the weight of the new system required a new mast in any case. Other revised data became displacement (*Texas*) 27,000t standard, 31,924t full load, beam 106ft (32.3m), draught 30ft 2in (9.2m) full load, secondary armament 16-5in/51 SP, 8-3in/50 AA, complement 1290.

Like the earlier reconstructions, the ships were wet and quite stiff. Moreover, they apparently performed poorly at sea due to their reciprocating

engines; they showed particularly severe torsional vibrations, bad enough to threaten to crack their propeller shafts, at the standard fleet cruising speed of about 12–14kts. Changes during World War II were confined to additional AA weapons; in 1945 they retained 6-5in/51 and 10-3in/50, and had 10 quadruple 40mm, 44 single and 1 twin 20mm guns as well. *New York* survived both atom bomb tests in 1946.

*Texas* March 1942.
CPL

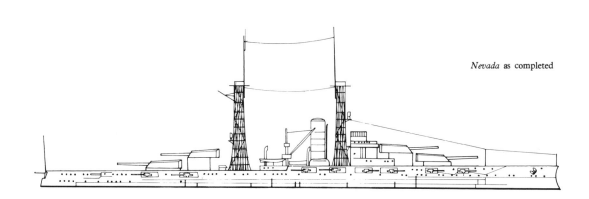

*Nevada* as completed

This was a revolutionary design, introducing 'all or nothing' protection. Since armour-piercing shells did not burst when penetrating thin plating, the designers reasoned that there was nothing to be gained from using thin armour which would serve only to detonate shells. Better to choose either the thickest armour, which would not be penetrated, or no armour at all; hence the name. The *Nevada*s were the first ships designed to General Board Characteristics (staff requirements), and they reflected the new demands of very long-range battle: heavy deck armour and highly centralised fire control.

In the previous *New York* class, the

## NEVADA class *battleships*

| | |
|---|---|
| **Displacement:** | 27,500t normal; 28,400t full load |
| **Dimensions:** | 575ft wl, 583ft oa × 95ft 6in × 28ft 6in |
| | 175.3m, 177.7m × 29.1m × 8.7m |
| **Machinery:** | *Nevada* 2-shaft Curtis turbines, 12 Yarrow boilers, 26,500shp = 20.5kts |
| | *Oklahoma* 2-shaft VTE, 12 Babcock & Wilcox boilers, 24,800ihp = 20.5kts. Range 8000nm at 10kts |
| **Armour:** | Belt 13.5in–8in (343mm–203mm), deck 3in (76mm), turret faces 18in (457mm) and 16in (406mm), sides 10in–9in (254mm–229mm), top 5in (127mm), rear 9in, barbettes 13in (330mm), CT 16in, top 8in |
| **Armament:** | 10-14in (356mm)/45 (2 × 3, 2 × 2), 21-5in (127mm)/51, 2-21in TT sub (beam) |
| **Complement:** | 864 |

| No | Name | Builder | Laid down | Launched | Comp | Fate |
|---|---|---|---|---|---|---|
| BB36 | NEVADA | Fore River | 4.11.12 | 11.7.14 | 11.3.16 | Sunk 31.7.48 |
| BB37 | OKLAHOMA | New York SB | 26.10.12 | 23.3.14 | 2.5.16 | Sunk 7.12.41 |

*Nevada* in 1944.
*CPL*

*Nevada* 1943

*Nevada* as completed.
*CPL*

*Oklahoma* between the wars.
*CPL*

central fire control station had to be placed above the relatively thin protective deck, since all of the hull volume below that deck was occupied by machinery and magazines. It was, therefore, enclosed in light splinter armour. In theory, shells would strike the 'lower casemate' and burst before they could reach the 'central', and its thin armour would defeat the splinters. As expected battle ranges increased, however, shells might well pass *over* this upper belt, to strike the 'central' directly. The first step in the *Nevada* design, then, was to move the main armoured deck to the top of the upper belt, with a splinter deck placed below

it to protect the machinery and magazines from shells bursting after penetrating the main armoured deck. It followed that the upper and lower belts might as well be merged into a single armour belt. Similarly, the upper casemate armour, which in earlier designs had protected the off-side secondary guns and the uptakes, was abandoned in favour of heavy armour round the funnel bases. Armour could also be used more efficiently, because the main battery was concentrated into four rather than five turrets. The splinter deck was 1.5in (38mm) slopes, 1in (25mm) flat.

The total weight of armour was

11,162t, of which 3291t was deck armour; the equivalent figures for *New York* were 8121t and only 1322t respectively.

At the same time, oil fuel was introduced, after tests in *Delaware*. Its advantages includes a reduction in the engine-room complement, and a consequent saving in berthing. However, there was no longer any coal protection to the machinery spaces, and a new form of underwater protection was required. In fact no truly satisfactory type of underwater protection was developed until 1915, in the *Tennessee* class.

These two ships were built with

competitive powerplants, turbine in *Nevada* and reciprocating in *Oklahoma*. Both ships were stationed at Bantry Bay, Ireland, from late August 1918.

*Nevada* and *Oklahoma*, like the five later battleships of the *Pennsylvania* and *New Mexico* classes, were deficient, at the end of World War I, only in underwater protection and in the maximum elevation of their heavy guns; they were reconstructed under the FY28 programme. The gun elevation was increased to 30 deg; apparently Britain and France no longer opposed such improvements. 6 Bureau Express boilers were fitted to

increase the depth of underwater protection being provided by bulges. *Nevada* received the Parsons geared turbines originally fitted experimentally to the scrapped *North Dakota*. 2in armour was added to the second (heavy) deck. This figure does not of course indicate the extent to which the new multi-layered decks were not the equivalent of single thicknesses; the figures quoted do not give equivalent thicknesses. The former rather wet secondaries were replaced by a deckhouse arrangement similar to that built into the *New Mexico*s, with 8-5in/25 AA and 2-5in/51 SP guns in open mounts above the deckhouse. The

lattice masts were replaced by heavy tripods. Other revised data became: displacement (*Oklahoma*) 29,067t standard, 31,706t full load, beam 108ft (32.9m), draught 29ft 8in (9.0m) full load, 25,000hp = 20.5 knots, secondary armament 12-5in/51 SP, 8-5in/25 AA, complement 1374.

*Oklahoma* was hit by five torpedoes and a bomb at Pearl Harbour, becoming a total loss. The first three torpedoes caused a rapid list of 25–30 deg; the last two hit on or above the belt armour as the ship was capsizing. The wreck was righted and refloated in 1943, and, after preliminary dismantling work *in situ*, sank on 17 May

1947 while on tow to San Francisco for scrapping. *Nevada*, the only battleship to get under way during the attack, was hit by one torpedo and five bombs, badly damaged and beached; reconstruction between 1942 and 1943 involved the replacement of the former mixed secondary battery by 16-5in/38 in twin gunhouses, the addition of a large number of 40mm and 20mm AA guns, the elimination of the tripod mainmast in favour of a squat tower, and the removal of the conning tower to save weight. The former two-tiered fire control position on the tripod was cut to one by the elimination of the secondary control position (and the

installation of two Mk 37 directors for the 5in guns). The addition of a small raked funnel extension above the casing provided an instant aid to recognition. *Nevada* ended the war with ten quadruple 40mm guns and 5 single and 20 twin 20mm, the fruits of a programme of AA improvement through the replacement of single by twin mounts. After surviving atom bomb tests 'Abel' and 'Baker' in 1946, and subsequent use as a target for battleship and cruiser gunfire, she was subjected to other tests before being finally sunk by torpedo bombers on 31 July 1948.

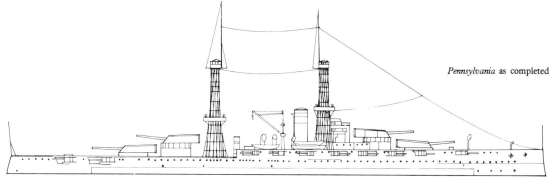

This was essentially an enlarged *Nevada*, with four triple turrets rather than the previous two twin and two triple mounts. This was what the General Board had originally wanted for the *Nevada* class; Congress had been unwilling to appropriate enough money. In addition, the secondary battery was increased from 21 to 22 5in/51 guns, the weapon right aft being abandoned because it was too difficult to assign for fire control purposes.

This class also incorporated special underwater protection, consisting of a 3in torpedo bulkhead 9ft 6in inboard of the shell plating, with a remaining bulkhead 30in inboard of it. Tests

*Pennsylvania* March 1942.  *CPL*

## PENNSYLVANIA class *battleships*

**Displacement:** 31,400t normal; 32,567t full load
**Dimensions:** 600ft wl, 608ft oa × 97ft 1in × 28ft 10in
*182.9m, 185.4m × 29.6m × 8.8m*
**Machinery:** 4-shaft Curtis (*Arizona* Parsons) turbines, 12 Babcock & Wilcox boilers, 31,500shp = 21kts.
Range 8000nm at 10kts
**Armour:** As *Nevada* class
**Armament:** 12–14in (356mm)/45 (4 × 3), 22–5in (127mm)/51, 4–3in (76mm)/50, 2–21in (533mm) TT sub (beam)
**Complement:** 915

| No | Name | Builder | Laid down | Launched | Comp | Fate |
|----|------|---------|-----------|----------|------|------|
| BB38 | PENNSYL-VANIA | Newport News | 27.10.13 | 16.3.15 | 12.6.16 | Scuttled 10.2.48 |
| BB39 | ARIZONA | New York N Yd | 16.3.14 | 19.6.15 | 17.10.16 | Sunk 7.12.41 |

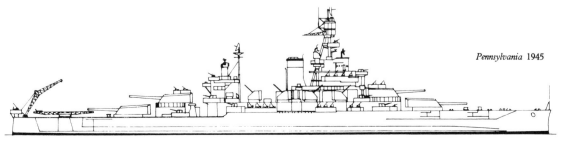

*Pennsylvania 1945*

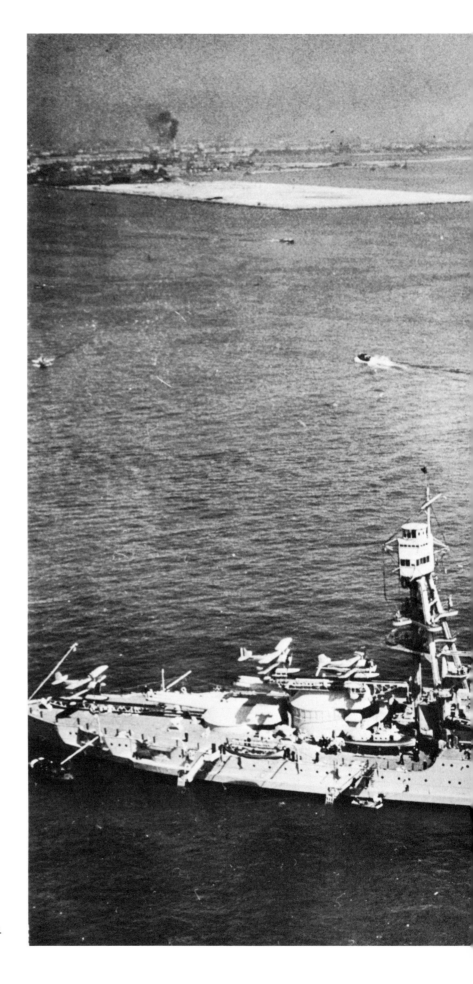

*Arizona* about 1935.
CPL

showed that this system could withstand about 300lb of TNT. The fuel oil was stored in the double bottom compartments; as it was considered very inflammable, the protective system was designed to keep torpedo explosions as far away as possible.

*Pennsylvania* was ordered as a flagship, with a special two-level CT. She was flagship of the Atlantic Fleet 1916–18, and escorted the liner carrying President Wilson to France for the Peace Conference, arriving in December 1918. *Arizona* joined the 6th Battle Squadron, Grand Fleet, just after the Armistice. She landed marines to guard the US Consulate at Constantinople on 14 May 1919 during the Greek occupation of the Turkish capital. *Pennsylvania* embarked 400 US marines to persuade

Panama to accept American mediation in her border dispute with Costa Rica on 18 August 1921.

Both ships were reconstructed under the FY30 programme, with changes to machinery, underwater protection, armament and rig generally as for *Nevada*. With 6 Bureau Express boilers and Curtis geared turbines (machinery originally ordered for the scrapped battleship *Washington* was split between the two ships), performance figures became 33,375shp = 21kts. 1.75in armour was added to the second (heavy) deck. Other revised data became: displacement (*Pennsylvania*) 33,384t standard, 35,929t full load, beam 106ft 3in (32.4m), draught 30ft 3in (9.2m) full load, secondary armament 12-5in/51 SP, 8-5in/25 AA, complement 1052. The recon-

struction made the pair a nearly homogeneous class with the originally very similar *New Mexico*s.

*Arizona* was totally destroyed at Pearl Harbour, with the loss of 1177 lives; the impact of 8 bombs and one torpedo led to the explosion of one of the forward magazines, tearing the ship in two. The sunken remains were dedicated as a national monument in 1962. *Pennsylvania*, the long-time flagship of the US fleet, was moderately damaged by a single bomb while in dry dock. After repairs, she operated for some considerable time in 1942, before being refitted at Mare Island. Changes were again much as for *Nevada*, with a 16-5in/38 dual-purpose secondary armament and two Mk 37 directors, numerous 40mm and 20mm AA guns, and modernised rig

and superstructure. Light armament at the end of the war was 10 quadruple 40mm AA, with 27 single 20mm and 22 twin 20mm. *Pennsylvania* survived both post-war atom bomb tests to be used for various experiments and then as a target ship, being finally destroyed at Kwajalein by aircraft attack on 10 February 1948.

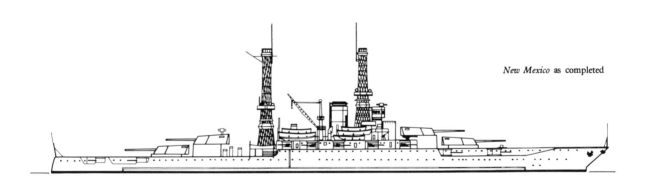

*New Mexico* as completed

In 1913–14 the General Board called for an entirely new battleship design, displacing about 35,500 tons, and armed with ten 16in guns in five twin turrets. Josephus Daniels, the Secretary of the Navy, refused to countenance any substantial increase in tonnage, and decided that the FY 14 battleships would essentially duplicate the *Pennsylvania*s, with whatever improvement that could be incorporated at minimum cost. Two were involved.

First, there was the old complaint of wetness. These ships had a clipper bow, and 12 of their 22 5in/51 guns were mounted in a deckhouse, ie one deck level above the secondaries of the previous class. They still retained 4

## NEW MEXICO class *battleship*

| | |
|---|---|
| **Displacement:** | 32,000t normal; 33,000t full load |
| **Dimensions:** | 600ft wl, 624ft oa × 97ft 5in × 30ft |
| | *189.9m, 190.2m × 29.7m × 9.1m* |
| **Machinery:** | 4-shaft Curtis (*Idaho* Parsons) turbines, (*New Mexico* General Electric turbo-electric drive), 9 Babcock & Wilcox boilers, 32,000shp (*New Mexico* 27,000shp) = 21kts. Range 8000nm at 10kts |
| **Armour:** | As *Nevada* class but 3.5in (89mm) armour deck |
| **Armament:** | 12-14in (356mm)/50 (4 × 3), 14-5in (127mm)/51, 4-3in (76mm)/50, 2-21in (533mm) TT sub (beam) |
| **Complement:** | 1084 |

| No | Name | Builder | Laid down | Launched | Comp | Fate |
|---|---|---|---|---|---|---|
| BB40 | NEW MEXICO | New York N Yd | 14.10.15 | 23.4.17 | 20.5.18 | Stricken 1947 |
| BB41 | MISSISSIPPI | Newport News | 5.4.15 | 25.1.17 | 18.12.17 | Stricken 1956 |
| BB42 | IDAHO | New York SB | 20.1.15 | 30.6.17 | 24.3.19 | Stricken 1947 |

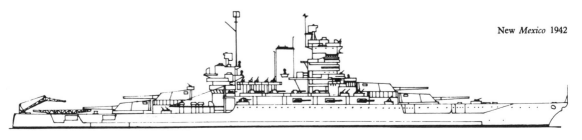

*New Mexico* 1942

Top: *Idaho* 1937. Above: *Mississippi* 1934
CPL

guns in the forecastle deck forward, and 4 more right aft, below the main deck; another pair was in the open, atop the deckhouse. One of the three ships was actually completed with all 22 guns, but by that time American experience in the North Sea was showing that only the deckhouse guns would be usable in a seaway. The bow and after positions were soon plated in, reducing the number to 14.

The other major improvement was in main battery gunnery: these ships introduced a new 14in/50 gun, and the weapons elevated independently, in contrast with earlier classes.

A series of detail weight economies permitted the designers to thicken the armoured bulkheads from 13in to 13.5in, and the main armour deck from 3in to 3.5in, both of which figures became standard for later US dreadnoughts.

One ship, the *New Mexico*, tested the turbo-electric drive system advocated by General Electric as an alternative to gearing. The collier *Jupiter*, which became the aircraft carrier *Langley*, had already served as a test platform. The Bureau of Steam Engineering wanted turbo-electric drive for economy, and to do away with astern trubines, which were giving trouble. C&R saw the new system as a means to improve subdivision, and employed it in all of its later dreadnoughts and battlecruisers. It was abandoned after World War One only because of its excessive demands on weight and internal volume.

Two ships were originally planned, but proceeds of the 1914 sale to Greece of the pre-dreadnoughts *Mississippi* and *Idaho* paid for a third ship.

The class was reconstructed under the FY31 programme, changes being generally as for *Nevada*. All received entirely new Westinghouse geared turbines and 6 (BB40 4) Bureau Express boilers, for performance figures 40,000shp = 22 knots. 2in armour was added to the second (heavy) dock. Other revised data became: displacement (*New Mexico*) 33,420t standard, 36,157t full load, beam 106ft 3in (32.4m), draught 31ft (9.4m) full load, secondary armament 12-5in/51 SP, 8-5in/25 AA, complement 1443. The tripod masts originally planned for the

*Idaho* 1942

reconstruction were replaced with tower bridges, justified primarily on the basis of resistance to blast and to shellfire. During World War II, there were little further alterations, except in detail. *Idaho* ended the war with a new secondary battery of 10–5in/38 in enclosed single mounts, fitted after battle damage; in 1945 she also had 10 quadruple 40mm and 43 Oerlikons. *Missis-* *sippi* was refitted at her captain's insistance at Pearl Harbour following Kamikaze damage; at the end of the war she had no 5in/51, but 16–5in/25, 13 quadruple 40mm, and 40–20mm. *New Mexico* was far less extensively altered, and in 1945 had 6–5in/51, 8–5in/25, 10 quadruple 40mm, and 46 Oerlikons. *Mississippi* was fitted out as a gunnery-training/experimental ship in 1946–47 to replace *Wyoming*, retaining only No 4 triple turret and receiving a variety of medium-calibre guns, before being further rebuilt in 1952 as a test ship for the Terrier SAM system, with all 14in guns removed. The other two were deleted 1947 and BU 1947–48.

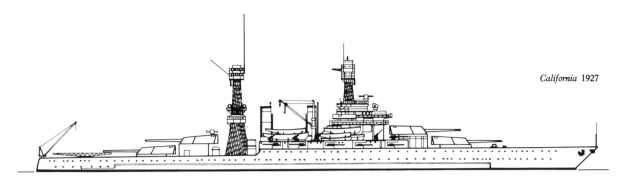

*California* 1927

These two ships were slightly modified *New Mexico*s, the principal changes being major improvements in underwater protection. A series of caisson experiments showed that a series of layers of liquid-filled and void compartments could absorb the explosive energy of even a substantial torpedo warhead; the system in these (and other US battleships of this period) was designed to resist 400lb of TNT. These ships therefore incorporated a series of five bulkheads on either side: the outermost compartment was left void, then there were three liquid-filled ones, and then an inboard void, into which the inner liquid layer could

## TENNESSEE class *battleships*

| | |
|---|---|
| **Displacement:** | 32,300t normal; 33,190t full load |
| **Dimensions:** | 600ft wl, 624ft oa × 97ft 5in × 30ft 2in |
| | *182.9m, 190.2m × 29.7m × 9.2m* |
| **Machinery:** | 4-shaft Westinghouse, (*California* General Electric) turbo-electric drive, 8 Babcock & Wilcox boilers, 26,800shp = 21kts. Range 8000nm at 10kts |
| **Armour:** | As *New Mexico* class |
| **Armament:** | As *New Mexico* class |
| **Complement:** | 1083 |

| No | Name | Builder | Laid down | Launched | Comp | Fate |
|---|---|---|---|---|---|---|
| BB43 | TENNESSEE | New York N Yd | 14.5.17 | 30.4.19 | 3.6.20 | Stricken 1959 |
| BB44 | CALIFORNIA | Mare Island N Yd | 25.10.16 | 20.11.19 | 10.8.21 | Stricken 1959 |

*Tennessee* in action about 1944.
CPL

*Tennessee* as completed.
CPL

burst in the event of a hit. By this time, designers had rightly appreciated that in the absence of oxygen oil fuel was not a fire hazard (cf *Pennsylvania* class), and could be used in the anti-torpedo system. Inboard of the torpedo protection, each boiler was in a separate compartment, the boilers themselves forming a kind of inner protective layer. Two large turbo-generators were on the centreline. The dispersion of the boilers showed externally in the adoption of two funnels, rather than the previous single trunked one.

The pilothouse and forward super-structure were considerably enlarged, the most prominent feature being a big air intake terminating under the pilot-house. The cage masts were of a new heavier type, and each carried a two-level enclosed top, the upper level of which was for main battery control, the lower for the secondary battery.

In addition, the elevation of the main battery guns was increased from 15 to 30 degrees. Both ships were completed in somewhat modified form, without hull-mounted secondary weapons, and with their hulls faired over the casemates of the original design.

*California* and *Tennessee* were among the most modern of the pre-World War II fleet, forming with the *Maryland* class the 'Big Five', homogeneous except for their main batteries. Inter-war modernisation plans for both classes were deferred first because of the Depression and then because the ships were too urgently needed; however, it was planned to fit them with bulges to restore buoyancy and so to lift their belts out of the water, given the extra weight they had accumulated since completion.

*California* was hit by two torpedoes and two bombs at Pearl Harbour and severely damaged, sinking in shallow water because flooding could not be contained (manhole covers in the torpedo defence system had been loosened off or opened for inspection); she clearly required major reconstruction. *Tennessee*, hit by two bombs and only slightly damaged, was operated for some time in nearly her original configuration, before being chosen as the prototype for major reconstruction. The scheme was based on that adopted for *Nevada* but included the provision of new main battery directors (Mk 34 diverted from light cruisers being converted to light carriers) on modern-style tower masts. In addition, the heavy conning towers removed were replaced by light ones taken from *Brooklyn* class cruisers. The principal addition of armour was

3in of STS over the magazines and 2in elsewhere; the turret tops were also reinforced. Much wider bulges were fitted, in a radical attempt to restore the armoured freeboard, estimated as 2.5–3ft below the optimum for gun engagements if *Nevada*-type hull alterations had been followed. Other revised data became; displacement (*Tennessee*) 34,858t standard, 40,345t full load, beam 114ft (34.8m), draught 33ft 1in (10.1m) full load, secondary armament 16-5in/38 (8 × 2), 40–40mm (10 × 4), 43–20mm (as fitted to *Tennessee* 1943), complement 2375. At the end of the war these ships differed in their light batteries; *Tennessee* was armed as in 1943, while *California* had 14 quadruple 40mm and 40 twin 20mm.

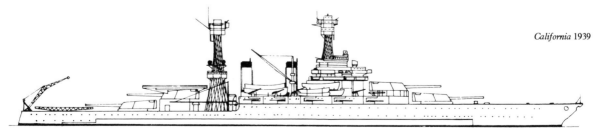

*California* 1939

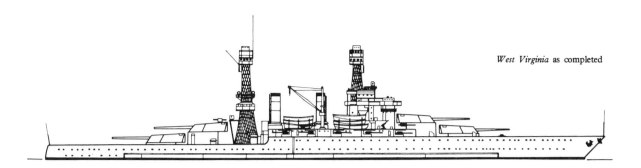

*West Virginia* as completed

This was a repeat *Tennessee* design with twin 16in/45 guns in place of the earlier triple 14in/50; there was no other substantial change, although for many years there were unofficial claims of a considerable increase in belt armour, from the 14in erroneously credited to the *Tennessee* to an equally incorrect 16in. The 16in/45 guns fired 2100lb shells at a muzzle velocity of 2600ft/sec, for a penetration of 18.9in armour at 12,000 yards (the corresponding data for the 14in/50 guns in *New Mexico* and *California* were 1500lb, 2800ft/sec and 13.6in armour at 12,000 yards). The electric installation was increased, every possible item of equipment being run by electricity.

## COLORADO class *battleships*

| | |
|---|---|
| **Displacement:** | 32,600t normal; 33,590t full load |
| **Dimensions:** | As *Tennessee* class |
| **Machinery:** | 4-shaft turbo-electric drive, 8 Babock & Wilcox boilers, 28,900shp = 21kts. Range 8000nm at 10kts |
| **Armour:** | As *New Mexico* class |
| **Armament:** | 8-16in (406mm)/45 (4×2), 14-5in (127mm)/51, 4-3in (76mm)/50, 2-21in (533mm) TT sub (beam) |
| **Complement:** | 1080 |

| No | Name | Builder | Laid down | Launched | Comp | Fate |
|---|---|---|---|---|---|---|
| BB45 | COLORADO | New York SB | 29.5.19 | 22.3.21 | 30.8.23 | Stricken 1959 |
| BB46 | MARYLAND | Newport News | 24.4.17 | 20.3.20 | 21.7.21 | Stricken 1959 |
| BB47 | WASHINGTON | New York SB | 30.6.19 | 1.9.21 | — | Sunk 25.11.24 |
| BB48 | WEST VIRGINIA | Newport News | 12.4.20 | 19.11.21 | 1.12.23 | Stricken 1959 |

*West Virginia* 1944.
CPL

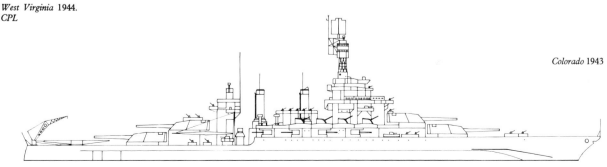

*Colorado* 1943

*Maryland* in the late 1920s.
CPL

One ship, the *Washington*, was suspended under the Washington Treaty on 8 February 1922, when 75.9 per cent complete, with side armour and barbettes in place but without boilers or machinery. In November 1924 she was used successfully to test the sandwich-type protective system against underwater explosions, before being sunk by 14 14in shells from *Texas*.

*West Virginia* was hit by six or seven torpedoes (four on the belt as she was listing heavily) and two bombs at Pearl

Harbour, and badly damaged, but sank on an even keel; refloated in 1942, she underwent reconstruction as for the *California*s, including extra horizontal armour, deep bulges and a new secondary armament. *Colorado* and *Maryland* received only the more limited modernisation planned prewar and described under the *California* class; the former was under refit at the time of Pearl Harbour and the latter received moderate damage from two bombs. At the end of the war these three ships varied greatly in their light

batteries. Only *Colorado* retained her prewar 5in/51s (8) and 5in/25s; she also had 8 quadruple 40mm, as well as 39 single, 8 twin, and 1 quadruple 20mm. *Maryland*, damaged by a Kamikaze, was refitted in 1945 with 8 twin 5in/38 in standard gunhouses, as well as 11 quadruple 40mm, 20 twin and 1 quadruple 20mm.

*West Virginia* had 10 quadruple 40mm and 58 single, 1 twin, and one quadruple 20mm.

*West Virginia* 1945

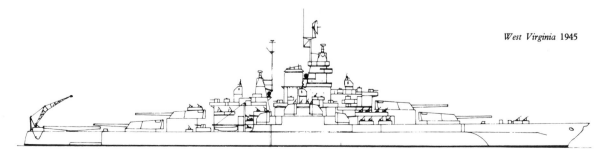

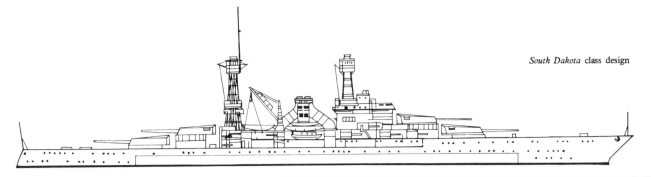

*South Dakota* class design

## SOUTH DAKOTA class *battleships*

**Displacement:** 43,200t normal
**Dimensions:** 660ft wl, 684ft oa × 106ft × 33ft
*201.2m, 208.5m × 32.3m × 10.1m*
**Machinery:** 4-shaft turbo-electric drive, 12 boilers, 50,000shp = 23kts. Range 8000nm at 10kts
**Armour:** As *New Mexico* class
**Armament:** 12–16in (406mm)/50 (4 × 3), 16–6in (152mm)/53, 4–3in (76mm)/50, 2–21in (533mm) TT sub (beam)
**Complement:** 1191

| No | Name | Builder | Laid down | Fate |
|---|---|---|---|---|
| BB49 | SOUTH DAKOTA | New York N Yd | 15.3.20 | Cancelled 17.8.23 |
| BB50 | INDIANA | New York N Yd | 1.11.20 | Cancelled 17.8.23 |
| BB51 | MONTANA | Mare Island N Yd | 1.9.20 | Cancelled 17.8.23 |
| BB52 | NORTH CAROLINA | Norfolk N Yd | 12.1.20 | Cancelled 17.8.23 |
| BB53 | IOWA | Newport News | 17.5.20 | Cancelled 17.8.23 |
| BB54 | MASSACHUSETTS | Fore River | 4.4.21 | Cancelled 17.8.23 |

With this class the General Board finally achieved what it had wanted since 1914, a jump in battleship capabilities and size. From the start, the board wanted 12–16in guns and a 23kt speed, the latter partly out of fear the Japan would acquire fast battleships (like the British *Queen Elizabeth*s) of her own. The board considered a 2kt increase an absolute minimum, given what it supposed was a general tendency towards higher speed. Finally, given a great increase in displacement, it was natural to go from the existing 16in/45 to the much more powerful 16in/50, and from the 5in/51 secondary gun to the new 6in/53. Armour thicknesses did not increase, largely because 13.5in was considered the maximum that could be manufactured with any certainty of consistent quality. Main battery elevation was increased to 40 degrees.

The design, then, amounted to an enlarged *Maryland*, with triple rather than twin turrets, and with all of the secondary battery above the forecastle deck. Visually, the most unusual feature would have been the massive trunked funnel, uniting four smoke-pipes emerging from the dispersed boiler rooms.

This design was frozen in the summer of 1918. At that time the US naval staff in London was much impressed by HMS *Hood*, and it proposed that the United States develop its own fast battleship, armed with 16in guns. Several sketches were prepared, but the General Board felt that to build them would make existing ships obsolete, and therefore would not be in the US Navy's best interests. It therefore persevered with the much more conventional *South Dakota* design.

Delayed by the emergency ASW program of World War One, the ships were not laid down until after the war, and none was very advanced at the time of the Washington Conference, when all were suspended (8 February 1922); progress ranged from 38.5% (BB 49) to 11% (BB 54) complete. They were cancelled on 17 August 1923, the date when the Washington Treaty was formally ratified and came into force, and BU on the stocks.

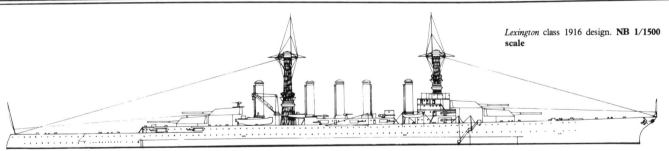

*Lexington* class 1916 design. **NB 1/1500 scale**

## LEXINGTON class *battlecruisers*

**Displacement:** 43,500t normal; 44,638t full load; 51,217t emergency full load
**Dimensions:** 850ft wl, 874ft oa × 105ft 4in × 31ft
*259.1m, 266.5m × 32.1m × 9.5m*
**Machinery:** 4-shaft turbo-electric drive, 16 boilers, 180,000shp = 33.5kts. Range 12,000nm at 10kts
**Armour:** Belt 7in (178mm), turret face (280mm), side 6in (152mm), barbette 9in–5in (229mm–127mm), CT 12in (305mm)
**Armament:** 8–16in (406mm)/50 (4 × 2), 16–6in (152mm)/53, 4–3in (76mm)/50, 8–21in (533mm) TT (4 aw)
**Complement:** 1297 (1326 as flagship)

| No | Name | Builder | Laid down | Fate |
|---|---|---|---|---|
| CC1 | LEXINGTON (ex-*Constitution*) | Fore River | 8.1.21 | Became carrier CV 2 |
| CC2 | CONSTELLATION | Newport News | 18.8.20 | Cancelled 17.8.23 |
| CC3 | SARATOGA | New York SB | 25.9.20 | Became carrier CV 3 |
| CC4 | RANGER (ex-*Lexington*) | Newport News | 23.6.21 | Cancelled 17.8.23 |
| CC5 | CONSTITUTION (ex-*Ranger*) | Philadelphia N Yd | 25.9.20 | Cancelled 17.8.23 |
| CC6 | UNITED STATES | Philadelphia N Yd | 25.9.20 | Cancelled 17.8.23 |

The General Board considered building battlecruisers in 1912, to counter the four Japanese *Kongo*s, but it withdrew them from its proposed programme because Congress was unwilling to buy enough battleships, which it considered a more urgent requirement. The ships contemplated at that time would have been relatively heavily armoured, and as such were much closer to fast battleships than to the 'battle scouts' approved in 1916. The *Lexington*s were ordered as part of the large 1916 programme, as a major element of a 35-knot scouting force to support a large battlefleet; other elements of the scouting force were the flush deck destroyers and the *Omaha* class cruisers. As 'battle scouts', the *Lexington*s would be ships powerful enough to press home reconnaissance in the face of enemy battlecruisers. The design was in effect scaled *up* from a series of designs for cruisers displacing about 10,000 to 14,000 tons, and so would have been much more lightly built than contemporary US battleships, a maximum stress of 14 tons per square inch being accepted on the usual assumptions. The 1916 design, for a ship of 34,800t normal displacement, was complicated by the relatively limited steam output of existing boilers: there was not enough space below the armoured deck for the 24 units needed to make 180,000shp. Hence the very unusual design initially adopted, in which half the boilers were above the protective deck, inside armoured boxes on the centreline. The remaining boilers were in individual compartments outboard of the generators. The uptakes were trunked into no less than seven funnels, of which only five showed in profile, as four were in widely spaced pairs abeam. Armour was very light: 5in belt, bulkheads, barbettes and conning tower, with 6in-2.5in turrets. The armoured boxes round the upper boilers were listed as 8in in contemporary descriptions. The main battery comprised 10-14in (356mm)/50 guns in two twin and two triple turrets,

the triples superfiring over the twins, and the secondary armament was 18-5in (127mm)/51 guns. The displacement was 36,350t full load., 40,734t emergency full load, on dimensions 850ft wl, 874ft oa × 90ft × 35ft 5in (max). Design requirements included provision for aircraft, which probably explains the break in the main deck right aft: when these ships were designed, the only US catapult was the fixed straight-deck type in the old armoured cruisers. Although trainable catapults were designed immediately after World War One, no later sketches show them in the final design.

This design would have been adopted, had not all American capital ship construction been suspended in favour of merchant ship and ASW programmes in 1917; the delay was used progressively to upgrade and refine the design. In 1917 the main armament was increased to 8-16in guns, because the 1916 authorising law required ships with 'as powerful armament as any vessels of their class'; battlecruisers with 15in guns were building in Europe while Japan was projecting even larger 16in-gunned ships. A reduction in the number of boilers to 20 enabled all to be located below the protective deck, so that the number of

funnels could be reduced to five, of which only three showed in profile. The secondary armament was increased to 14-6in (152mm)/53 guns. These changes increased the normal displacement to 35,300t at 31ft 3.5in draught; the beam remained at the 90ft of the 1916 design, and power and speed were also unaltered.

The next modification (1918) was to improve protection by widening the hull to incorporate an anti-torpedo protection system and by increasing the (vertical) belt armour to 9in. In a further step, the hull depth was then increased, probably for strength purposes, and the armour belt was reduced in thickness and sloped outwards. With the appearance of small-tube boilers, their number could be further reduced to 16, and the uptakes would have been trunked into two large, oval funnels. Increased displacement and reduced speed were accepted.

The final version of the design, presented in the table, owes much to US reactions to HMS *Hood*, even though it was still very lightly armoured, and so still reflected the original operational concept. The Bureau of Ordnance argued, moreover, that on the basis of British analysis of Jutland,

the loss of the battlecruisers had been due, not to their lack of armour, but to their poor anti-flash protection: the battle, then, did not imply that more armour was needed, but rather that better magazine arrangements were in order. The choice of a sloping belt owed much to British practice, as (probably) did the decision to provide four abovewater TT to supplement the four underwater ones.

All six were cancelled under the Washington Treaty, two being completed as large aircraft carriers. However, it appears that they were considered obsolescent even before the negotiations, since early in 1921 there were studies of conversions to carriers, and also of the use of material collected for the *Ranger* to build a carrier designed as such from the keel up. Progress when construction was suspended on 8 February 1922 varied from 29.4% (CC 3) to 4% (CC 4) completed; a contemporary report noted that only 4 million dollars were allotted to the four most advanced units in 1921–22, and less for the other two, meaning a 5–6 year building period unless funding were to be more generous thereafter.

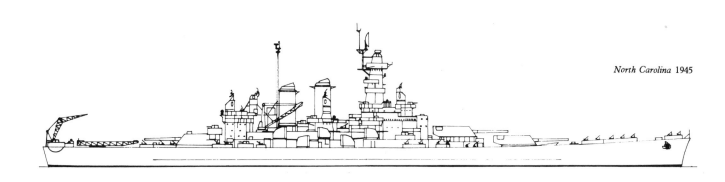

*North Carolina* 1945

The two *North Carolina*s were the first battleships the US Navy built after the expiration of the Washington Treaty 'building holiday'. As such they were the outgrowth of a long and tortuous process of design evolution, which began not with fast battleships but rather with an updated version of the traditional US type, concentrating on firepower and protection at the expense of speed. In 1935, however, the US Navy General Board decided that it would be useful at least to explore the type being built abroad, ie a fast but well-armed and well-protected ship. What decided the issue in favour of the fast ship was the need to operate carrier task forces; at one point it was suggested that two fast battleships combine with each of the

two big carriers (*Saratago* and *Lexington*) to form a task group. The threat presented by the three 26kt *Kongo*s was also an important factor. The General Board therefore approved a 30kt, 9-14in gun ship, protected against 14in fire, using much the same arguments that would later be made in favour of the *Iowa*s. At virtually the last minute, however, the Chief of Naval Operations rejected this design, preferring a more traditional 27kt type, armed with 11-14in guns (later 12in, in quadruple turrets), and it was his design which was ultimately adopted.

Although 16in guns had figured in the earliest sketch designs, the London Treaty of 1936 limited new battleships to 14in guns, and it was this latter

calibre which determined both the battery and the protection designed into the new ships; they were to be immune against 14in (1500lb) shells between 20,000 and 30,800yds (reduced on the inner edge to 19,000 against barbettes, and extended to 33,000 against magazines). The design made specific allowance for replacing the new quadruple 14in turret with a triple 16in turret, in the event that an escalator clause in the London Treaty had to be invoked; this latter referred to Japanese acceptance of the 14in limit. Japan, as it turned out, refused to agree to this limitation, and the US government invoked the escalator clause, so that in fact all the new US battleships were armed with the 16in gun. What such invocation could not do was change the armour

distribution, which was basic to the design. Thus against the 2250lb 16in shell (which was less effective than the 2700lb shell actually adopted), the *North Carolina* immunity zone was only 21,000–27,000yds over magazines, and 23,200–26,000yds over machinery (as of November 1937).

Both ships entered service just before the outbreak of war, although they were not fully effective until early 1942, due in part to severe propeller vibration difficulties. *Washington* was the only modern US battleship to engage an enemy capital ship: she sank the Japanese battlecruiser *Kirishima* on the night of 14–15 November 1942. On 15 September 1942, *North Carolina* was hit by a Japanese torpedo containing the equivalent of 960lb

TNT, outmatching the anti-torpedo system, designed for only 700lb; the system failed, but not catastrophically, although the ship's capabilities were significantly reduced. Damage included the main search radar, incapacitated by shock, and required two months to repair.

It appears in retrospect that from an operator's point of view the *North Carolina* design was superior to the later, more cramped, *South Dakota*. At the end of the war each ship had 15 quadruple 40mm mounts; *North Carolina* had, in addition, 20 single and 8 twin 20mm, her sister 63 single, 8 twin and one quadruple mount. *North Carolina* herself was refitted and employed briefly postwar as a training ship, unique among the US treaty battleships.

# NORTH CAROLINA class *battleships*

| | |
|---|---|
| **Displacement:** | (*Washington*) 37,484t standard; 44,377t full load |
| **Dimensions:** | 714ft 6in wl, 728ft 9in oa × 108ft 4in × 32ft 11.5in full load |
| | *217.8m, 222.1m × 33.0m × 10.0m* |
| **Machinery:** | 4-shaft General Electric turbines, 8 Babcock & Wilcox boilers, 121,000shp = 28kts. Oil 6260t, range 17,450nm at 15kts |
| **Armour:** | Belt 12in–6.6in (305mm–167mm) on 0.75in (19mm) STS, deck 5.5in–5in (140mm–127mm) with 1.45in (37mm) weather deck and 0.62in–0.75in (16mm–19mm) splinter deck, bulkheads 11in (280mm), barbettes 14.7in–16in (374mm–406mm), turrets 16in (406mm) face, 7in (178mm) roof, 9.8in (250mm) side 11.8in (300mm) rear, CT 14.7in–16in (374mm–406mm) with 7in (178mm) roof |
| **Armament:** | 9–16in (406mm)/45 (3 × 3), 20–5in (127mm)/38 (10 × 2), 16–1.1in (28mm) (4 × 4), 12–0.5in (12 × 1), 3 aircraft |
| **Complement:** | 1880 |

| No | Name | Builder | Laid down | Launched | Comp | Fate |
|---|---|---|---|---|---|---|
| BB55 | NORTH CAROLINA | New York N Yd | 27.10.37 | 13.6.40 | 9.4.41 | Preserved 1961 |
| BB56 | WASHINGTON | Philadelphia N Yd | 14.6.38 | 1.6.40 | 15.5.41 | Sold 24.5.61 |

*North Carolina* running trials 1941.
*CPL*

## SOUTH DAKOTA class *battleships*

| | |
|---|---|
| **Displacement:** | (*South Dakota*) 37,970t standard; 44,519t full load |
| **Dimensions:** | 666ft wl, 680ft oa × 108ft 2in × 35ft 1in full load |
| | *203.0m, 207.3m × 33.0m × 10.7m* |
| **Machinery:** | 4-shaft General Electric turbines, 8 Babcock & Wilcox boilers, 130,000shp = 27.5kts. Oil 6959t, range 15,000nm at 15kts |
| **Armour:** | Belt 12.2in (310mm) on 0.875in (22mm) STS, lower belt 12.2in–1in (310mm–25mm) on 0.88in (22mm) STS, deck 5.75in–6in (146mm–152mm) with 1.5in (38mm) weather deck and 0.62in (16mm) splinter deck, bulkheads 11in (280mm), barbettes 11.3in–17.3in (287mm–439mm), turrets 18in (457mm) face, 7.25in (184mm) roof, 9.5in (241mm) side, 12in (305mm) rear, CT 16in (406mm) with 7.25in (184mm) roof |
| **Armament:** | 9–16in (406mm)/45 (3 × 3), 20–5in (127mm)/38 (10 × 2), 12–1.1in (28mm) (3 × 4), 12–0.5in as designed, 3 aircraft. See notes |
| **Complement:** | 1793 |

| No | Name | Builder | Laid down | Launched | Comp | Fate |
|---|---|---|---|---|---|---|
| BB57 | SOUTH DAKOTA | New York SB | 5.7.39 | 7.6.41 | 20.3.42 | Sold 25.10.62 |
| BB58 | INDIANA | Newport News | 20.11.39 | 21.11.41 | 30.4.42 | Sold 6.9.63 |
| BB59 | MASSACHU-SETTS | Bethlehem, Quincy | 20.7.39 | 23.9.41 | 12.5.42 | Preserved 1965 |
| BB60 | ALABAMA | Norfolk N Yd | 1.2.40 | 16.2.42 | 16.8.42 | Preserved 1964 |

The four *South Dakota*s were an attempt to achieve effective protection against 16in shellfire on a displacement limited to 35,000 tons by the London Treaty, without any sacrifice of the speed achieved in the *North Carolina* design. It was also important to protect them against underwater hits, which were expected at very long range; ultimately an immune zone (against the 2250lb 16in shell) of 18,000 to 30,000yds was required. The design solution was a combination of very steeply sloped internal side armour and a heavy armoured deck; in order to save weight the length of the vitals was reduced as far as possible, and some considerable cramping of upper-works (such as blast interference between secondary guns and light AA) was accepted; even when these ships were being designed in 1937, the General Board considered them potentially uncomfortable. The steeply sloped belt, no thicker than that of the *North Carolina*s, was continued into the armoured bulkhead of the torpedo protection, a novel system which had not been tested when the ships were laid down. Subsequent caisson experiments suggested that it was not entirely satisfactory, but by then not only the four *South Dakota*s but also the *Iowa*s had received it. Yet another unusual feature was the 'tunnel' stern, in which the two outboard propellers were encased in massive skegs, with the two inboard units revolving in the tunnel thus formed. Among the functions of the skegs were torpedo protection for the propellers on the other side, and hydrodynamic refinements which permitted enough hull volume

abreast the after magazines to provide sufficient torpedo protection there.

*South Dakota* was unique in that she was fitted as a Force Flagship, with an extra conning tower level; as topweight compensation, she received only 8 twin 5in/38 mounts, although she had 20–1.1in (5 × 4) compared with her half-sisters. Originally only she and *Indiana* were authorised under the FY 39 Naval Appropriations Act; designs for the *Iowa*s were begun under the designation 'BB59'. However, a Deficiency Appropriations Act of 25 June 1938 authorised two more 35,000-ton battleships and these were ordered as *Massachusetts* and *Alabama*, even though at that time work was already well advanced on the *Iowa* design.

As much as had been sacrificed in order to bring these ships to acceptable standard of protection against 16in fire, in 1939 the Bureau of Ordnance developed a new 2700lb 16in shells which required, once more, a new standard of protection: it was estimated that the *South Dakota* immune zone would shrink to 20,500–26,400yds, as would that of the *Iowa*. In effect the *Montana* began as an attempt to design a ship, unlimited by Treaty, which would have roughly the characteristics of the *South Dakota* but against the new 2700lb shell, which the Bureau claimed had more effectiveness than an 18in shell of more conventional form.

During the second battle of Guadalcanal, 14–15 November 1942, *South Dakota* was hit at ranges of 5800–7000 yards by 1 14in and 26 8in, 6in and 5in shells from the Japanese battlecruiser

*Kirishima* and two cruisers. Damage was largely superficial and centred on the superstructure, neither strength, stability nor buoyancy being much affected, but the communications, radar and fire control systems were badly hit, destroying the ship's electronic and night fighting capabilities. *Massachusetts* was not hit during her duel with *Jean Bart* at Casablanca in the same month.

All four ships were withdrawn from service immediately after World War II, although *Massachusetts* was refitted for further service. Her refit included considerable reductions in automatic weapons, presumably incident to a reduction in operating personnel. None of the four had seen really arduous service, and through the 1950s a variety of schemes to utilise their hulls was proposed. For example, for a short time it was suggested that one of these ships, rather than a cruiser, become the first US fleet missile ship. *South Dakota* (and *North Carolina*) class hulls were also proposed as satellite-launching ships, as fast replenishment ships, and as helicopter assault ships – none of which appeared to be particularly economical. There was even a brief study of what it would take in the way of boost power to bring one of these ships up to the new fleet speed of 33kts, but that proved astronomically expensive.

In August 1945 BB58 and 60 each had 12 quadruple 40mm mounts, BB57 17 and BB59 18. They also had, as 20mm batteries: 72 single (BB57); 48 single plus 4 twin (BB58); 31 single, 1 twin and 1 quadruple (BB59); and 56 single (BB60).

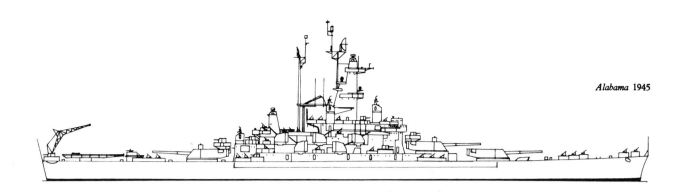

*Alabama* 1945

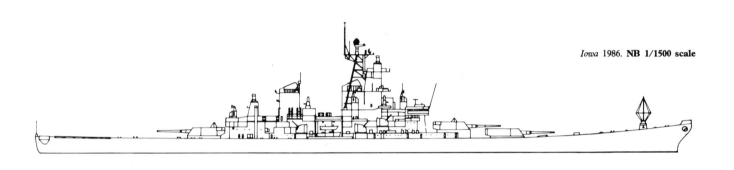

*Iowa* 1986. **NB 1/1500 scale**

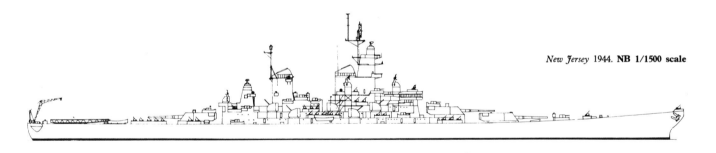

*New Jersey* 1944. **NB 1/1500 scale**

## IOWA class *battleships*

| | |
|---|---|
| **Displacement:** | (*Iowa*) 48,110t standard; 57,540t full load |
| **Dimensions:** | 860ft wl, 887ft 3in oa × 108ft 2in × 36ft 2in full load |
| | *262.1m, 270.4m × 33.0m × 11.0m* |
| **Machinery:** | 4-shaft General Electric turbines, 8 Babcock & Wilcox boilers, 212,000shp = 32.5kts. Oil 7621t, range 15,000nm at 15kts. |
| **Armour:** | Belt 12.1in (307mm) on 0.88in (22mm) STS, lower belt 12.1in–1.6in (307mm–41mm) on 0.88in (22mm) STS, deck 6in (152mm) with 1.5in (38mm) weather deck and 0.62in (16mm) splinter deck, bulkheads 11.3in (287mm), barbettes 11.6in–17.5in (295mm–439mm), turrets 19.7in (500mm) face, 7.25in (185mm) roof, 9.5in (241mm) side, 12in (305mm) rear, CT 17.5in (445mm) with 7.25in (184mm) roof |
| **Armament:** | 9–16in (406mm)/50 (3 × 3), 20–5in (127mm)/38 (10 × 2), 80–40mm (20 × 4), 49–20mm, 3 aircraft. See notes |
| **Complement:** | 1921 |

| No | Name | Builder | Laid down | Launched | Comp | Fate |
|---|---|---|---|---|---|---|
| BB61 | IOWA | New York N Yd | 27.6.40 | 27.8.42 | 22.2.43 | Extant 1987 |
| BB62 | NEW JERSEY | Philadelphia N Yd | 16.9.40 | 7.12.42 | 23.5.43 | Extant 1987 |
| BB63 | MISSOURI | New York N Yd | 6.1.41 | 29.1.44 | 11.6.44 | Extant 1987 |
| BB64 | WISCONSIN | Philadelphia N Yd | 25.1.41 | 7.12.43 | 16.4.44 | Extant 1987 |
| BB65 | ILLINOIS | Philadelphia N Yd | 6.12.42 | — | — | Cancelled 11.8.45 |
| BB66 | KENTUCKY | Norfolk N Yd | 6.12.42 | 20.1.50 | — | Sold for BU Sept 1958 |

*Wisconsin* 1952.
CPL

The four *Iowa*s were the largest and fastest battleships completed for the US Navy during World War II; in principle they were *South Dakota*s lengthened for higher speed, the increased displacement being used also to pass from 45 to 50cal 16in guns. In view of the past US preference for protection instead of high speed, 10,000 tons seems a very high price to pay for the jump from 27 to 33kts. However, the motivation, which parallelled that for the original 30kt *North Carolina* design, was the need for ships to form fast carrier task forces. US prewar strategists expected Japan to form such task forces out of her carriers and her large heavy cruisers, for attack upon US lines of communication to the Western Pacific prior to a decisive battle near the home islands; they felt that any fast carriers assigned to action against such task forces would have to be covered by heavy units capable, for example, of defeating the three Japanese *Kongo* class battlecruisers which might well be detached from the Japanese Battle Force as cover for the carriers – which indeed occurred in 1941.

Design work began in 1938, after rumours of Japanese 46,000-ton battleships led the United States, Britain, and France to agree to invoke the Escalator Clause of the 1936 London Treaty, to raise the limit on displacement from 35,000 to 45,000 tons; in fact the *Iowa*s as built exceeded the latter limit. The existence of three

*Kongo*s (the refit of the training ship *Hiei* was apparently unsuspected as late as 1940) set a lower limit of three *Iowa*s, with a fourth as insurance against the unavailability of any one of them, and similarly against requirements in the Atlantic. Indeed, in 1940 it was expected that battleship construction would soon revert to the more traditional heavy type, and the first studies of what would become the *Montana* were made under the designation 'BB65'. However, on 19 July 1940 Congress passed a very large emergency construction programme, and the Secretary of the Navy decided that a large part of it would simply duplicate the latest classes already on order, as a means of saving time. Thus two more battleships, BB65 and 66, were ordered as *Iowa*s rather than as a new class.

Only four out of the six ships were ever completed, and they served in the Fast Carrier Task Force in the latter part of the war. *Iowa* was built with an enlarged conning tower; to balance its topweight, she was never fitted with a quadruple Bofors gun on No 2 turret. Ironically, although she was thus designed as a Force Flagship, in fact her sisters also proved quite suitable for that role, *New Jersey* serving as Fifth Fleet flagship in 1945. *Iowa*'s 20mm and 40mm outfit differed from her sister's: she carried 60 of each. Wartime modifications included some extensions to the bridgework and major additions of light anti-aircraft

weapons; surely an unexpected dividend of the great length adopted for high speed was the ease with which light weapons could be added without interfering with the arcs of fire of 16in and 5in guns. In 1945, *Iowa* had 19 and her sisters 20 quadruple 40mm mounts. Their 20mm batteries varied: *Iowa* had 52 single mounts, *New Jersey* 41 single and 8 twin, *Missouri* 49 single, and *Wisconsin* 47 single and 2 twin. The extra mounts in *Iowa* were atop No 2 turret in place of the 40mm.

*Illinois* was cancelled in 1945; her engines were later installed in two Fast Replenishment Ships (AOE). Her sister *Kentucky* was suspended and ultimately launched to clear the building dock at Norfolk; during the 1940s and 1950s she was redesigned several times as a missile-launching battleship (BBG), but ultimately she was scrapped instead. Of her four sisters, all but *Missouri* (training ship) were laid up before the Korean War; they were then reactivated, and served for a time as fire support ships and Force Flagships before again being consigned to reserve in 1955-57. *New Jersey* alone was reactivated (and refitted) for fire support duty off Vietnam, 1967-69.

By all accounts the four *Iowa*s were comfortable, fast ships, capable of making their somewhat extraordinary designed speed and unusually manoeuvrable for their great length, thanks, perhaps, to their twin-rudder design. However, the long, narrow bow adopted for high speed made

them somewhat wet, as did their limited freeboard due to large weight increases both during construction and due to wartime additions of anti-aircraft weapons. They were the only US battleships fast enough to keep up with fast carriers and proved useful as specialised flagships in a postwar world in which there were no longer targets suitable for battleship engagement. However, they were expensive to operate and so were soon deactivated in peacetime.

To help reach the target of a 600-ship navy in the 1980s, all four were recommissioned 1982-88 as cruise missile carriers, with secondary battery reduced to 12-5in/38, but with 8 × 4 Tomahawk cruise missiles, 4 × 4 Harpoon SSM, as well as 4 Mk 15 20mm Phalanx Close-In Weapon Systems. Further plans for greatly increased missile batteries and facilities for VSTOL aircraft (with removal of No 3 turret) are now unlikely to be realised. The main air search radar is an SPS-49 forwards, with LAMPS data link antennas above it, and satellite antenna and SLQ-32 countermeasures just below the forward main battery director (Mark 13). *New Jersey* was reactivated 1981-82, *Iowa* 1982-84, while *Missouri* recommissioned in 1986 and *Wisconsin* is scheduled for 1988, all modernisation being done at Avondale Shipyards in Louisiana, under a subcontract from Ingalls.

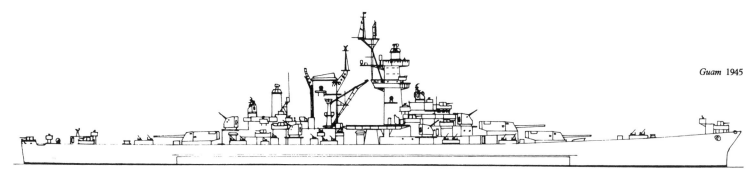

Although these large cruisers are often considered capital ships (in view of their main batteries and their general appearance) in fact they were simple developments of US cruiser doctrine and requirements; they were in effect, heavy cruisers finally unencumbered by the Treaty limits of 8in guns and a maximum displacement of 10,000 tons. They are often described as white elephants, since by the time two out of the six originally ordered finally appeared in 1944 the tactical concepts which had inspired them had been completely superseded. However, that is not to deny their validity in the context of 1940, when nearly all senior US commanders afloat enthusiastically supported a 'super-cruiser' to replace the existing 8in type. It is often said, too, that these ships were imposed on the Navy by President Roosevelt, but such statements are at best difficult to verify. What is clear is that a 12in cruiser project surfaced in the Bureau of Construction and Repair as early as 1938, and that the President may well have inspired it on the basis of his notions of foreign 'battlecruiser' and 'supercruiser' development. Later discussions always began with the 12in ship, often designated CA2 to distinguish it from a conventional heavy cruiser (CA1) as one alternative in a spectrum of possible future cruisers.

Cruiser practice shows in the provision of one rather than two rudders (which, unfortunately, ensured a very large tactical diameter) and in the requirement for enclosed stowage for aircraft. This latter was responsible for the unusual aircraft arrangement: hull depth aft was too restricted to permit a hangar in the conventional location there. However, it should be noted that the abortive light and heavy cruiser designs of 1940, which were related to this one, also showed aircraft amidships; the Bureau of Aeronautics flirted briefly with this idea, but ultimately rejected it. In 1945–46 there were proposals to remove the two catapults and replace them with an additional pair of twin 5in/38 gunhouses; a single catapult (no hangar) was to be fitted on the fantail.

The 12in/50 guns were a new design and, because they were unique among wartime US ships, they were the most expensive heavy US guns of their period. The initial *Alaska* design called

## ALASKA class *large cruisers*

| | |
|---|---|
| **Displacement:** | (*Alaska*) 29,779t standard; 34,253t full load |
| **Dimensions:** | 791ft 6in wl, 808ft 6in oa × 91ft 1in × 31ft 10in full load |
| | *241.2m, 246.4m × 27.8m × 9.7m* |
| **Machinery:** | 4-shaft General Electric turbines, 8 Babcock & Wilcox boilers, 150,000shp = 33kts. Oil 3619t, range 12,000nm at 15kts |
| **Armour:** | Belt 9in–5in (228mm–127mm) belt, deck 3.8in–4in (97mm–102mm) with 1.4in (36mm) weather deck and 0.62in (16mm) splinter deck, barbettes 11in–13in (280mm–330mm), turrets 12.8in (325mm) face, 5in (127mm) roof, 5.25in–6in (133mm–152mm) side, 5.25in (133mm) rear, CT 10.6in (269mm) with 5in (127mm) roof |
| **Armament:** | 9–12in (305mm)/45 (3 × 3), 12–5in (127mm)/38 (6 × 2), 56–40mm (14 × 4), 34–20mm |
| **Complement:** | 1517 |

| No | Name | Builder | Laid down | Launched | Comp | Fate |
|---|---|---|---|---|---|---|
| CB1 | ALASKA | New York SB | 17.12.41 | 15.8.43 | 17.6.44 | BU July 1961 |
| CB2 | GUAM | New York SB | 2.2.42 | 12.11.43 | 17.9.44 | BU Aug 1961 |
| CB3 | HAWAII | New York SB | 20.12.43 | 11.3.45 | — | BU Jan 1960 |
| CB4 | PHILIPPINES | New York SB | — | — | — | Cancelled 24.6.43 |
| CB5 | PUERTO RICO | New York SB | — | — | — | Cancelled 24.6.43 |
| CB6 | SAMOA | New York SB | — | — | — | Cancelled 24.6.43 |

*Alaska* 1944.
USN

for eight guns in two triple and one twin turret, and the design finally adopted (three triples) was justified in part because it would simplify turret production. Armour was designed to assure immunity against the 12in 1140lb shell between 18,000 and 24,000yds at target angle of 60° – a requirement typical of prewar cruiser practice. The original Characteristics specified the protection of machinery spaces only against 8in (cruiser) fire, but in view of the positioning of the 5in magazines in way of these spaces, the designers had to provide uniform protection against 12in fire there too.

Neither ship was modified during the war, and both were laid up soon afterwards. *Hawaii* was retained incomplete, at first for conversion to a missile ship; later she was very nearly converted to a command ship, a kind of larger sister for *Northampton*. They were expensive to maintain, and a poor substitute for a battleship; moreover, in the postwar naval world, even a *Baltimore* could quite overpower any Soviet cruiser, so that there were no more potentially hostile 8in cruisers to overwhelm – not to mention that, with a plenitude of carriers, surface commerce raiders presented rather less of a threat than prewar planners had imagined.

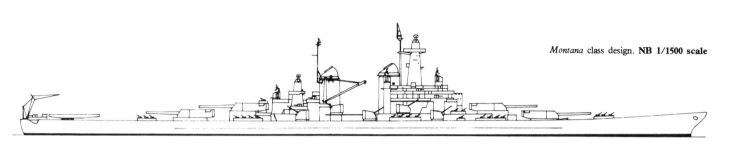

*Montana* class design. **NB 1/1500 scale**

## MONTANA class *battleships*

| | |
|---|---|
| **Displacement:** | 60,500t standard; 70,500t full load |
| **Dimensions:** | 890ft wl, 925ft oa × 121ft × 36ft 8in full load |
| | *271.3m, 281.9m × 36.9m × 11.2m* |
| **Machinery:** | 4-shaft turbines, 8 boilers, 172,000shp = 28kts full load. Oil 7300t, range 15,000nm at 15kts |
| **Armour:** | Belt 16.1in–10.2in (407mm–260mm) on 1in (25mm) STS, internal belt 7.2in–1in (182mm–25mm), deck 6in–7.35in (152mm–187mm) with 2.25in (57mm) weather deck and 0.62in–0.75in (16mm–19mm) splinter deck, bulkheads 15.3in (389mm), barbettes 18in–21.3in (457mm–541mm), turrets 22.5in (572mm) face, 9.15in (232mm) roof, 10in (254mm) side, 12in (305mm) rear, CT 18in (457mm) with 7.2in (184mm) roof |
| **Armament:** | 12–16in (406mm)/50 (4 × 3), 20–5in (127mm)/54 (10 × 2), 32–40mm (8 × 4), 20–20mm (20 × 1), 3 aircraft |
| **Complement:** | 2149 |

| No | Name | Builder | Laid down | Launched | Comp | Fate |
|---|---|---|---|---|---|---|
| BB67 | MONTANA | Philadelphia N Yd | — | — | — | Cancelled 21.7.43 |
| BB68 | OHIO | Philadelphia N Yd | — | — | — | Cancelled 21.7.43 |
| BB69 | MAINE | New York N Yd | — | — | — | Cancelled 21.7.43 |
| BB70 | NEW HAMPSHIRE | New York N Yd | — | — | — | Cancelled 21.7.43 |
| BB71 | LOUISIANA | Norfolk N Yd | — | — | — | Cancelled 21.7.43 |

The *Montanas* are the clearest proof that the *Iowa* design was a departure from normal American practice: slow ships (by the standards of their day) protected against the new 2700lb 16in shell, and provided with extra weapons largely on the basis of the extra displacement required to provide that protection. The design process was a long one, extended by the 1940 decision to build two repeat *Iowas* instead of ships of a new design. At first an 18in gun scheme was considered, but quite early twelve 16in/50 (at first in quadruple turrets, to save length) were adopted, with protection against the 2700lb shell. The design was not feasible until the outbreak of war had removed the 45,000-ton limit; then it grew very rapidly to the figure shown.

The final design showed a reversion to the externally armoured, bulged hull form of the *North Carolinas* and the adoption of a new 5in/54 secondary gun in twin enclosed mountings. The former change was adopted because of a strong feeling that the more steeply sloped internal armour would be extremely difficult both to fit and also to repair after battle damage; moreover, damage to the skin of the ship would cause local flooding. In a ship of very greatly increased displacement and beam, it would be possible to accept the heavier external belt. However, the resulting ship would not be able to pass through the existing locks of the Panama Canal. This last was no serious limitation because money had already been appropriated for a third set of locks quite wide enough for a *Montana* to pass through. As for the new secondary gun, it had been designed to provide more stopping power against destroyers; some loss in rate of fire against aircraft was acceptable. The new twin 5in/54 was specified for several wartime projects, including (at one time) the *Midways* and a new anti-aircraft cruiser; ultimately it was superseded by the now-familiar Mk 42 automatic (single-barrel) version.

Although the General Board thought in terms of four ships (one division) in fact five were authorised under the Act of 19 July 1940; all were to have been built in Navy Yards. They were suspended at Presidential direction in April 1942, owing to an apparent steel shortage; the same reason was given for cancellation of the new Panama Canal locks. The General Board was later to claim that 'this shortage was more a matter of proper distribution and priority assignments rather than an actual shortage', but all five ships were finally cancelled on 21 July 1943.

The *Montana* design was one of a generally ill-fated generation of US warship designs produced just as Treaty restrictions were given up: they included new large 8in and 6in cruisers, a new 7500-ton anti-aircraft cruiser – and the *Alaskas*. All died because just as the Treaty limits expired, and large amounts of money for new construction became available, it also became obvious that time was very short and that it was far better to build ships for which plans were in existence, than to build the (far more effective) ones which had yet to be designed in detail – hence the decision in favour of repeat *Iowas* for BB65 and BB66. Similar decisions were made for cruisers and for destroyers. However, the design work which produced the *Montanas* was not totally wasted; for example, the machinery arrangement adopted for the *Midways* was quite similar to theirs.

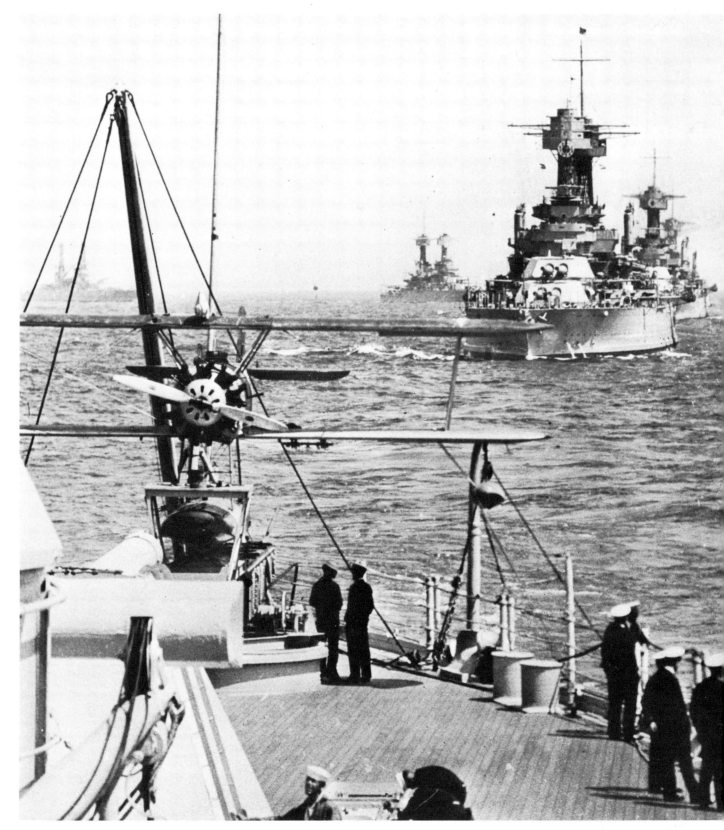

The American Battle Fleet off San
Pedro California in 1930.
*CPL*

# Index